Close to the Edge

ABOUT THE AUTHOR

Alec Lom has worked as a writer for the past 20 years, as a Fleet Street journalist, television script writer and author. He specialised in show business while working on newspapers like the *Daily Mirror* before joining BBC TV's entertainment department. He is married with two children and lives in London.

JIM DAVIDSON

Close to the Edge

WITH ALEC LOM

EBURY
PRESS

First published in Great Britain in 2001

10 9 8 7 6 5 4 3 2 1

Text © Jim Davidson 2001

Jim Davidson and Alec Lom have asserted their right to be identified as the authors of this work under the Copyright, Designs and Patents Act 1988

First published by
Ebury Press
Random House, 20 Vauxhall Bridge Road, London SW1V 2SA

Random House Australia (Pty) Limited
20 Alfred Street, Milsons Point, Sydney, New South Wales 2061, Australia

Random House New Zealand Limited
18 Poland Road, Glenfield, Auckland 10, New Zealand

Random House South Africa (Pty) Limited
Endulini, 5A Jubilee Road, Parktown 2193, South Africa

The Random House Group Limited Reg. No. 954009

www.randomhouse.co.uk

A CIP catalogue record for this book is available from the British Library

Designer: Dan Newman/Perfect Bound Ltd
Jacket photo: Steve Poole
All photos © Jim Davidson unless otherwise credited.
Plate section design: Seagull

ISBN: 0 09 188104 8

Papers used by Ebury Press are natural, recyclable products made from wood grown in sustainable forests

Printed and bound in Great Britain by Clays Ltd, St. Ives Plc

For Lea.
Now you'll know.

Who is stronger?
Wine, women
Or a king?

Contents

Foreword

In a rage, Tracy picked up the shepherd's pie and smashed the heavy plate down over my head. It crowned me and fitted like a soggy wig. It was a perfect shot and the hot mince and mash slowly dripped down all over my eyes and face. Well, actually, it didn't really *drip* all that much because, well, there wasn't any gravy with it ... and, you see, that was the cause of the problem and all the fuss in the first place. We'd never really been violent with each other until that day, until that shepherd's pie. It was Christmas 1993. I'll never forget it. It wasn't the remotest bit funny, or like slapstick in a situation comedy, like a pie in the face. This was nasty. A plate is hard and when it's smashed on to your head – it hurts!

We were living in Ewhurst in Surrey, in a little house that Tracy and I had bought when we first got together. I had changed the original name of the house to The Old Forge. There used to be an old forge stuck on to the side of the house and I'd crammed it with all my books and TV and hi-fi equipment. It was somewhere I could creep off to and isolate myself when I wanted to. I'd go and watch all my favourite *Star Trek* videos and distance myself from the real world. I quite liked the house because, up the hill from us, Pitch Hill, was the famous Windmill pub, which was a fabulous place.

I enjoyed going to the Windmill so much that I used to pop in there nearly every lunchtime and every night. We formed a little clique of mates, which was really nice. There was Roger from the brickworks down the road, Cedrick, who was a car dealer and a bit of a mystery, Dick, Jonathan and all the guys. It was just like that bar in *Cheers*.

Round the corner lived Eric Clapton. He used to be a regular there but when he stopped drinking, the pub almost went skint – luckily I made up for the shortfall in Eric Clapton's money by drinking the place dry!

There was a fantastic atmosphere there and it always puzzled me that Tracy never wanted to join me and my friends down the pub. She just didn't want to go there and I started to feel a bit miffed by that.

'Christ, I'm turning into my Dad!' I found myself thinking.

My Dad would regularly go to the pub and Mum would go to Bingo regularly, too – and they'd lead separate lives. But it wasn't as if Tracy was going to Bingo or anything. She would just rather do nothing than come to the pub with me. And it really pissed me off.

'Oh, she's lovely, your wife,' everyone at the pub used to say to me.

'Well, if she's so lovely,' I'd secretly be thinking to myself, 'then *why* isn't she here?!'

I really put all the blame on her. Around that time, I didn't have any businesses to run. I was just a stand-up comic, so I decided that, rather than sit around feeling bored at home, I'd go down to the pub. This seemed fair enough to me.

That Christmas Eve afternoon, I'd had a meeting with all the boys in the pub and I'd drunk a few whiskies and felt quite good. When I got home, Tracy was busy pottering around in the kitchen, like she did when her mother was over. I got back and popped up to The Forge to watch some of my *Star Treks* for the afternoon. I had another little drink, then I fell asleep.

I woke up about seven o'clock in the evening and sat up as Tracy came in with some dinner for me. She placed a large shepherd's pie on my lap.

'Aren't we going out tonight?' I asked.

'No!' she replied.

'It's Christmas Eve,' I said. 'Everyone's meeting up the pub, come on! Everyone likes to see you, we'll have a great time. Come to the pub.'

Tracy was determined to dig in.

'No, no,' she insisted, 'I'm staying here with Mum. It's a big day tomorrow.'

This was driving me mad.

'I *know* it's a big day tomorrow,' I said, 'but this is Christmas Eve.'

She wouldn't budge.

'Well, *I'm not going!*'

So there I was, sitting with this huge shepherd's pie on my lap, having a row. I looked down at my it and I realised there wasn't any gravy with it …

'And another thing, this shepherd's pie is *crap!*' I said to her.

Ridiculous really, now I look back on it. Actually, it was probably quite a nice shepherd's pie and I was starving. I hadn't eaten for a couple of days but because she wasn't coming to the pub the shepherd's pie was 'crap'!

As it turned out, within seconds I was wearing it.

The pie absolutely covered me. After I'd scraped the worst off, I jumped up and started to have a moan. I ran round complaining and shouting and doing all that irate husband stuff. It was nothing really to do with the shepherd's pie. It was just that I'd had enough of being on my bloody own all the time. If I wasn't spending my time sitting in The Forge watching *Star Trek* videos on my own, then I was in the pub on my own. In the pub, there was always a crowd but I was always there on my own thinking, 'Why doesn't the wife come here with me?'

An hour or so later, Tracy and I had a laugh about the shepherd's pie incident and so I asked her again.

'Look, come out with me tonight.'

But once again, she wouldn't budge.

'No, no, I'm not coming.'

'Well, do you mind if I go out, then?' I said.

Then Tracy really started on me. 'I'm sick of you being pissed,' she ranted and raved. 'I'm sick of this whole house smelling of booze,' and so on.

So I promised that I wouldn't get drunk that night and then, full of good intentions – but still slightly miffed that she didn't want to come with me – I went upstairs to get ready to go out. At least, she'd let me out and I didn't have to sit there at home, gagging for a drink, feeling awful unless I had half a gallon of whisky inside me.

For some unknown reason, I decided to get changed into my Davidson tartan kilt.

'Bugger it,' I thought, 'I'm going to go out and celebrate.'

Somehow, I knew that, later, I was going to get melancholy and miss Mum and Dad. That's what I always used to do. This was probably down to the fact that I loved them dearly and I felt terribly alone without them, having no-one to share my triumphs with. I often turned melancholy because I was so full of whisky or brandy that I couldn't reason things out. I'd just sit there and feel sorry for myself.

When Tracy and I lived in The Old Forge, every New Year's Eve would find me pissed, every birthday would find me miserable. One year, I even slept up a tree with a bottle of brandy because I was feeling so melancholy about absent friends and relations who'd died. I just climbed up a tree.

I think it really was a cry for attention. I was trying to make Tracy come and comfort me and tell me everything would be alright. That didn't happen. Instead, I put on my kilt anyway and went out on the piss and stood by for the inevitable.

If I wasn't happy, I'd make myself miserable. I would self-indulge myself and put on sad records, then go and sit out in the garden with a bottle of brandy and moan, 'Where's all my dead family gone?'

So that night, I somehow knew that a bit of that melancholy mood was going to hit me later on. Putting on my kilt somehow forced me down that route.

I set off for the pub, met up with the gang, started having a few drinks with them and just stayed on the large whiskies. Everyone there was in fine spirits but then they all started asking about Tracy.

'Go on, phone her up. Phone her up,' they were all urging me.

I used to ring Tracy from the pub all the time. So I did again. And I asked her again to join me.

But she was still having none of it.

'No, I'm going to bed in a minute,' she replied.

Again, I couldn't fathom it. Why didn't she want to be in the pub with me and the lads? I'd had a couple of drinks, I was in a great mood, it was great there.

As I put the payphone down in the corridor, I'd head back to the bar and the lads would ask, 'Who was that on the phone?'

'Oh, no-one. I couldn't get through.' I was just too embarrassed to say that my wife wouldn't come up the pub with me.

I made my way home just before closing time. After all that fun, warmth and friendliness I'd revelled in at the pub, I went home to a silent house. Tracy was already in bed, asleep. I just lay there on the bed, wide awake and wanting to party.

It was about eleven o'clock by the time I got home that night. I had promised not to get drunk and I was … er … drunk. And crazy! I stormed straight into the bedroom where Tracy lived when she wasn't in the kitchen and tried talking with her. But she really didn't want to know. She just started complaining that I was staggering drunk.

At that point, I pulled the blankets and sheets off her and got quite violent. I've never hit Tracy. We just had a huge row and I told her to go stuff herself.

I retreated back down to my *Star Trek* videos in my Little Forge, which had been fitted with my own little cinema and a little bar (the obligatory bar that Davidsons always build in their houses – no matter how small the room is, half of it is always taken up by a bar).

I grabbed myself whatever I could find to drink and slumped down in a chair to watch as many *Star Treks* as I could.

Pretty soon, I'd fallen asleep.

The next morning was Christmas Day and I got up feeling rough. My idea of what Christmas should have been like was having the house decorated beautifully, like a little chocolate box house, with a tree up and presents round it. Everyone would be there with their video cameras, ready to film the children opening their presents, a log fire would be burning and a bottle of champagne would be popped by someone. This was what Christmas *should* have been about.

This Christmas I got up and no-one was talking to me much. I felt awful. It was eleven o'clock, so I went upstairs, stormed around, grabbed all my stuff from the house and headed back to the pub. Actually, I didn't take *all* my stuff, just some shirts. But they were enough for me to do the whole token bit of storming out past everybody.

I slung them in the back of the Range Rover and drove off to the pub. What a state of affairs – and on Christmas Day too.

I went in and the lads were all there with their wives. The boys all had on their new Christmas jumpers and socks. Everyone was smelling sweetly of the after-shave they been given for Christmas. And there was me, Billy No Mates, feeling terrible, knowing that I'd cocked up at home but not knowing a way out of it.

If only Tracy had come to the pub with me, had shared a laugh and joined in. But then again, women don't do that. Mum never used to go to the pub with Dad, well, only on Saturday nights when there was a sing-song. Mum didn't really want to be with Dad, she just wanted to have a sing-song.

Looking back now, I think *that's* what niggled me. Why didn't Tracy want to be with me? I was paying for everything. Her mother was there. So too was her girlfriend Jackie, the kids' nanny.

I was paying for the Mercedes and the bloody house and the God knows what else. I was working my arse off.

And, in my mind, it kept coming back to, 'Why won't she come with me to the pub?'

As luck would have it, or as *unluck* would have it, I bumped into two girls in the pub. They were 'singly' girls who used to join our little gang every now and again. We got chatting, then got extremely pissed on champagne.

I'd known them for a quite a while and they'd become quite good friends. They were, sort of, two of the lads, really. I had nowhere to go and I knew that if I left the pub all I had was shit when I got home, so I reckoned I might as well stay with the girls in the pub.

Suddenly, they started to look more attractive. I mean they weren't unattractive. They were pretty girls. But after a bottle of champagne, they turned into Miss Worlds.

These girls joined in. They were the sort of girls I wanted. I loved Tracy and I didn't want to change her but I felt it would have been nice if she'd been a little more like these two girls.

'So, Jim, where are you going now?' they asked me.

'I've left home,' I replied, making things a little bit more dramatic than they were. 'I've been slung out!'

And when the girls said, 'Do you want to come back for the afternoon?' it was the Halleluiah Fucking Chorus opening up.

That was that.

I went back to their place. I think it was their Dad's place. There was me and the two girls and some guy I'd never met before. By now, we were all pissed and sitting round drinking even more.

When I went out to the loo, I found some bloke taking some coke and I thought, 'Oooh! Now that will *really* get me out of trouble.'

I hadn't taken cocaine for years and years, since I was quite adolescent. But I thought, 'Right! This'll do me.'

I bent over, looked down at the lines and sniffed hard. And that was it. I remember nothing much after that. I just recall grabbing a bottle of brandy and trying to get oblivious to everything. I woke up in one of the girls' beds on Boxing Day and was greeted with a 'look'.

It wasn't a *'How-did-you-get-here?'* kind of look. It was a look of, *'Whoa! Whoa! Whoa! Are YOU a lunatic!'*

I didn't know what she meant. Had I delivered the performance of a lifetime, made love to one or both of them … or had I murdered someone? I wasn't going to hang around to find out what was what! I just remember that look when I woke up in bed next to her.

'Oh, fuck,' I thought. 'What have I done?'

By now, I really was feeling awful. I also felt totally lost. I had a terrible hangover, plus that awful cocainey feeling. I really don't know how people take coke regularly. Coke always took much more away from me than it gave me. I had that terrible hollow feeling inside.

It occurred to me that I was in a strange house, with two girls who *used to be* my friends. I didn't exactly know what I'd done to the two of them, or to one of them.

All I knew was that they were looking at me as if I was Dr Crippen! And the bloke from the night before was nowhere to be seen. I was checking the floor for bloodstains!

It may seem a bit over-dramatic now but really I could have done *anything* the night before. I'd suffered a total blackout.

I didn't get blackouts very often. But they are terrible things because I'd be desperately trying to fit all the pieces together about what had happened. The last thing I wanted was for someone to tell me what I'd done. I wanted to remember it myself. The last thing I wanted was for someone to say, 'Oh what an arsehole you were last night.'

I jumped back in my car and drove back to the only place where I knew I was welcome, the only place I could go – the pub! Amazing, isn't it?

I couldn't go home. I felt that my life there had been removed from me. Now I was just overcome by a desire to wrap myself in the warm, rosy glow of that cheery, smelly pub and the nice, friendly people there who didn't seem to care about who I was, or my family, or my income, or whatever. They just liked me to be part of the team.

As it turned out that Christmas, I felt they were my *real* family – Cedrick, Roger, Dick, Jonathan, just ordinary guys in a pub.

When I walked into the bar, they all surprised me with their reaction.

'Christ! You look awful!' they said, 'where have you been?'

'Don't ask,' I replied, somewhat startled.

'Go on, tell us.'

'No, really, don't ask.'

Instead, I had a much better idea. I ordered some champagne.

By now it was Boxing Day and I *still* hadn't been home.

Boxing Day, I pondered, imagining a glittering Christmas tree, covered in fairy lights and surrounded by presents waiting to be opened.

Then, I looked out of the pub window and saw Tracy's car drive past as she went off to see her mates for the day, probably to get out of my way. She had the kids with her, and her mother.

And I thought, 'Well that is it. That is the end now. She does not need me at all now.'

There's always been a nagging insecurity in my mind, ever since the day I met Tracy.

'Does she need me at all?'

Hmmm.

Then into the pub came a couple I knew. She was a beautiful girl, about my age, and he was a nice guy and, like me, used to drink a great deal. I was always thinking what a lucky bloke he was. *His* wife was always with him in the pub. They were always drinking together, getting out of it and having loads of fun with their friends. I was dead jealous of that.

They saw I was on my own so they asked me to go back to their place.

'Great!' I thought, 'Boxing Day with a real family.'

We went back to their place and some other guy turned up. He also had some illegal stuff, some powder. I mean there must have been a fete on down the road – Colombian Marching Powder –Special Offer!

'Has Ewhurst turned into the drugs capital of the world?' I wondered, and couldn't believe my luck.

'Fantastic! God has come to my rescue!' I reckoned. 'More oblivion!'

So, a couple more nosefuls of the Colombian Marching Powder and some more champagne and … I instantly fell in love with this woman!

I knew I had a beautiful wife, and girls were two-a-penny really if you fancied them. But I fell in love with this woman because, ironically – and I know this sounds crazy – because, to me, she seemed such a 'good wife' to the bloke!

I wanted to know why my missus wasn't like that? Why wouldn't *my* missus come to the bloody pub with me, party up and drink champagne all afternoon?

After all that coke and champagne, I stayed there until the early hours of the morning, trying to whisper sweet nothings into this bloke's wife's earhole, telling her how lucky her husband was.

Then I came to my senses instantly. I'd gone from a lovelorn gibbering cocaine freak back to the drunk and sicky feeling again. That always used to happen to me as a lad, when I used to take cocaine. I'd be waffling away to some awful dragon of a woman, telling her how much I loved her and how I could never leave her side … and then, suddenly, the drug would just stop working. I'd be faced with the reality of it all. What I'd do then, of course, was run off and have another couple of nosefuls.

But this wasn't like that. I just knew I had to be at home. Ironically, here I was being made to feel welcome by all these people and having fun, while I knew going back to the place where I really wanted to be – where I knew that, because of my behaviour, I would be unwelcome – would be awful.

I staggered home the next morning. We must have been up all night because it was eight o'clock in the morning when I got back. I walked up and down the gravel path of our house like a caged animal. I really was too frightened to go in. I felt a bit jittery. It had been a massive four-day bender.

I didn't think anyone was up yet, so I hung around outside, pacing about and trembling. I hadn't eaten much for a couple of days and I had that awful hollow shaky feeling. I couldn't quite focus as my eyes were blurred. I felt dreadful and had a horrid taste in my mouth. I didn't know what to do.

Then I remembered something awful. I had been booked to do a gig that night in a club in Birmingham. The owner was a great mate of mine but I knew I had to let him down.

Terror gripped me, the fear that occasionally sets in when I know I don't feel up to the job of going on stage – but I've got to.

That day though, it was a case of 'No way, José. Not today.'

I clearly wasn't up to it. I looked and felt like shit. So I wasn't going. Instead, I phoned up my friend Kevin, who's been my roadie for the past twenty years and told him I couldn't make it. Kevin was a big boozer himself but I think he realised the shit I was going through or the shit I was causing myself.

Inside the house, I started roaming round in the larder looking for something to drink, without realising I had turned into one of those awful winos. I was feeling sorry for myself. It was a case of the old saying, 'Poor me, poor me, pour me a drink!'

I felt so awful and I just wanted to get some booze inside me to make myself feel better. Physically and mentally, I was now at my lowest ebb. I grabbed an awful old bottle of brandy from Cyprus, a bottle I'd had for years and never touched, bunged on a *Star Trek* video and fell fast asleep.

'Are you still here?'

That was the greeting from Tracy when she came in around lunchtime. I looked at her and, in my head, I blamed her for everything. I had already told her that I was leaving her, that I didn't want to see her again and that we were getting a divorce.

'What's the fucking point of being with you,' I tried to explain to her, 'if you don't want to be with me?'

'I don't want to be with a drunk,' she said.

'I'm only getting drunk because I feel so upset and fucking lonely. So now, if you don't want to be with me, I'm going to leave you.'

That wasn't much of a threat, I know. In my confused state I had no idea why she didn't throw her arms up in horror when I rejected her like this. Didn't she realise how rotten I felt when I was in such a hole? – I never thought of her problems, only mine.

As it was, Tracy took the car keys and went off back to her friends. I was left all alone in the house. And I carried on swigging at that awful old bottle of brandy. Slowly, I fell asleep once more.

Some time later that evening, Tracy came in and found me lying on the floor with the brandy bottle next to me on the carpet. Understandably, she disowned me. We exchanged a few sharp words and I told her to piss off.

Tracy went up to bed and I went to the toilet and threw up, not just because I'd had too much to drink but because I knew the end was inevitable. I was overcome by the fear of it all ending. I was in that toilet with my head down the loo, knowing that everything I'd worked for right from *New Faces* was going down the pan ...

They say your life flashes in front of you. Well, it does to an extent. I thought of Mum, of what would happen to me if I couldn't go on any more.

'What if I just stay in this toilet for the rest of my life?' I thought. 'I can't face the rest of the world. All I can face is this regurgitated brandy.'

I knew that, in a minute, I'd feel like death because there was nothing else to drink in the house.

It was about half past nine when Tracy normally went to bed. I staggered after her, up to the bedroom, feeling like death.

I somehow felt that, this time, my life really had ended. Certainly, my *marriage* had ended. I knelt down now at the end of the bed and bowed my head on the covers.

At first, she just sighed and gave me a look as if to say she'd had enough. Slowly, her look changed to compassion and I begged her for help. She was the only person that could have helped me, and more importantly, she was the only person I *wanted* to help me – even if it meant I had to die at her feet right there and then.

I just wanted to hear her to say, 'I will miss you,' or 'I do love you.' All I wanted was for her to put her arms round me and say, 'It'll be OK.' If she had done that before, then I wouldn't have been in the position I was in now. I had convinced myself of that.

Tracy leant over and rested her arms gently on my head. Then she cradled me in her arms.

'I know you've every reason to hate me,' I blurted out, and I remember these exact words, 'I know you've got every reason to hate me … but unless you help me now I am going to die tonight.'

1

A change for the better

I gently rested my head in Tracy's arms and she gave me a friendly cuddle.

Suddenly, there was a gentle little knock at the door. It creaked open and the Prince of Wales stuck his head round.

'Will this room be OK for you?' he enquired.

We were at Highgrove and this was the year 2000, seven years on. I'd been invited to spend the night at Highgrove with the Prince of Wales and I had taken Tracy along. It was amazing how my life had changed. I had stopped drinking, I'd been successful in various projects in my life, and even when I hadn't achieved what I'd set out to, people didn't frown at me, people realised that I hadn't cocked up for the sake of it. People didn't think, 'Oh, it's Jim being a bit headstrong and grandiose ...'

I had made something of my life. Now, I was clean, sober and I'd started to become accepted. People had begun to realise that I was taking my life seriously.

When I'd formed the British Forces Foundation to raise money to entertain the troops, I had written to Mrs Thatcher and, unbelievably, she'd arranged a meeting at her house for me to explain it to her. Then the Prince of Wales had agreed to become Patron. The Prince of Wales has always been a bit of a hero to me. I like him as a man, not just as my Prince. He turned up and played a few games of polo for us at the Foundation.

And now I'd been invited to spend the night at Highgrove as his guest. But they say there's no such thing as a free lunch, and certainly, there is no such thing as a free night at Highgrove.

It was all Jethro's fault really. Jethro is one of my favourite comedians in the world. Actually, I have two – one is Bradley Walsh and the other is Jethro.

I love Jethro and he likes me. Jethro's a great chap and more than a little larger than life. He owns so much land in the West Country, I reckon he owns more of Cornwall than the Prince of Wales.

If the *Bismarck* was a pocket battleship, then Jethro would be a pocket Brian Blessed. Just a smaller version, with the same beard, but with a great Cornish accent.

Jethro is so funny, he's probably the only man I know (with the possible exception of Dave Allen) who can just read the telephone book to you out loud and have you in stitches. He has become probably the most successful stand-up in the country.

A while ago, I went down to see Jethro in Cornwall. He's bought a barn, which he's turned into what he calls a coach house. He's named it 'Jethro's Coach House' and made it his cabaret venue.

Now Jethro's a mean bastard (I mean he's *really* mean – he's still got his paper round money) and when he first became a stand-up comedian, he carried on running his own building business.

'Jethro, you can't do *both* jobs,' I said to him one day. 'You're getting quite famous now.'

'Look Jim,' he replied, 'you've got all these celebrities these days paying good money to go and lift weights down the gym. Well, I can lift a hod of bricks up a ladder three times a day and at the end of the week I've got a bungalow.'

And that's the kind of bloke he is. He's really odd – and I love him.

I had discovered that Jethro had decided that his hobby would be show horses. He became very successful at it. He'd bought hundreds and hundreds of show horses ... well, OK, about 50 of them, to be truthful. And they were worth a fortune.

Jethro was a great horseman and when I came to visit, he brought out this great horse.

'This here is my horse and it's a bloody marvellous horse,' he declared proudly. 'This horse and me are *as one*.'

Whereupon, he promptly galloped off round the paddock – and fell off.

Well, I don't think I have ever laughed so much in all my life. I have never seen a bloke get back on a horse quicker than he fell off it. Honestly, he defied gravity.

To this day, I'm sure that my dear friend Jethro got his own back on me for laughing at him – by getting me to do this job for the Prince of Wales.

Every year Jethro used to appear at the Beaufort Hunt, a group of people who go out hunting in the Cotswolds.

It's also rhyming slang. It's not generally very nice to be called 'a bit of a Beaufort' – which is exactly what Jethro must've felt like when he fell off his horse.

Of course, I was dead jealous because Jethro used to tell me stories as if the Prince of Wales was his mate.

On one occasion when I met the Prince of Wales at a 'do,' the Prince said to me, 'Do you know Jethro?'

'Yes, I do, sir,' I replied.

'He's marvellous,' said the Prince. 'He comes down and does all these jokes for us. He's disgusting. He's absolutely fabulous.'

So, then Jethro said to me, 'Listen, Jim. I've had five years of doing the Beaufort Hunt. They do it in a big indoor arena at Badminton. Two thousand people turn up with their own beer and sandwiches and the atmosphere's great. But they've heard all my jokes now and the last time I did it, I died on my arse.'

'Jethro,' I said, 'you've *never* died on your arse.'

'No,' he insisted, 'it was bloody awful – and I wouldn't wish it on anybody … so I've told the Prince of Wales that *you* are doing it next year.'

Well, right, cheers, mate …

One Sunday morning, I was wandering around at home at the farm down in Dorking, half naked, cooking my breakfast, reading the *News of the World,* finding out which of my mates was being exposed that week.

I finished reading about Michael Barrymore – poor old Michael – and I'd bunged a couple of fried eggs on and popped some bacon under the grill when the phone rang.

'Hello, is that Mister Jim Davidson?' said a posh voice.

'Yes,' I replied.

'This is So-and-So from St. James's Palace,' said the posh voice. 'The Prince of Wales would like a word with you.'

All the moisture drained from my mouth immediately. I stood to attention in the kitchen. I did. I swear to God I stood to attention like an idiot. In my baggy underpants. And when he came on, I said, 'Morning, your Highness.'

'Hello,' said the Prince of Wales.

And then he started to ask me whether I would be prepared to do this gig at the Beaufort Hunt. I felt that it was unbelievable that this man, my Prince, was calling me and speaking to me at home. If only he'd seen me seven years previously, pacing up and down in the garden, throwing up in the rhododendron bushes, he wouldn't have spoken to me. Actually, he probably would have asked if I was alright and tried to find a way of making me feel better.

I stood there in my kitchen ramrod straight as I was speaking to him – and I looked down and one of my knackers was hanging out of my pants. For some unknown reason I thought, 'Cor, how disrespectful.'

At the same time, my eggs had now started to fizzle and pop everywhere. I had to take action.

'Will you excuse me a second, sir?' I asked him quickly.

'Yes, of course,' he said, 'what's up?'

'I've just got to turn my eggs down.' I mean I didn't tell him I wanted to tuck my bollock in. I thought that was a bit too much.

The Prince is such a kind man that he immediately said to me, 'Oh dear, would you like me to call back?'

Now imagine that! Do you think I was going to say, 'Oh yeah, *do you mind* not bothering me when I'm in my underpants frying my eggs in the morning.'

'Oh no, sir,' I replied instead, 'it's fine, thanks.'

So I hurriedly turned down my eggs.

'It's in July, on a Saturday night. Will that be alright?' he enquired.

'Well, whatever I've got on, sir,' I said, 'I'll cancel it.'

He sounded surprised. 'Well can you do that?'

'Certainly,' I replied. 'I'll just say it's by Royal Appointment.'

The Prince chuckled. 'What a good idea,' he said, 'I'll have to try that one myself. It will mean so much to these people in the country,' he added, 'because they're having such a hard time at the moment.'

I said I'd be delighted to oblige. The call ended.

The Prince of Wales hung up. He'd said he'd seen me at the polo and I immediately wanted to run round the house and tell somebody. I just couldn't believe it. There was I, in my pants, now with both knackers hanging out in shock, my eggs were burnt and I had no-one to tell. That's the sad thing about being alone, I had nobody to tell. My eldest daughter Sarah wasn't in, I had no real mates, no-one I wanted to share that news with anyway.

I'd resigned myself to taking on the Beaufort Hunt job. I was so thrilled that the Prince had asked me to do it. But it was rather like the Prince asking me if I'd jump off a cliff to instant death.

'Well, if that's what you want me to do, sir,' I'd have to say, 'I'll do it ...'

But I knew I would die on my arse and I knew it would be one of those awful gigs with a rotten PA system that kept going on the blink. I knew that I'd be faced with the Prince before the show saying, 'Thank you for doing it,' and then afterwards having to say to him, 'Well, I'm sorry, sir, I tried my best.'

I felt sure he would have been fine about the whole thing ... but then again I would have felt such a prick.

Dear Jethro was now phoning me every other day to warn me that something dreadful was going to happen. The PA system was crap, he said. They'd all be drunk, he said. The audience wouldn't laugh because the Prince of Wales was there, he said. And Jethro warned me that I mustn't be blue. He was winding me up rotten.

Then I received another phone call from the Prince of Wales's office saying the Prince would like to know if I'd like to stay at Highgrove that night.

A few years previously, I thought my life was going to end when I was stuck in that clinic. Now I'd got someone whom I loved, adored and respected beyond belief inviting me to stay at his house.

Before I knew it, the Prince was on the phone to me again.

'Jim, are you coming to the polo at Sandhurst?' he asked.

Luckily I wasn't frying my eggs that time and I had a pair of trousers on.

'Yes, sir,' I said, 'I am due to present you with a cheque for money that's been raised for the Prince's Trust.'

Because the Prince was the Patron of the British Forces Foundations, someone had offered to donate money to the Prince's Trust and it was thought it might be a good idea for me to present it to him.

'Ooh good,' replied the Prince, sounding pleased. 'Perhaps then you can follow me down because I'll be driving back and you can join the convoy. Do you still have a licence?' he added jokingly.

Luckily I did.

'And will you be bringing your wife with you?'

It was at this point that I realised the Prince of Wales had not completely read my CV. How was he to know that I'd been married four times?

'Err, yes, sir, I will,' I blurted out, committing myself. I would now have to take a wife with me – but which one?

I couldn't take a girlfriend, I couldn't take the little dolly bird I'd just picked up, and I couldn't take someone I didn't particularly know that well. I could just imagine the headlines in the *News of the World*:

'HOW I WAS BONKED IN HIGHGROVE'

'HE WAS HUNG LIKE A HAMSTER'

How I hate that shit. So I rang Tracy and asked her.

Tracy and I had recently divorced and she had a boyfriend, Noel the vet. But nevertheless I still asked her.

'Would you like to come with me to the polo and then come down to watch me do the Beaufort Hunt and stay with the Prince of Wales at Highgrove?'

'I'd be delighted' Tracy replied, without a second's hesitation.

Now this was the woman who would never come to the pub with me, never sit and have dinner with me and would never sit and chat to me. But now that we were divorced and I'd asked her to come to Highgrove with me, she'd said, 'I'd be delighted.'

Hmmmmm.

But I still liked Tracy. I still love Tracy to this day.

And anyway, we were off to see the Prince.

A week later, I picked Tracy up and off we drove to Sandhurst and watched the polo. Being there was sensational. Champagne was drunk, lots of Pimm's, and I presented the Prince with a cheque for £50,000.

'Oh Jim,' he said, turning to me, 'follow me down, I'll be driving the Aston Martin. You can't miss it. I'll be surrounded by policemen.'

Then a detective came over and asked me which car was mine. I pointed ours out.

'Right,' said the detective, 'you just follow us along. The Prince is driving himself.'

This sounded fun. 'Oh, do we go through red lights, then?' I asked.

The detective laughed. 'Only if he wants to.'

We all drove off in convoy. The Prince in his Aston Martin, followed closely by a car full of detectives with guns and God knows what. And then me and my ex-wife. What a sight.

The Prince drove the Aston Martin on his own with the roof down, and when we stopped in traffic, people were driving past, looking right at him. I could see their lips moving and I could read what they were saying and it was,

'Fuck me! It's the Prince!'

And the Prince just smiled and nodded. Occasionally, he looked back to see if I was still there. Of course I was. My arse was gripping the seat in anticipation. I had mixed feelings really, knowing that I was so privileged to be in this convoy but also knowing that, later on, I would die a death.

Finally, the convoy left the main road and, as the lanes narrowed, we began to slow down. It was clear we were arriving at Highgrove. Slowly, we drove up to a breathtakingly beautiful house. Various people, all dressed very smartly, were there to meet the Prince, plus more detectives.

Tracy and I got out and someone asked me, 'Will you give me your keys, sir, so I can park your car round the back?'

Someone else took our luggage away and we walked into this wonderful house. Once inside, the Prince, who was still wearing his polo gear, enquired, 'Jim, would you care for a cup of tea?'

Tracy and I were then shown upstairs and into our room. It was the most magnificent room you have ever seen. It had a gigantic four-poster bed and fantastic pictures on the walls. I mean *so much class*. It was like the best hotel room you have ever, ever stayed in in your entire life.

I couldn't believe it. It was like being in a fairy tale. It was amazing. I only wish I'd *really* had someone there to share it with me. Tracy was a good friend but I wanted someone to rush into my arms and say, 'I'm so proud of you.'

Instead Tracy, bless her, said, 'Isn't this a nice room?' and, 'Oh, God, they've folded up my knickers and put them in a drawer.'

It was good to have her there though.

Then there was knock on the door and the Prince of Wales came in with a smirk on his face. He knew it was a sumptuous room but he asked us, 'Will you be alright here? Will this room be alright?'

He chuckled as he said it. 'I'll see you downstairs,' he said softly. Then he left us.

I walked into the bathroom to discover that the bath had been run for us and our bags had all been unpacked. To my horror, I also found that my overnight wash bag had been emptied. So now, the Prince of Wales's staff knew that I'd got emergency condoms in my bag.

Great...

Tracy and I had been allocated a double bed. We both had a giggle but seeing as we hadn't make love much when we were married, it didn't really matter now that we weren't.

A woman came in and asked Tracy (whom she addressed as 'Ma'am') what dress she would like to wear that night.

I wore a stagey suit I'd brought along for the show. Downstairs, we were met by the Prince and Mrs Parker Bowles, who had turned up to come to the do with us. I'd met her once or twice before, the last time being at a dinner. I'd found her really charming and not a bit like the papers always say she is.

We started talking about the countryside, about the house, and about horses. Mrs Parker Bowles was really warm, friendly and down-to-earth. I also found the Prince like that. They are caring, nice people. When they asked you a question and you told them the answer, they *listened to you*.

The Prince and Mrs Parker Bowles really put me at my ease. He must have known I was shitting myself about the show that evening.

While we were nattering away in the drawing room, Prince William and Prince Harry turned up. I was in the middle of this royal family gathering and I thought I was in a dream.

If only Mum and Dad could have been in that same dream, I could have said, 'You see, we've made something of ourselves. Look! Look who it is!'

We only ever got to see these people on stamps.

The two princes said they were going down to the show with their mates. They'd reserved a table very near the stage.

As I chatted to them as informally as I could, I didn't know whether to call them 'sir,' 'Your Highness,' 'Prince,' 'Harry,' 'William' or what.

I hadn't got a clue.

I mumbled when I spoke to Prince William. I was dithering around, looking at the floor and my mouth had gone dry. And the young prince, all of 18 years of age at the time, had this wonderful way of making me feel a little more at ease with him. He just smiled and raised his eyebrow, as if to say, 'Yes, I know it's difficult, isn't it?'

He's going to be a great man.

But really, they were just like two normal young lads. Prince William is a big, tall, handsome boy – the same age as my own son, Cameron. He wore a pair of trainers and jeans and looked really cool and confident.

As for young Harry, he had a mischievous twinkle in his eye.

The Prince of Wales was showing even more concern now, because he began to realise how frightened I'd become. I just didn't want to die in front of them when I went on stage later.

'Look Jim, about tonight,' he said. 'You don't have to worry about me being there. You just go for it and have a go. The audience will be fine.'

I could see Prince Charles was searching for a way to describe the audience.

'They like it,' he said, '... they like it ... '

And Prince Harry cut in, 'They like a bit of dirt.'

Well, that made it a lot clearer. I started laughing and the Prince of Wales turned to admonish his son.

'Oh Harry, don't encourage him,' he said.

I smelled a rat. All these nice people were being so kind to me for one reason and for one reason only – because they knew that I was going to die on stage tonight in front of two thousand people.

The future King had sentenced me to death by comedy and by being polite and kind he was apologising to me for it.

'You will have your head chopped off in The Tower, Jim, or the equivalent. But I am really sorry, I can think of no-one else better to die than you.' Nonsense, of course. He really hoped I was OK and reassured me repeatedly.

By now, I didn't feel inadequate because I was concentrating on the job ahead and I knew the Prince really wanted me to do well. So I just mucked in.

At Badminton, in the indoor arena where they stage the showjumping, there were at least two thousand people. They were all sitting on wooden benches wearing jeans and jackets. To set the scene, think of the noisiest beer-swilling happy bunch you've ever seen in your life. You could have flown Concorde through there and you wouldn't have heard it. They'd all brought along barrels of beer and great big hampers of food. The noise in this big tin shed was absolutely staggering.

I decided I wasn't going to drink a great deal, so I immediately poured myself the largest glass of red wine ever and sat down at a table. Opposite me sat the Prince, with Mrs Parker Bowles next to me. Tracy sat next to her. All these various lords and ladies were milling about as the young princes came over to say hello. They flung their arms round their Dad.

Food appeared and our table started tucking into some salad. But I couldn't swallow any of it because I was so nervous. I was looking round apprehensively, checking out the scene. The PA system wasn't that clever and the lights were pretty ropey and the stage was thirty feet wide by four feet deep. More like a load of pallets than a stage. I was definitely going to die here.

Then, a voice announced, 'And now will you please welcome our support act this evening.'

Everyone applauded as a beautiful young black girl got up and started to sing. She was only supposed to do twenty minutes but she was pretty good and because she was going down so well with the audience, who were so up for enjoying themselves, she carried on.

The Prince started clapping along. I was shaking, and, of course, this was the Royal Variety Show for the girl singer. This was the best gig she'd ever done in her life. So she stayed on stage for an hour. And I was sitting there thinking, 'I should be on any minute, I should be on…'

Finally, the singer came off stage to a standing ovation. There was a ten-minute gap before my turn was due to arrive and, as the minutes ticked by, the Prince looked up at me with a look that said, 'I'm really sorry.'

The noise was deafening because this audience was now warmer by an extra hour's drinking time. The man on the microphone introduced me and the adrenaline kicked in.

I walked out to the middle of the stage to a big cheer. I smiled but inside, I was terrified. Every pace I took from the wings, striding towards the middle of the stage, my heart was beating faster. It was pounding in my chest. I felt like it was taking me for ever to get there.

'Your Royal Highness, ladies and gentlemen … Jethro, says bollocks to all of you.'

That was my opening line and it brought the house down. I didn't look at His Royal Highness in case I'd offended him. I thought best not to know.

When the laughter died down, I started my little act. I thought I might keep it a bit clean, so I talked about the countryside, about the foxes and a few other bits and pieces.

I was going down really well and I felt brilliant. These people loved me. The people were liking me and I liked them …

And then I put my foot in it.

'Yes,' I said, 'and what about the Queen?'

And everyone looked at me.

Oh no, I thought to myself. *I've mentioned the Queen. How do I get out of this one?*

I knew which story I was about to tell. But the audience didn't know this yet. As I uttered the words, '…and what about the Queen?,' something inside me said, 'You *can't* tell this joke.'

I started arguing with myself. One bit of me said it'd be fine, but on the other hand I was worrying that if I went ahead, I'd be locked up in the Tower and have my head chopped off.

So I looked at the Prince of Wales and he looked up at me and I took the plunge. '…Yeah, what *about* the Queen?'

And with that, I walked ten paces to my right and looked down from my four-foot high stage. Below me I saw Prince Harry, Prince William and their chums, who were now staring up at me with that open-mouthed expression. The facial expression from that great clip in that movie *The Producers*, when that Jewish audience heard 'Springtime for Hitler' for the first time. Before me, there was this gaping-mouthed audience, all waiting for me to offend the Queen, whom they all loved – and I did too. So I thought, 'Well, in for a penny, in for a pound.'

I turned to the young Princes.

'Don't you tell your grandmother I'm about to talk about her, will you.'

That broke the ice. I ploughed on. I told a story. It was either going to go one way or the other.

'Bollocks to it,' I thought to myself. 'Here we go. If I end up in The

Tower, then I end up in The Tower.'

And the joke went like this....

The Queen and the Duke of Edinburgh arrive in Australia and the anti-royalist prime minister at that time, Paul Keating, puts his arm round the Queen. He slides his arm round her back as she gets off the plane and he says to her,

'Let me introduce you to a few mates, Yer Majesty. But before we go any further I'd like to tell you that we are soon to be a Republic and we're gonna get rid of the monarchy, no offence. We're gonna call ourselves The Principality of Australia.'

'But you can't do that,' Her Majesty says to him. 'You're not a prince.'

'Ah well, alright then,' says Keating. 'We'll call ourselves The Kingdom of Australia instead.'

'I'm afraid you can't do that either,' she says. 'You're not a king.'

'So what do you suggest?' Keating pipes up.

And the Duke of Edinburgh says, 'Why don't you just continue being a country?'

Now the roar of laughter from that was incredible. I've never heard laughter like it. They cheered the place down. Once again, I didn't dare look at His Royal Highness in case I had offended. I swerved away from looking at him, fearing I was going to end up in The Tower. After my act, the Prince got up on stage and thanked everybody. He went down exceedingly well. They cheered him to the rafters. Then he turned, looked at me and said over the microphone, with gratitude and relief in his voice, 'Jim, it was my idea that you came here tonight. Thank God you were funny!'

So instead of going to The Tower, I got the OBE.

Result!

Well, who'd have thought I'd get the OBE?

I couldn't believe it myself. I surely wasn't destined to get it, especially not under a Labour government and after I'd been slagging off Tony Blair all over the place.

I did eventually receive my OBE, even though amazingly they faxed it to my old factory. They faxed this official letter to an old factory where I used to keep my sound equipment – but *five years* previously.

Maybe, the Prime Minister imagined, begrudgingly, 'Oh well, we'll give him a bloody OBE but we'll send it somewhere remote and hope he doesn't reply. Then we'll put it down that he doesn't want one.'

We've spoken about royalty. Now let me tell you about prime ministers.

I have never met Tony Blair in person, although I did write to him once. It was when his son was found slightly the worse for wear in London's Leicester Square. I thought he did really well. I always believe these things happen to all of us, so I decided to write him a letter.

'You know I'm a staunch Conservative BUT …,' I began.

Then I wrote something like, 'It's funny how we're both in show business together really. We have to speak to lots of people. When my mother and my father died, I had to carry on and go up on stage on both occasions,' and I ended the letter by saying, 'I think you've done really well.'

He wrote back to me funnily enough, in blood.

Only joking. He actually sent me back a kind little handwritten letter, on Downing Street notepaper, saying, 'It's nice to see that some things transcend politics and thank you for your letter.'

I'm sure he's a nice man. He just doesn't get my vote.

I also met Margaret Thatcher back in 1982, after I'd been to the Falklands. When I returned, I put together a leukaemia charity and I met Mrs Thatcher at the cheque presentation. She showed me the room where they'd decided to retake the Falklands. Then she sent me off to Beirut to entertain the troops.

Later, I had the idea to form the British Forces Foundation. I thought the person to get on board as a trustee was Mrs Thatcher. So I wrote to her and went along to her house.

'I'd be happy to help, Jim,' she told me, 'so long as you don't make me work *too* hard. I'm getting on a bit now, you know.'

She always speaks about what great things I do. That's unbelievable coming from her, really. Sometimes I think to myself, 'Am I doing all this just so that people will say nice things about me?'

Mrs Thatcher won the Falklands War – with the help of the soldiers, of course. She's a strong person, she's everything that Britain needs – and doesn't have at the moment.

On a personal note, we share a laugh and people say that she cheers up when I turn up in a room – because I can be a bit rude about people. She doesn't take herself that seriously and she works hard. All the time.

I said to her once, 'You do so much.'

'What else would I do?' she replied.

Another prime minister I met was John Major. We were introduced by the then Deputy Chairman of the Conservative Party, Jeffrey Archer. John Major later phoned me at home after I'd performed at a 'do' in his constituency.

I had settled down with my son Charlie to watch an Arnold Schwarzenegger action-adventure film called *True Lies*. Out of the blue, someone shouted out, 'The Prime Minister's on the phone for you.'

'Yeah, yeah, *sure*, course he is,' I shouted back, thinking it was another practical joke by one of my mates.

I picked up the phone and the Prime Minister said, 'Jim, it's John Major.'

Well, once again, I stood to attention. Like I do.

'Thanks for coming to the constituency,' he went on, 'and please give Tracy my regards.'

Suddenly, there was a loud burst of machine gun fire in the room. It came from the film I was watching on the video.

'Are you under attack?' the PM asked.

He'd heard the noise.

Now I'd got Arnie in one ear and the Prime Minister in the other.

'No sir, I'm not,' I said hurriedly. 'I'm watching a film called *True Lies*.'

'Ah, thank heavens,' said Mr Major. 'I saw that film and I thought I was under attack.'

I was quite surprised that the Prime Minister shared my taste in movies – and we shared a good laugh about it on the phone.

I've been in William Hague's company a few times. He's always been slightly preoccupied as he has had a lot on his mind, running around with his beautiful wife Ffion, trying to meet as many people as he can. He's a great speaker although I've been accused by some people in the Press of writing his jokes. Well, it's not the case – but I have stolen some of them.

It's a shame that he resigned after the General Election but what could he do? I suppose he just couldn't carry on any more. His energy had gone. I wish him well and I think his departure is the country's loss. It's amazing that people can say, 'I love what he stands for but I can't vote for him because he doesn't look attractive enough.' People are so fickle.

He's got a great sense of humour. When the Labour Party conference was on last year, if you remember, when Tony Blair gave his speech, he absolutely sweated to death. He famously took his jacket off and his shirt was soaked in sweat.

I decided to copy that. Before I went on, I was waiting in a back stage room. William was preparing his speech and I was preparing my shirt. I started pouring Perrier water all over it. William saw what I was doing, looked up and said, 'You're not doing the sweaty shirt joke, are you?'

'Yes, I am,' I replied.

'Right,' said William, 'well, get some more water on it then.'

So then, he put down his speech papers and started helping me to prepare my shirt. He helped me by directing me.

'You need a bit more water up there and a bit more on there.'

I can't say he poured the water on himself. I'd *like* to say that he did but it would only annoy him. So there is the Leader of the Opposition, ready to go on and deliver what was probably the most important speech of his life, and instead of boning up on his speech, he took time out to help me with my shirt.

I just drenched myself and put my coat back on over my shirt. I walked on to the stage, secretly hoping I wasn't going to dry out. Then I said to the delegates, 'Ladies and gentlemen and Shadow Cabinet, before I start, I'd just like to take five minutes to stand at this pedestal because, frankly, I fancy myself as Prime Minister. You see, I've got all the necessary credentials …'

And, with that, I took my coat off.

And the place roared.

Afterwards, William thanked me and we shared a laugh. Ffion was there. She is a very sexy-looking girl is Ffion, with two 'ffs'. I always get a bit nervous with them though. I never tend to get too pally. I always speak when I'm spoken to. But when I *am* asked to speak, then I don't shut up.

So, somewhere between the famous shepherd's pie incident and after I'd come out of the clinic, later in 1994, Jim Davidson changed. I turned away from the downward spiral of despair and all my drink-related problems into a new man with a fresh outlook on life, someone who was determined to sort himself out – and the result was that I became accepted and liked again. Suddenly, I found all these important people were phoning me up. Amazing, really.

So that's me now, I live in this farmhouse down in Surrey, not too far from The Old Forge, which is full of old memories. I haven't been in the Old Windmill for quite a long while now. For me, it's still too painful to go in there, thinking of that Christmas.

Something has definitely happened to me in the last ten years or so. Apart from turning 40 and going into the clinic, people realise that I take a little more concern about show business. I think I have proved to people that I am taking life a bit more seriously and that I have taken on fresh responsibilities. I look to the future now and think about how I'm going to end up, not tonight or tomorrow but in the longer term.

Also, since I turned 40, I can't do some of the things I used to, which is a shame. I still try occasionally, which is why some of this book has wobbly writing.

But my life has changed. For the better.

It's a bizarre life sometimes though. I can speak to pop stars. I bump into Robbie Williams and he says, 'Hello Jim.'

The other night, I went to a Charlton Athletic match and David Ginola, who scored a brilliant goal for Aston Villa against Charlton, came up to me after the game.

'Hello Jim,' he said, 'I am a big fan of yours.'

I couldn't believe it. I can speak to generals. I can get on board battleships and be saluted.

I reckon my career has been in two parts. First of all, there was 1975/76, when I won *New Faces*, when money was dropping out of the sky and all over me. The only responsibilities I had involved getting myself from one gig to the next.

Then, as I got older, I had a second bite of the cherry, a second chance: (a) when I sorted myself out and (b) when I was given the chance to re-invent myself as a family entertainer on television; I took that chance and I became an entertainer that the BBC could trust.

I think the BBC have finally come to regard me in the same way that the politicians do and the way the Royal Family do, to an extent. They realise that Jim's not going to vomit on anybody any more.

Suddenly I had a chance to do light entertainment. That's why I make *The Generation Game* really for young kids and families – because it gives me a chance to clown around and do things I can't on stage where it is expected that every other word I say will be 'fuck'.

Now that I'm 47 and aware that I'm fast approaching 50, I look back at what I have achieved and the journey I've taken. I always thought I would do this with my life. I don't see the way my life has developed as being a matter of 'destiny'. It's just that I have always had a feeling inside that I am *different* to everyone else.

I also feel sometimes that I am *cleverer* than everyone else. I have *always* felt that. Even when I was a young lad, I was captain of the football team. I was the one in the school play who landed the leading part, the one who was picked to appear in *The Gang Show*.

Everything I did, I did to extremes. I was never happy until I was the centre of attention, which meant being the captain or the lead player. My adult life and career today are really just an extension of all that.

I've finally packed up getting continually pissed – well, at least I don't drink 'to excess' too often nowadays. I am still making people money and people have come to recognise me as someone who's approachable, even with my chequered, colourful past, which people now laugh at.

They laugh at my always having struggled with money problems, and they laugh at the fact that I have had four wives. People find it *hysterical*. They love it. They say to me, 'Go on, Jimbo, go and get another wife.'

Nowadays, I have to keep up a balancing act between how people perceive me to be on stage and the real person. So many times, I've had people come up to me and say, 'Oh, you look miserable.'

It's just that on television, they only ever see me smiling and laughing. They don't realise all the other shit that goes on in my life, the tax, the worries, the children and the loneliness, asking myself, 'Why have I fucked up? Why have I had these four wives? Why is it that I can't have a drink like anybody else? Why is it when I want one drink I want ten? Why is it that one's too many and a thousand's not enough …'

But little by little, or as they say in AA, 'a day at a time', I'm getting better – and people realise that. I just need to stay away from those melancholy moments where I grab a bottle of brandy and climb up trees. Because if I really want to be down, I can get myself into such a big hole, there really is no way out, no way at all.

But for all that, lots of people have been good to me and I couldn't have done it without them.

Especially Tracy. My marriage to Tracy was a distant marriage, really. But I loved her. I would always tell her, 'You've got smiley eyes.'

Whenever I landed myself in deep trouble, Tracy would make it all better with those smiley eyes …

2

My Tommy Steele guitar,
The Gang Show ... and girls

I gazed into Tracy's smiley eyes, then slumped down on the bed and started sobbing. She held me close and suggested softly, 'Why don't I phone Christine?'

Christine was our local doctor, an Irish woman, a great doctor. She was always keeping on at me saying, 'One day, Jim, we will dry you out. One day, we'll get you off the booze.'

Right now, I wanted to get off the booze more than anything in the world. I also wanted my family back. I wanted to feel better – and Tracy's forgiving smiley eyes gave me some kind of hope.

Tracy got off the bed and called Christine. While she was on the phone, I lay there. I felt numb. I craved Tracy's forgiveness. I didn't really want to stop drinking. I just wanted it to be OK, whatever it was.

Christine told Tracy there was a drinks clinic, amazingly, right round the corner from where we lived in The Old Forge. It was located in a village called Ockley, about five miles down the road from us. Dr Christine told me it was a clinic where they treat you for alcoholism and drug addiction.

'OK great,' I said on the phone, 'I will speak to you in the morning.'

I collapsed back down on the bed and slung my arms round Tracy.

'I am so sorry for everything,' I told her. 'I'm so sorry for not being there, sorry I'm not the husband you want, sorry I'm not the guy in the Timberland shoes and the comfortable sweater who goes to the garden fête with all the other husbands and wives. I'm sorry I'm not the stockbroker with the nine to five job. What I am is what I am.'

Tracy understood. But understanding didn't make it OK. I'm sure she really

43

wanted one of those guys with the cord trousers who drank half a pint of beer instead of this lunatic who went through life with a struggle, struggles that I admittedly made myself.

She said it would be alright but it was far from fucking alright really. I wasn't sure who she was trying to convince – her or me. But right now those words of comfort were all I had and I took as many of them as I could.

I admitted to her I was frightened about what was going to happen but I acknowledged it was going to have to happen. Tracy tried to soothe me and calm me down. She said I'd be alright.

'Don't worry,' she said softly, 'we'll all stick by you.' That made me feel marginally better.

'You will definitely go, won't you?' she asked.

'Yup, I'll go.'

Tracy told me the doctor was going to come round in the morning and together they would take me down to the clinic.

'OK. Thanks Tracy,' I blubbed. 'I promise, I'll never do this again.'

I went downstairs, grabbed a bottle of brandy and took a couple of swigs, not because I was frightened, or wanted to fall into oblivion – it was just that I was desperate to stop myself wanting to throw up through fear. Then, for good measure, I took a sleeping tablet, one of those awful Valium pills that are shaped like a rugby ball. I climbed into bed with Tracy and, for the first time in four or five days, I slept a deep, heavy, albeit drunken sleep.

The next day, I was up early, still feeling rotten, looking dreadful and not knowing quite what to expect. The doctor came round at about 9.30 am. It was Tuesday, 28 December 1993 – the end of a four-day bender and I felt like hell.

But Tracy was helping me now and that felt good.

I was frightened like a little boy at the prospect of checking into the clinic. I didn't quite know what to expect. I had no idea what lay ahead at all. I packed my bags, pyjamas, a load of books and a couple of videos, in case I had access to a video recorder there. I mean for the price it was costing, apparently £1,000-a-week, I thought the place was bound to have a few facilities. I also took some sleeping tablets along with me as I imagined that, without a drink, I wouldn't be able to get to sleep.

We drove past the little gate house and there, down the drive, I saw for the first time Farm Place — my home for the next few weeks.

A big old fourteenth-century farmhouse, the 'clinic' is surrounded by beautiful grounds and a couple of lakes. I knocked at the wooden front door and it felt like I was wandering through into somebody's drawing room — except that there was a little reception desk built into one corner. Apart from that, it was just like a private house. The place seemed cosy enough. Smiley people milled about. One of them came up to me and suddenly a thought snapped in my head,

'Oh God, this is just like that film One Flew over the Cuckoo's Nest.'

Everyone was smiling at me far too much. All we were short of was the Mantovani piped music.

I parked myself on the sofa in reception and filled in a form which a nice lady handed me. Tracy was looking concerned and the doctor was fussing around. Then they led me off and I had to give them a urine sample. They also took a blood test.

Finally, they sat me down. Tracy sat next to me holding my hand. I must have looked like a lost little boy when they took a Polaroid picture of me. I didn't quite know what was going to happen next ... and then the bombshell hit me when the nice smiley people suddenly said to me,

'Right, Tracy is going to leave now and you won't be able see her for two weeks, I'm afraid. And you won't be able to speak to her on the telephone either. In fact, you won't be able to speak to anybody for a week.'

I was speechless. But that was that.

I kissed Tracy goodbye, shaking like a leaf as she went off. She told me later that she had cried all the way home.

When I heard that door shut, it also clicked in my head.

'Jim, you're on your own now, boy.'

I admit I was frightened to death.

I met some people and went out to a little room where people were sitting around smoking. Although I must have looked dreadful, but probably no more dreadful than the people around me, mainly unshaven men in jeans and old plimsolls and scruffy jumpers. The air was thick with smoke and it was like a doctor's waiting room, with newspapers everywhere — although I noticed there were no Suns or Daily Stars there, none of that excitement, none of the really exciting 'Let's go out, get pissed and shag a Page Three girl' stuff.

Instead, there were masses of books about alcoholics and how we had to deal with our lives. I took one look at that dishevelled bunch of people and shuddered to myself, 'Oh God, is this what I've turned into?'

I was given a couple of tablets, a drug called Heminevrin, which replaces the body's need for alcohol. The pills made my nose go a bit tingly and a bit woozy. Quite pleasant, actually. The nurse also gave me some vitamin tablets, apparently so that I didn't have a fit.

I teamed up with a guy called John and we went for a walk. He was very nice, a bit younger than me, with short, cropped hair. He came up and put his arm around me, which I thought was a bit odd at first but he said, 'Are you alright, mate?'

'Yeah,' I said, 'I think so.'

'Come on,' he said, 'let's go for a walk.'

So we walked out into the grounds of this beautiful Farm Place, with the duck pond, its grassy lawns and that brick road at the end of the driveway that led up to the exit — and back to normality.

I wondered if I'd ever be walking out of there. I wondered whether something magic was going to happen to me to turn me into one of those people that Tracy wanted. I wondered, more importantly, whether I wanted to be turned into one ...

John was an alcoholic and he spewed out his problems to me about how he could not have just one drink, about how he'd go out for a pint of beer and then wake up pissed in some doorway. Although I wasn't quite as bad as that, it made me think that maybe some other people are worse off than me. Maybe, it occurred to me, if this guy could do it, then maybe I could have a go as well.

We walked right up to the little coach house — the doorman's house as I imagine it would have been in the old days — right by the gate and we stood there looking out into normality. I saw the cars going past, people going about their normal daily lives, going to the pub with their wives and I thought, 'Why me?'

I turned to looked at John and he seemed to peer deep into my soul. He gave me a little smile and said, 'Come on, let's get back.'

That night I went upstairs to my little room, which had two single beds in it. There was an adjoining room to that, with two more single beds and a shared toilet. I was right at the top of this house and it was cold and dark. I put silly pyjamas on, a pair they'd made me bring, and I got into bed.

I pulled the blankets over my head and, as was fast becoming a habit, cried my eyes out like a baby.

I was still crying when Dad came into my bedroom, wearing only his 'Y' fronts.

'Get out of bed I'm not going to tell you again.'

I carried on my pretend crying.

'But Dad, I've got a really sore throat and I feel sick,' I pleaded.

'Right then, bloody well stay there,' he boomed, in his broad Glaswegian accent. He stormed out, back to his own room.

I knew that my ruse would work. I stopped my fake crying and lay there totally contented. I didn't have to get up and go to school that day and I knew that my mate Ray Sparks would be coming round as soon as he'd pulled the wool over *his* Dad's eyes – and then we would push off fishing down Horton Kirby. Greatest place ever.

That is all I seemed to live for in those days – just fishing, fishing, fishing. We used to visit some old gravel pits in Kent, just off the A20, down by Brands Hatch. I used to spend all my time there. We'd hop school and when we'd saved enough money, we'd grab our fishing gear, jump on a train to Dartford, walk or hitchhike to Horton Kirby where we would fish, come home covered in mud, muck and filth, smelling of fish.

'Where have you been?' Dad would ask me, when I got home.

'I fell in the school pond, Dad,' I'd say.

Little did he know we never *had* a school pond.

I was born on 13 December 1953. We lived at 118 Holburne Road, Blackheath, London SE3, a little council house that was built by Italian prisoners of war. We were three houses away from 'the dump', as it was called, which was really just an old field where we used to go digging, make camps and boil stews out of vegetables that we'd pulled up from people's allotments.

My best friend Tommy Elliot lived across the road and he was a great guy. We called him 'Professor', because he was always making bombs. He would get Cherry Blossom shoe polish tins and pack them full of gunpowder from fireworks and blow them up.

Or else The Professor would teach us how to make rocket fuel out of weedkiller and sugar. We'd make rockets, watch them explode and then vanish into thin air.

The Professor was always up to something. He always had some gadget or other that would come on if you plugged it in a light bulb socket or a switch. I was fascinated by him and his antics and he made great cocoa.

I had a funny upbringing really. My birth was in an upstairs room in our house, in what we knew as 'Dad's bedroom'. Mum was obviously bearing down quite heavily at the time – but Dad was doing something else heavily … drinking, down the pub in Woolwich.

Dad's younger brother, Uncle Bill, *was* in the house that night though. Bill was a very educated man and ex-Army, an ex-major in the Cameron Highlanders. He spoke various different languages and was a great graphic artist.

I still remember to this day the little drawings he did for me. He was playing 'Clair de Lune' on the piano downstairs, while my Mum was delivering me into the world.

I think Dad was absolutely delighted to have a son. Apparently, he got back from the pub, walked into the bedroom, pointed at his new-born baby son (me), tossed a bottle of whisky on the bed, and shouted, 'Give him a drink for me.'

Well, Dad, that did it alright.

Dad worked quite hard and I didn't see much of him. But when he wasn't working, and he did have time to be with us, I was his 'little soldier'. He used to take me around with him everywhere he went.

The house was always full of other children, like my sisters Eileen (the eldest), Jean (the next one down), then two years below her my brother Billy and two years below him, my brother John. After that came a ten year gap before I popped along.

I often wondered why that was. It was always a great puzzle to me, right up to the time when Mum died. To this day, I don't know what Uncle Bill's *real* relationship was with my mother, but I wondered whether he might have had something to do with me coming into the world. Obviously, though, he loved Mum and he was loved by everybody. While Dad was out working and drinking, Uncle Bill took over the role of our Dad.

Although I can't remember him now, my brothers remember Uncle Bill with great joy. He was a bit of a mad bastard who used to walk up to the shops in his kilt and pink scarf with his red hair flowing in the wind. He also used to write poems and paint wonderful oil paintings and watercolours.

Some days he would come home from work and grab my two elder brothers and say, 'Right. We're going camping,' and off they would go.

On my first birthday he apparently forgot it was my birthday and didn't buy me a card. But instead, he painted me a beautiful picture card, which I still have hanging up in pride of place on my wall at home. It's a watercolour which he signed, 'From his A-bu!'

'What does "A-bu" mean?' I asked Mum when I was older.

'You could never pronounce the words "Uncle Bill" when you were a tot,' she explained, 'so you used to call him "A-bu".'

After that, I just took it for granted. I used to ask Mum to tell me about him and she would tell me all about what an eccentric he was, what a great and clever man.

Uncle Bill was the intelligence officer of his battalion, the Cameron Highlanders, and he could speak Arabic fluently, also German. In fact, he was pretty much an all-round genius. Basically, he was a right Clever Dick, as they say.

When I reached the age of two, Uncle Bill disappeared. He went off to Thailand. Just like that. And he was never to be seen or heard of again. My brothers used to reminisce about him and say what a wonderful man he was but Mum used to clam up and Dad never mentioned his name. It was more than a bit odd.

After he'd left, I would often ask Mum to tell me more about him. A strange pattern began to unfold.

When I was about 24 or 25, much later on, I owned an old Austin 1800 car, which had an old coat hanger stuck in it for an aerial.

One night, I was listening to a record on the car radio. The song kept cutting out and I could hardly hear it because of my makeshift aerial. Then, the disc jockey started to announce what record it was – but just at that point, my coat hanger aerial gave up and all I could hear was static.

I was desperate to know the name of the song. I told my Mum what had happened and she suggested I phone up the radio station and ask them.

I called Capital Radio and they told me the track was by a Japanese keyboard player called Tomita and the number was called 'Clair de Lune', from the album *Snowflakes Are Dancing*. When I told Mum, she said, 'Ah, well, that's the tune you were born to. I wonder if that's why it stuck in your mind.'

That seemed a bit far-fetched to me. I said I just thought it was a nice tune. I couldn't wait to buy the record though and I quickly learnt to play it on the piano at home. When I played it to Mum one night, she burst into tears. Then she told me the story of how Uncle Bill used to play it.

'Why did Uncle Bill leave?' I asked her.

She said he'd just left because he couldn't stand the rows. 'Me and your father were having terrible rows,' she said. 'There were some awful bloody rows.'

That didn't seem enough though. I still couldn't understand why Uncle Bill left. 'But he never got in touch with the boys who he loved or the girls, or you again, did he?'

Mum just sighed. 'That's just the way he was,' she said. 'Uncle Bill just wanted to go away.'

I couldn't really get it. I couldn't understand. Until one day, I somehow sussed out in my mind that Uncle Bill might have had an affair with Mum.

I spoke about this a while ago to my sister Jean, who was over from America. She'd gone to live in America when I was aged three and still lives there now. I also mentioned my theory to my other sister Eileen, now sadly deceased.

One night, I put it to my sisters straight. 'I am sure Uncle Bill was my Dad, you know,' I said to them. 'I reckon that's what prompted all the fuss, what with him going away so abruptly, don't you?'

My sister Jean seemed genuinely shocked. 'How *dare* you insult our mother like that?' she said and she went on and on about it – until I ended up thinking, 'Well, I'm not bloody asking *that* any more.'

I also dared to ask Mum the same question and she also dismissed the notion out of hand.

'Don't be so ridiculous,' she scoffed. 'Your Uncle Bill couldn't have children. It was a known fact that he could not have children. He was infertile, just couldn't have them. So, don't be so ridiculous.'

When Mum died, she'd written a couple of things in her will. One of them was that she didn't want me to get drunk, but I did.

Me and my brother Billy walked into the church and as dear old Mum's coffin was sitting there and we heard 'Clair de Lune' again, this time coming over the tannoy. I immediately wondered, 'Is that a message to me from beyond the grave, my Mum sending me a signal about the true origins of my birth?'

I could never stop the doubt in my mind. Nothing ever added up and no-one would admit anything. And then, years after that, I was in Glasgow and, out of the blue, I received a message to call a woman called Jean Gibbons. She'd claimed to me on the phone that she was my cousin. So, being naturally curious, I agreed to meet her.

She drove up from Ayrshire and we met in my hotel. She took me completely by surprise.

'I am Uncle Bill's daughter,' she blurted out.

'Mmm,' I thought, 'here's a woman who is Uncle Bill's daughter but Eileen, my sister, said Uncle Bill *couldn't have children.*'

I must have said something that indicated I didn't quite believe her.

'Well, I *am* his daughter,' Jean insisted, 'don't you worry about that.'

We chatted on and she told me that she now lived with a nice man down in Ayrshire and that they were hill farmers. She said I must go and visit them some time. Then, all of a sudden, she reached into her handbag and pulled out a little book, about as big as a medium-sized photograph album.

In it were lots of drawings and poems, exactly the same as the ones shown me by my brothers. Jean's poems were also similar to the ones that

Uncle Bill had written for us. They were great verses, written in Robert Burns style.

This really intelligent Scotsman, whom I knew as Uncle Bill, clearly was her father. Then she got to the point.

'But what I could never understand is why he left my family for yours.'

Jean told me that Uncle Bill had left *her* home when she was also two years old. He'd left her family to come and live with *my* Mum and Dad.

'He also buggered off from *my family*,' I said, 'and I never knew him properly.'

'I could never understand why he left me for *your* family,' she replied.

I told Jean that Uncle Bill had eventually left us when I was two as well and also that I was told later on that he couldn't have children. I asked Jean what she'd been told.

She said they'd told her that Uncle Bill had always wanted a boy.

'If *I* had been a boy,' said Jean, 'my name was to have been Cameron.'

That truly was a bombshell! Because Cameron is actually my real first name. Gradually, another piece of the jigsaw puzzle was falling into place.

I still don't really know what to believe. Now I sometimes think to myself, 'Well, if I was a detective, I'd make that the case.'

But then I feel so awful even contemplating the idea, awful out of disrespect for my father Jock. There is so much of Jock in me but he and Uncle Bill were brothers, after all. I don't really know. Rather than dwell on it, I often push the issue aside. What is, is.

To this day, I *still* don't know the answer to the puzzle about who my father really was. But there is one piece of 'evidence' that is almost too neat. My very first birthday card, hand-painted for me by Uncle Bill, is probably the biggest clue I have. At the bottom, he signed himself off, 'A-bu'.

And I later discovered that in Arabic, 'A-bu' means 'Father.'

To sum up, yes, I do believe that Uncle Bill could be my real father. But sometimes, in my life, I have been really convinced that something was right – and it still turned out that I was wrong. However, on the other hand, I have also learnt over the years that if there is *any* doubt about something, then there is *no doubt*.

Dad was a Scotsman, John Davidson, from Bridgetown in Glasgow. He had a very broad Glaswegian accent and was in the Royal Artillery during the war. Dad was posted to Woolwich, where he met my Mum when she was about 16.

My Dad's father, whom I never met, was apparently a short ginger-haired Scotsman, who was always in trouble and drank like a fish. There were family stories about when the police came to get him. He was so small, he hid under the sink in the kitchen.

Dad's mother, who came to stay with us for a little while when I was about two or three, had terrible asthma and I called her 'Nanny Puff-Puff' because she was always having to squirt this puffer thing into her mouth to stop her from having asthma attacks.

To me, Dad was always a big scary bloke with a rough accent, who was hardly ever at home.

Mum, whose name was Emily Davidson, formerly Lewis, came from Woolwich. There was always a bit of confusion as to how old Mum really was because she thought she was born on 1 April 1919 but, as it turned out later, when she applied for her birth certificate to get a passport, she was actually a year younger than she thought and was born on 31 March 1920.

My earliest recollection of Mum was of her fur coat, which was obviously fake and had a strong smell of perfume to it. I would cuddle up to Mum and she was always smiling and happy.

My Mum was always a little happier than the other people in the street. She was a bit of a duchess and I think Uncle Bill used to call her that, 'The Duchess.' Mum always classed herself as Irish, even though her father was an Englishman called George Lewis. He had a big beer belly, grey hair and tough old hands that were constantly rolling Old Holborn, leaving bits of tobacco all over the kitchen table.

Mum's mother was Maggie Kieley before she married George Lewis, another Royal Artillery man. She came from County Cork and was a thin little Irishwoman who used to get her words all muddled up.

Nan and Grandad lived down in Woolwich, next to a pub called the Village Blacksmith. If you check there now, as I did the other night, there is a little bungalow on the site. But, in those days, it was an old ramshackled, dark, Dickensian building. I have vivid memories of going round there when I was a little kid and seeing my Nanny with her hair in a bun. My grandfather, Big George, was there too, although he was another one of these elusive characters who drank thousands of pints of beer and came home drunk.

Mum had lots of brothers and sisters. There was talk of eleven children. Uncle George, Mum's younger brother, who was in the Navy; Uncle Spike, the youngest, who was a big bruiser of a man; Auntie Peggy, and the brilliant Uncle Tony, who taught me how to 'not give a shit.' I can't remember them all though – it seemed there were hundreds of them.

Dad came home from work once – I think he was working for Wall's Ice Cream at the time – and I apparently ran up to him and flung my arms round him as he came walking down the street.

'Hello Dad,' I shouted, 'are you coming back to stay?'

Dad used to work every hour that God sent. And he drank all the whisky the Devil sent!

When I was five, I started going to school. Mum took me down for the first time to Kidbrooke Park Primary School, Hargood Road, Blackheath. It was near our home but when she stood outside and let me go into the classroom on my own, I thought, 'Oh my Gawd, this is awful. My Mum's leaving me here.'

But I quite liked it. I got on well at school and found that I was a pretty good footballer. I used to enjoy walking down to school, even though I didn't have proper shoes – just plimsolls. When I came home my Dad would whiten them. He had this whitener stuff in a little jar, which came with a sponge on the end of a bit of wire. The things you remember.

In the fourth year, before I left to go to secondary school, I decided that I particularly hated school dinners. I'd get my shilling to pay for my school dinner, and I'd tell the teacher I was going home for lunch.

Then, my friend Roger Mason and I would race down to the shops instead. We'd 'lig' around for an hour and just buy sweets. Once, I bought a cap bomb, an amazing thing that you don't get any more.

Finally we got caught, of course. I don't quite know how we were found out but Mr Offered the headmaster gave us the cane and Christ did it hurt! Three whacks on each hand. I'd never felt pain like it in my life and I didn't fancy it again.

Luckily, I wasn't too bothered because I'd just fallen madly in love with a girl called Susan Sergeant, a beautiful redhead who lived opposite the gates of Kidbrooke Park Junior Mixed, in Hargood Road. Susan was my first-ever romance. I don't think I ever kissed her or anything. I was just in love with her.

Susan and I lived about 500 yards apart, as the crow flies from her back garden. In the evenings, I used to sit in my Dad's bedroom and flash the room's light on and off, while Susan used to flash her Mum's light on and off. We were 11 year olds, making love by Morse code. They were great times.

By the time I was in the third year at school I was the first boy in my year to get into the proper school football team. I loved football so much and it was great to be known as being good at something.

We had two trees in Holburne Road, one on each side of the street, which served as our goalposts. Most days I'd get home, bolt down my tea, then play football.

I quite often came home from school to find a note waiting for me. There was a key on a bit of string, dangling down the inside of our front door letterbox. On the end of the string, I'd find a note asking me to pop up to the shops to buy Dad a pork chop or a nice chump chop for his tea. I thought there was an animal called 'a chump'.

After I'd got the tea, I would be home alone until Mum got back from work. She worked at Woolworth's in Lewisham, so she would get home at about 5.30 pm. Dad would get home a lot later in the evening.

One night, we heard his motorbike and sidecar pull up. He'd spent all night in the Sun in the Sands pub, at Shooters Hill. He was pissed and had driven home on his motorbike. With all that drink inside him, I think that motorbike used to drive Dad home on its own. He stood there swaying outside our house as my brother Billy opened the door for him

… at which point, my Dad's trousers fell off. It was the highlight of brother Billy's life explaining that magical moment to his friends.

Billy my elder brother was very close to me and he still is to this day. All my family are really, but Billy was a very deep soul. In fact, if Mum or Dad ever told me off, I would cry and Billy would sit on the stairs and cry with me. When I was a bit older, Billy went off to join the Royal Navy. He came back after a couple of years but it seemed to me like he'd been away for a lifetime. He brought me back a cap gun, a real solid 'go-faster' cap gun which he'd bought for me in Hong Kong. I would run around Blackheath shooting everyone. I was a real little soldier.

I had a great life as a kid, full of adventures. We couldn't afford to buy a new bike, so the kids in our street used to make their own transport. We'd make things called 'trolleys' but they were more like a couple of old pram wheels knocked together with a soap box.

We would play hide-and-seek and get up to lots of mischief. We'd go camping in my friend Ronnie Lee's back garden, about four of us in a tent.

As soon as the adults went to bed, off we would go on these great adventures, climbing over people's gardens and scrumping their apples.

Mrs Lewis, who lived opposite, had a pond full of beautiful goldfish. We nicked them all, and then climbed up a tree next day to watch what happened when she came out to try feeding her fish – in vain.

I also liked to collect birds' eggs. I don't know if it's allowed nowadays, but back then we all used to go up the woods and collect birds eggs. We'd usually end up with a blackbird's egg first. I also bagged loads of chaffinch eggs. We would take them home and empty them, by putting a pin in either side of the egg and blowing them through. Then we'd varnish them and put them on display. I used to love getting my collection of eggs out and counting how many I'd got.

It was a riot on Bonfire Night. We would head up to the woods, about a mile up the road, and pull old trees back to our dump, where we often played. Then we'd go round knocking at people's doors, asking, 'Anything for the bonfire?'

We'd set the bonfire, then build a little camp on the side and sit in it. If someone had set fire to it, we would have been burnt to death.

I always looked forward to Bonfire Night more than anything else. Some silly bastard from the rival bonfire down the road would sometimes come and set fire to ours, ages before it was time to burn it, just because he was annoyed that we'd dared to have a bigger bonfire than theirs.

I was a bit hacked off that I didn't have any shoes. The 'tally' man came round, Mr Leggit, on a Thursday night and he would get money or a provident cheque, I believe it was called.

When you got the cheque, you could go and spend it in the shops that would accept them. Then you would pay on the 'never-never'. Mum bought me a pair of shoes and the night I got them I went down on the bus to Greenwich to go swimming with the Scouts. I couldn't stop looking at these shoes. I thought, 'I've cracked it.'

I looked the absolute bollocks! When Susan Sergeant saw these new shoes, she'd fall into my arms. They felt quite uncomfortable actually because I was always used to wearing plimsolls. But now we had shoes, I'd turned the corner. I was growing up and I didn't look like an extra for *Tom Brown's Schooldays* any more. I'd arrived – in size fours.

We weren't *really* that skint. I didn't have a great many presents but I had tons and tons of love from Mum – and Dad as much as he could give, I suppose.

Saturday nights, when my parents went out together, were great because they would get ready at 7.30 pm and then head off to the pub, leaving me there with my cousin Julie, Uncle George's daughter.

Mum and Dad would get home at about 11.30 pm and bring a crate of beer with them. Often, some other people would come back too and I used to love that. People dancing and singing and putting records on.

Since I can remember, I was always very fond of drumming and tapping things. Mum and Dad saved up and bought me a drum kit. It was red and I used to bash the hell out of it all the time. I would like showing off to Mum, and it must have sounded awful. I'd also play drums while miming to some Beach Boys records that I was really in to at the time.

The only thing I was short of … was a *show* really. Even as a little kid, after my parents had bought me a little Tommy Steele guitar, I'd sit up by our front gate, entertaining passers-by. I guess I was a little lad who just wanted to show off.

At school, I'd become a bit of a teacher's pet. At the age of eleven I'd gone on to St Austen's Catholic School. The rest of my family were brought up as Catholics and, although I was never baptised, Mum was determined that I would go to a Catholic school.

We went down there for an interview with a Mr Sankey, who was my brothers' teacher in Woolwich all those years ago.

'So long as Cameron learns to become a Catholic, he can join,' he said.

So I was sent round to another kid's house in Kidbrooke to learn all about the Bible. It was a nightmare.

One of our first family holidays was to a place in Norfolk called Potter Heigham. We used to pack Dad's van full of kit and all sorts of camping and fishing gear and off we'd go, me, Mum and Dad.

Dad, of course, would go to the pub in the evening and I'd sit outside with my half of cider and fish. One year, I headed up to Great Yarmouth with him, camping. That's when we met these couple of blokes from Durham, who were drinking in the pub where we were. They asked Dad to go back and have a drink with them on their Hoseason's boat.

While we were there, Dad said to me, 'Go on Cameron, do some impressions for them.'

So I did a few impressions, told some jokes and was generally showing off. I don't know where my ability to do impressions came from. I seemed to just be able to do people's voices. It all started when I discovered how much I enjoyed taking the mickey out of my teachers at school.

Later, my voices extended to people I'd seen on the telly. When everyone came home from the pub, I would get them all laughing by doing impressions of people like Dudley Moore and Peter Cook, especially his deadpan E.L. Wisty character. I also did a mean Kenneth Williams and I got his 'Oooooh Matron, Nooooh' down to a fine art.

The guys asked me if I was in the Scouts. I nodded and then they asked me, 'How would you like to be in *The Gang Show*?'

I'd seen *The Gang Show*, that marvellous show full of boy scouts, because it was on once a year on TV. But I didn't realise that for two weeks a year it also ran as a proper theatre show at the Golder's Green Hippodrome.

The next thing we knew, my parents received a letter asking if they could they bring their son Cameron to the London Palladium. So Mum and Dad took me up to London to perform an audition for *The Gang Show*. They took a photo that day and I still have the picture hanging on my wall at home.

Down in the bar at the Palladium I met the great Ralph Reader. I did all my impressions all over again just for him. Then we got *another* letter saying, 'Will you please turn up at Baden Powell House, Kensington and come to rehearsals?'

I wore a white T-shirt, blue shorts and The Gang Show scarf they sent me. I had wondered how the hell I was going to get there but they'd said there was a scout leader in the show who lived round the corner from us in Kidbrooke. He was called Gerry Hart and he used to pick me up in his Anglia car. After rehearsals, he took me home, as well.

That was in 1965 when I was twelve, the age I got my first break in showbiz.

I'll never forget my first appearance at the Golder's Green Hippodrome. I went there on my own, got on the train at Kidbrooke, travelled up to Charing Cross, then caught the Northern Line to Golder's Green – every night, in my boy scout's outfit.

My little spot on the show involved walking out on stage and introducing ... er ... nothing really. My job was just called 'introducing'. Out on stage strode this little kid (me), and I just did my five minutes of impressions. They were pretty much rubbish really but I suppose it looked a bit novel. I was only twelve but I thought to myself at the time, 'This is great. Show business is marvellous.'

At home, I kept practising my other showbiz skills and continued playing with drums in the front room. I also told them at school that I had been picked to be in *The Gang Show* and, come October, I'd have to finish school early.

I used to run home, get myself changed and then belt down to Golder's Green Hippodrome. Once, my set master Mr Trinder came down to see the show.

Mum and Dad were obviously very proud of my role in *The Gang Show*. They didn't imagine that it would lead anywhere but they were delighted to come and watch the performances.

'I'll be in the audience tonight, so look out for me,' Dad said.

We drove up in Dad's van. I had to join in singing a song, which was being sung by Peter Straker who, funnily enough, I still know. Peter's song was called 'Freedom'. We were all dressed as slaves, trying to look as brown as we could.

'During the song, flick your lighter,' I said to Dad, 'so I'll know where you're sitting in the audience.'

Well, he did – except that he flicked the lighter *and left the flame on*. From the stage, I could clearly see my Dad's face lit up grotesquely in the darkness.

All my family liked me being in the show – not that there was any money in it, not even a tenner. But it wasn't a huge deal to us.

'You may be in *The Gang Show*,' Dad would say. 'You're quite a talented lad but keep your bloody feet on the ground, son, and think about getting a job.'

The following year, when I was 13, as well as doing *The Gang Show*, I also went along to ATV for *The Billy Cotton Band Show* and Lesley Crowther was on the bill. Terry Scott was there too, doing that 'Cor, my bruvver' thing.

I had to do a little single spot with Billy Cotton. He was a famous name in broadcasting and a great big man who had a nose on his face that looked like it had been soaked in two bottles of gin for 30 years. He ran a big band and was also a bit of a comedian-cum-celebrity in the late 1950s, and early '60s. One of his offspring, Bill Cotton Junior, ended up as one of the big cheeses running the BBC. They were a very big show business family.

The late Leslie Crowther was a great old comedian whom I went on to work with in later years. He was a very charming man.

They asked for someone to do a line and I immediately stepped forward. I forget what the line was but I stood there and looked up at Billy Cotton's nose – and delivered my little line.

'There ya go,' I thought, 'stardom.'

Then one day, they wanted me to go up to London for an audition for *Oliver!* Someone wrote to me and said, 'We'd like you to come to an audition for the film based on Lionel Bart's hit West End musical.' I did my audition and I sang a song called 'Alicante', from *The Gang Show*. Unfortunately, it was a key too high for me and it sounded horrible. Plus, I couldn't dance.

But the casting director, who was a nice woman, said to me afterwards, 'We think you'd be a good Artful Dodger rather than an Oliver.'

Time went by and Mark Lester ended up playing Oliver and Jack Wild was picked for the Artful Dodger. Me? I played hookey from school and started smoking. I went fishing for most of the rest of my fourth year, really.

I left the scouts because I got fed up with them. I decided that fishing and playing the drums were more interesting that prancing around like one of those prats in *The Gang Show*.

I'd still much rather go fishing than have to stand on a stage telling people jokes. I mean I admit, yes, I enjoy receiving the adulation of the public. But you can get a bit bored with that after a while.

However, telling jokes also leads to other things, like nice houses and prettier women. But I didn't want a house or women back then. I just wanted to fish. And being in *The Gang Show* didn't help catch bigger fish. So I quit.

Towards the end of my fourth year at school, in about 1968, I started going to acting school, down in Woolwich. This move was instigated by my teacher, Mr Wray, whom we all thought was a bit of a hippie. He was actually a nice guy. Everyone in my class nicknamed him 'Bango' for some unknown reason.

I bumped into my mates as I stood at the bus stop one day, waiting to catch a bus down to Woolwich to go to stage school. 'Where are you going?' they asked.

I said I was going to guitar lessons. I was too embarrassed to admit to them that I was going to night school to learn how to act.

We used to hop off school quite a bit. At lunchtime me and my friend Danny Scott would go down to Manz's Pie & Mash shop in Woolwich. Afterwards Danny would go round and have his hair done at the hairdressers, a local salon named Maison Maurice, which was run by two young guys, one of whom was called Terry, the other Malcolm. I quite liked the atmosphere in there, so I asked them if I could be their Saturday boy. They agreed and that's what I did.

I used to get into trouble at school all the time. I was dropped from the football team for smoking and, in the end, I just decided I couldn't be bothered with it all.

I was just about to get the cane from my class teacher Mr Scripture and I thought, 'Oh, sod that.'

That guy could cane for England. 'Bend over,' he said.

'No, sir, I'm not doing that.' I replied. 'I'm off.'

And, with that, I walked out.

I'd been ordered to report to the headmaster's room. But between leaving Mr Scripture's classroom and reaching the headmaster's, I decided, then and there, that I'd had enough. Instead of knocking on the headmaster's door, I walked straight out, got on a bus and went to Catford, where Mum worked in a laundry in Brownhill Road. When I arrived, I told her straight.

'I'm not going back to school again, Mum,' I said. 'That is it. I can't stand it any more. I'm not learning anything. All I'm doing is getting the cane and messing about. I'm not even in the football team any more. I'm not in *The Gang Show* any more. What is the point? Let me leave and get a job.'

I just wanted to explain to Mum that the sooner I was grown up the better. Like all mothers, she was concerned. But then in those days, most kids were leaving school at 15. I was just leaving a little bit earlier. Mum was fine about it and, in the end, I just stopped going to school altogether. I'd finally had enough.

I don't think we told Dad. I just went fishing for a couple of months.

When I got my first job, stacking shelves in the Co-op, I still kept playing the drums at home and on Saturday nights, when Mum and Dad started going to a new pub called the Director General in Woolwich, I sometimes used to go down there with them.

There was a woman drummer there who I used to watch. The band had a pianist, a lead singer named George, and this woman drummer who was absolutely useless. But my Mum loved her.

One night, I jumped up and gave her drum kit the Full Monty, and ended on a bit of a drum solo as well. The crowd in there loved it and at the end of the night, when the woman had packed up and left, I tried my luck with the governor of the pub, who, I used to joke, looked just like the African Grey parrot he kept on the bar.

'I'll play drums for you,' I said to him, 'but you've got to buy me a drum kit.'

To my great joy, he agreed to lend me £70 to buy a drum kit – and, into the bargain, he paid me £4 a night to play there. Mind you, he docked £2 a night of it to go towards paying him back the £70.

And that was that.

I played drums there for ages. I used to finish playing drums at the pub on a Saturday night at 11 o'clock, run like hell down to Woolwich Arsenal to catch the train to Dartford, then walk the three-and-a-half miles to Horton Kirby to go fishing overnight for carp.

Earning a few quid playing drums of an evening was all well and good but I needed to save up more money to pay off that £70. One day my mate Tommy came up with a solution.

'I've got a great job in the West End,' he said. 'Why don't you clock on with this employment agency in the West End and see if you can get a job?'

It sounded interesting, so I went along to the agency on Charing Cross Road and fixed myself up with a job as a messenger for ten quid a week. That meant a rise from £4.

I was working for Mill Bank Travel, 104 New Bond Street and – do you know what? – I *still* bump into people today who remember me from there.

By the time I turned 16, I was playing drums in the pub and working for Mill Bank Travel as a messenger boy, walking all over London delivering people's tickets. I used to love walking round London taking in the architecture and all the sights. I always managed a bit of a fiddle.

'You'll have to deliver these tickets *really quickly*,' my boss would say.

'Can I have a taxi fare, then, sir?' I'd reply.

'Yes. Here's five bob for a taxi,' he'd always say.

Then off I'd run as fast as I could and keep the five bob. It was a neat scam.

While I was working for Mill Bank Travel, my biggest claim to fame was that, during my two weeks' holiday, I went to Horton Kirby, my old haunt from my school days, and caught a 21.5 pound carp. It was the record for the lake at the time. There's a picture of it in the paper. A proud day for me.

I landed something else at around that time, equally impressive – my first proper girlfriend.

Her name was Jane. She was the most beautiful girl I had ever seen. She made Susan Sergeant look like Sid James. Jane had really short hair, was always chewing gum and had a boyish sort of face. She had a bit of a flat chest but had a great figure. She used to wear these great big flared trousers and was so full of confidence, she'd walk along like a man magnet. Actually, she was Terry Honeyman's girlfriend. Terry was my big mate from up the road, and I nicked her off of him. I had my first leg-over with Jane and it was *great*. I was 15 at the time.

Afterwards, one of my mates said to me, 'Did you know that when you've had your first shag, your dick gets bigger.'

So, I quickly wandered into the toilets to have a look.

And I'm still looking.

One day, Jane took me by surprise.

'I think I'm pregnant,' she announced.

'Great,' I replied. 'That's it.'

I was thrilled. I could stay with this woman for the rest of my life, I thought, and have my own family. She could never leave me now. She was having my baby ...

That was the start of it, I think. That was the first time I can remember thinking, 'If you're madly in love, have a baby, get married and then they won't leave.' That's taking them hostage really, isn't it?

But Jane was winding me up – she wasn't pregnant at all. I don't know why she said it. She probably just missed her period or was just trying to fish to see whether I was in love with her.

Jane and I drifted apart and, about the same time, something else significant happened. I started to drink pints. When I started playing drums in the pub, I'd sussed out that when people asked me, 'Do you want a pint?' or 'Do you fancy a drink?' if I said, 'Yes please, I'll have a brown ale,' I used to get just one bottle of brown ale, which is a half. And if I said I wanted a pint of brown, it would look as if I was greedy. But if I said I wanted a brown and mild, it would mean they'd have to give me a pint. Ha ha!

I quite enjoyed the beer. I liked the taste of it although I could never drink more than about three pints before I got pissed.

It made me feel grown up. Also, around this time, I'd started to wear cardigans, like my uncle's, and roll my own cigarettes, again to try and be grown up. I just wanted to stop being a kid.

My next brainwave was to join the Navy. Looking back now, I don't really know *why* I wanted to. I was just fed up. There was nothing doing for me around there. I'd had my chance in *The Gang Show* and that had fallen apart. I'd had my chance to marry Jane after she'd said she was pregnant – but then she said she *wasn't*. So, I thought to myself, 'You're getting nowhere here, Cameron. Do something with your life.'

I was fed up with being a messenger boy and one day, when I was delivering a parcel up in town, I headed up to the Royal Navy building Fleet House, in High Holborn and picked up some forms. Later, I spoke to my brother Bill, who'd been in the Navy for twelve years and loved it. I filled in my forms and turned up for my medical.

I will never forget the doctor looking up my arse with a torch. To this day, I couldn't tell you what he was looking for. Locker space probably.

So, there I was, all set to join the Navy. I told all the mates I was hanging around at the time with that I was off to join the Navy and then, out of the blue, I bumped into this girl, who said, 'Cameron, whatever you do, *don't* join the Navy.'

I went all twinkly-eyed when I saw her beautiful face and so I said, 'Er ... OK.'

And with that, I gave up my career in the Navy. Just like that. All for this girl whose name I can't even remember now. It was all *your* fault, you nameless girl, you.

Wanting to join the Navy was a cry for help, I think. I know it sounds ridiculous but it was like a suicide note. 'If you don't get your act together, Mum and Dad ...' or 'If I don't get a girlfriend who loves me' (because Jane had gone) 'I'll join the Navy. That'll teach you all.'

I threatened them with joining the Forces and then I met this girl and instantly fell in love. Then I didn't have to join the Navy any more. I could just have this girl and she'd make me happy. All the miserable times at home would be made up for in the back of someone's car with this girl.

I was footloose and fancy free but I didn't want to be. I was desperate to settle down. I mean all my life I've been lovelorn. All my life, I've been looking round the corner, looking for maybe something that doesn't exist. Even if I've got everything I need, like people tell me I now have, they still look in my eyes and say, 'Jim, there's a sadness there.'

I think that started years ago, a sadness for something that I don't have ... and I don't know what that something is.

So I was still working for Mill Bank Travel but eventually I handed in my notice. The terribly nice managing director, Mr Tampin, took me to one side – we used to call him Mr Tampax, by the way, but I digress – and he said to me, 'If you're not going to join the Navy, then why don't you come back and learn to be a printer? Do our Rank Xerox course and you can handle all our printing.'

So, that's what I did. I sat a course – I've still got the certificate hanging up in my loo at home – and that was me fixed up. Then they said to me, 'How about a job as an air ticket clerk?'

So I went and worked for this bloke called Pierre, a French bloke who was based on the first floor. He was a great laugh. For lunch, he ate chicken and coleslaw French bread sandwiches, washed down with a gin and tonic. Together we used to spend our days writing out air tickets.

Also during that time, in the same office as Mill Bank Travel, I met Mr Bryce. He was a nice man, who set up something called the Transatlantic Brides Association. You could buy cheap air tickets and fly to America.

Through that company, Mum and Dad got on an aeroplane (for the first time in Dad's life) and flew to America to visit my sister Jean, who lived in Cleveland in a place called Sheffield Lake.

Mr Bryce took me to the airport to wave them off. I'd never been on a plane myself and I used to have these brilliant ideas about stealing plane tickets from the bottom of the pile, stamping them up, writing myself out a ticket to somewhere exotic. While I was gone, I imagined, no-one would know I'd been away.

The trip to America was brilliant for Mum and Dad. I knew how nervous Dad was going to be. He started drinking *a whole week* before he had to turn up at Heathrow.

Everything was panning out fine in my life. I was now an air ticket clerk. I had a bit of money. I could go fishing. I played the drums and got bought drinks. The trouble was, I couldn't wait to spread my wings. I decided living at home wasn't for me. Mum and Dad were constantly arguing and Dad's drunkenness was getting on my nerves. They never spoke to one another – she never went to the pub with him – and that made for a dodgy atmosphere at home.

I argued with them all, although the rows never turned nasty. I decided I was going to pack up working for Mill Bank Travel and try and move on.

At a party one evening, I met a girl called Sue Walpole, who seemed very nice. I was going out with an Indian girl at the time, named Darleen, but the next thing I knew, Sue started phoning me up and I saw her once or twice.

I had another row with Mum and Dad, and said, 'Oh, nuts to you all!' and I went to live in Brockley with my brother John and his wife Barbara.

John found me a job at Wall's Ice Cream, where he worked. I became the cashier. When all the ice cream men came back in, I'd cash up all their money. I was totally useless at it. John would get in late every day because he had to drive over from Brockley. From south east London all the way to Barking. The job quickly became a nightmare.

I started going out with Sue and she came to stay with me at my brother's a couple of times.

Then, one day, Sue asked me, 'Why don't you ask my Mum if you can stay with me at our house in Woolwich?'

I asked her Mum, who was a widow and she agreed. But she said I'd have to sleep on the sofa. That was better than nothing.

Suddenly, life was great again. Sue and I were together. I was still seventeen when two things happened – I got a new job and Sue became pregnant.

I had a job working for a company called Thomas Moore's in Chancery Lane. I'd really landed it because I'd learnt how to work a Xerox machine. I think I was on about £17 pounds a week then, which wasn't much considering the financial responsibilities that lay ahead, with Sue being pregnant.

I just said right out to her, 'OK, that'll do me. We must get married, then. We'll have to get married.'

We were married in November 1971 at Woolwich Town Hall. On the way there, I asked Dad, 'What shall I do, Dad?'

'Keep the fucking cab going past the Register Office,' he replied.

I did the deed, tied the knot, and then, in April the following year, Sarah, my daughter, arrived.

With Sue being pregnant came more problems. She became very possessive, to the extent that she got upset when I had to go to work in the morning. She'd run down to the station, chasing me in her nightdress and slippers, shouting, 'Don't leave me, don't leave me!'

It was all a little bit much for young Cameron but I was looking forward to the birth of my daughter. It would mean I'd become a man.

Sarah was born down in Plumstead. When I took Sue into the hospital, she was in agony. I felt so helpless and I was so in love with her. The nurse told me nothing would happen for ages, so I told Sue that I'd drive home, have my tea and then come back. So in my little Triumph Herald that I'd bought for £70, which had no tax or insurance, I drove to Mum and Dad's to get something to eat.

By the time I got back to Plumstead, Sue had had the gas and air.

'I'm still in pain but the pain's miles away,' she said.

Then, in the early morning, I watched Sue give birth. She was pushing and shoving, and the nurse said, 'Look! There's a lovely little crop of red hair popping up.'

Awful. Then out came little Sarah and I gave Sue a kiss. They put the baby in Sue's arms for a while, then placed her gently in a little crib in another room.

As I went to leave, I stared down and saw her little ears all folded over and I just thought it was wonderful. There was another little me in the world. I didn't know then that it would all end and be taken away. At that moment, I felt that God was smiling at me ... until I went back to the car park and found that my fucking battery was flat!

Dad had to come and pick me up in his van at six in the morning. He drove me home. Exhausted, I sat down in the kitchen and Mum put a big pile of bacon and eggs down in front of me.

'You're a man now,' she said.

Some man ... I burst into tears!

Not that I was home much. Like my Dad, I seemed to spend time working or in the pub. I was still playing the drums and I was now working for Rank Xerox in Store Street, just off Tottenham Court Road. Trouble was, it was night work. My shift ran from 5.30 pm to 1.30 in the morning. Not ideal.

I used to drive up there in my old Cortina and come back at 1.30 in the morning. After three months of that Sue cracked.

'I've had enough,' she said. 'That's it.'

We just didn't get on. We'd stopped sleeping together or having sex and she just wanted a bit more than I could offer. She was a year older than me. I was just 18 – and 18-year-old boys are like 14-year-old kids, while 18-year-old women are ... quite delicious, actually. So therein lay the problem.

I was living with her Mum. Then we tried living with *my* Mum and Dad, and then she went back to *her* Mum's and I stayed with *my* Mum and Dad. But it was no good. Within a few months, less than a year, we'd drifted apart.

It was all a bit of a mess and a terrible upheaval. But I just put a brave face on it and blamed her for all sorts of things. Then she started to see another guy called Tony who eventually went to live with Sue and brought up my daughter Sarah quite well, even though he was a West Ham fan.

I thought I'd got the rest of my life in front of me. I felt my daughter would always be there for me. But I just couldn't bring myself to go back and visit. I resigned myself to the fact that I'd turned a page in my life and I had to get on with it.

Then, out of the blue, I got a letter from the council saying we'd been given a flat at Thamesmead. So I raced back to Sue and said, 'Look, come on. Let's get it together.'

But she wouldn't give it a go. It was a pretty traumatic moment for me. I knelt down on the old kitchen floor and begged and cried. All to no avail.

Recently, we talked about our break-up.

'Sue, why did you bin me?' I said.

'Well, you were going with other women.'

'I swear to God I wasn't.'

'Well, you probably weren't – but you *wanted to*.'

What chance does that give you!?

I was 18 now and I didn't have anywhere to live. I was still working nightshifts and still playing drums in the pub. I'd been out of school for three years. I'd realised my marriage hadn't worked but there was nothing I could do about it.

'And in the end,' I thought to myself, 'I've got to get on with my life.'

So what could I do? I could play drums, therefore, I wanted to be famous. I wanted to be a famous drummer. It was the beginning of the Seventies, and we were all into Roxy Music. My favourite band, Emerson Lake and Palmer had just formed. They were my idols. My mates – Tommy, Larry, Ronny – and I used to go to our local pubs, watch the bands play and dream that, one day, we'd be famous.

I had long gingery awful wavy hair. So I thought I would turn myself into Brian Connolly. Not the comedian, the singer from Sweet. So I had it cut shortish on the top but I kept it long. It was well down below my armpits and I dyed it from a peroxide bottle, bright blonde.

I must have been nine and a half stone, I had long blonde hair, down to my arse nearly, and I used to wear those black hugging jeans and high heeled boots. I looked a right freak – and on top of that I used to drive a truck for National Carriers, in Barking. When I pulled up somewhere to deliver a parcel, all these lorry drivers would blow kisses at me. But I didn't care. They were just lorry drivers – but I was a drummer who just happened to be driving a lorry.

I also bought myself a little motorbike 'on the never never'. I signed up for the motorbike and said my brother Billy would be guarantor. Billy went mental at me when he found out what I'd done. He said he could lose his job. But the deed was done. I used to drive over to Barking every morning and in the evenings, meet up with my friends.

I'd sit around with them and I'd smoke the odd joint. I'd go and buy a pound deal somewhere and smoke all these bloody drugs. It seemed to be the thing to do. It was fun.

I sold my motorbike, without even paying off the rest of the debt, and with the money I raised, I was able to put down a deposit on a flat, 216 Burridge Road, for me, Kevin, Ronny and Tommy to live in.

Then I decided that I'd start to buy grass. I went down to this place in Brownhill Road, opposite where Mum worked, and bought what used to be called 'a quarter of a weight' – I'd imagine that was hippie talk for a quarter of a pound of grass in a big carrier bag. I'd make it up in little envelopes and sell it to the guys in the pub. Just my mates, I wasn't hanging round the street corners or the schools. But people used to complain.

'Oh no, not *grass* again,' they'd say. 'Ain't you got any black? Ain't you got any Red Leb? You're useless, you are!'

If the truth be known, I wasn't a very good drug dealer.

I had great times in that flat. I was my own boss. Ronny brought in his hi-fi system, which was fantastic.

We all liked the same music, bands like Emerson Lake and Palmer, King Crimson and Pink Floyd. You could sit round, smoke these joints and then get some speed, these wonderful amphetamine tablets. I used to buy them off people in a pub in Shooter's Hill, where I used to live. I loved those pills. They turned me into Superman.

I thought, 'Christ. These are great. I'll take ten of these.'

They were only £1 for ten. So, I asked the bloke who sold them to me, 'How much and where do you buy 'em from?'

'I get 'em from Erith,' he replied. 'Erith is the drug centre of the world,' he told me, which seemed unlikely, but there you go.

He suggested I buy a thousand pills for forty quid. Well, I worked out that was sixty quid profit and I decided that grass was for kids. I was *now* in the pill business.

Off I went with my money and bought probably a couple of thousand pills. I spent all night wrapping them up into little piles of ten, each wrapped in silver paper.

Staying up all night didn't bother me, of course, because I'd taken all these bloody pills myself.

What made matters worse for me was that I was never one of those people who could have *one* of anything. So when it came to drugs, for example, while other people took ten tablets, I took *twenty*. And *one* of these tablets would keep you awake all night.

It was the fear of not feeling good that made me want to take more than other people. As soon as this drug started to wear off, I couldn't *bear* the normality. I think it was something about the rush of those speed tablets starting to work that got me. You could talk absolute bollocks to people and make yourself exciting and listen to their bollocks back and find that just as exciting.

It was like being the life and soul of the party. You were slightly breathless all the time, slightly in a state of euphoria. Everything about you was fine, except for your dick, which shrivelled up, of course. My music tastes changed as well. Instead of sitting round listening to Melanie, I really got into ELP and Roxy Music.

I even had my hair cut much shorter like David Bowie and had red streaks put in it. It looked like someone had hit me over the head with a pint pot and cut my head open. I loved it. I really looked forward to taking those ten tablets and getting on with it. The night lasted for ever and every bit of it was exciting. One weekend, I took *250* amphetamine tablets. Understandably, I ended up in the local hospital because my throat had completely swollen up. I couldn't swallow and when the nurse stuck a needle in my arse, she asked me why I'd taken so many drugs.

I didn't really have an answer for her. I said to this nurse I wanted a treatment. I didn't want her opinion. I wanted to be able to take drugs, not to stop taking them.

I just didn't want to die in the process.

3

There's no business ...

'I just don't know why I took so many drugs!'

'How old were you?' she said.

'Nineteen,' I replied.

'And how old are you now?' the nurse asked me again.

'Forty,' I replied, feeling humble.

'And how long has it been since you've taken speed?'

'Well, I haven't taken any drugs for ages and ages,' I said, 'not until this Christmas when I decided they would help me get out of the nightmare I was in with my wife.'

Day Two in the clinic

I got up and had to report for an interview with Anne the nurse, a woman with a constant look of concern on her face, even when nothing was wrong. She seemed to me to be utterly determined to prove to everyone that they were addicted to everything in the world.

To this day, I still think that was how she regarded her job. You'd check into the clinic with an alcohol problem and come out addicted to sex, you'd be bulimic, you'd be anorexic, you'd be co-dependent, you'd be a drug addict, and so on. If you weren't she'd convince you otherwise.

You had to own up to every single little tablet that you'd ever taken in your entire life. You had to confess it all to this woman.

At first, I didn't know whether to lie or make it up, so I just told her the truth. I told her that I'd been married at 17 — so she put me down as a sex addict.

Then she asked me, 'What tablets did you take? ... How many did you take?

... When did you have your first ever drink?' and 'When was your first blackout?'

I told her that my first blackout was when I went to a party in Woolwich with Terry Honeyman, my friend from Holburne Road. His ex-girlfriend Jane had been there and she was now my girlfriend. Terry had got a bit nasty towards me. (Isn't it funny how guys who've been great mates for years can still fall out over a women? They've got you, haven't they, these girls?!)

We shared a half bottle of whisky. We went to get it from the pub and we sent our mate Micky Hill to get it because he looked the oldest. We started to drink it and it was fucking horrible tasting. I can imagine the first man who ever invented whisky. How on earth did he not spit it out and say, 'Back to the drawing board'?

But most of all the taste reminded me of the smell of my father.

I was on top of a bus and throwing up. The next thing I knew I was waking up on Jane's settee. Her Mum and Dad came down in the morning and said I must have been in Jane's bedroom during the night because there was some sick on the bed. All they could hear all night was the toilet lid being slammed down.

That was my first ever recollection of feeling really awful and having a blackout. It was half way between being unconscious and conscious. You just drink so much that you should be unconscious and asleep but you're just unconscious and walking around. In this case, I was on a bus – apparently. I could have been on Concorde and not known.

I told the nurse all this and she made a careful note of all the things I'd said and done.

Next, I met the person who was going be my counsellor. His name was Steve. He had reddish hair and looked quite fit. He had a smiley face and used to grin quite a bit. I think that was part of his training. He really seemed to enjoy his job. But it seemed to me that his bedside manner towards me was different. He wasn't nice to me like other people were. I mean, come on, I was famous, I was Jim Fucking Davidson. Why didn't this bloke treat me with a bit of respect? He knew his job, this guy, and I referred to him as 'council public toilet paper' – he took no shit.

At first, I thought he must be a doctor, or one of the trainee doctors. He sat me down for a one-to-one chat and we began talking.

'Hi,' he said. 'I'm Steve and I'm an alcoholic as well.'

I was a bit shocked and confused.

'Sorry mate,' I said, 'I thought you were a doctor!'

'No, there's no doctors here,' he said. 'You saw the one doctor who examined you when you checked in. They did tests on you and we'll await the results of your liver test later. But I'm no doctor. I'm just an alcoholic, same as you.'

You could have knocked me down ... How could a clinic be run by alcoholics?

'Well what are you doing here?' I asked.

'I'm a counsellor now because I've gone through it.' Steve explained. 'I'm here because I want to help you get through what you're going through.'

'So, can you give me the pill to make me stop doing all this then?'

'No.'

And then Steve began to explain what alcoholism is all about. And this is the amazing thing that struck me. He explained to me that if you're an alcoholic, you have to first admit to yourself that you are an alcoholic and your life is unmanageable. Well, frankly, I already knew my life was unmanageable! But an alcoholic doesn't quite truly understand that at first. Obviously, I preferred life being pissed to life being sober, so I suppose that put me into the bracket.

Then Steve said something that quite baffled me. 'Thing is, Jim,' he said, 'alcohol is only a symptom of the illness.'

'Well, that's a bit obvious, isn't it?' I said.

'Alcoholism is really all about personality disorders,' Steve went on. 'They are what create the alcoholism and they manifest themselves in the various things you do. You spend too much, you run around saying, "I want it! I want it now! I've got to have this now or my life will end! I've got to be the centre of attention! I've got to have that warm rosy glow around me all the time otherwise life is just unbearable." Who have you met in here so far?' Steve continued.

'I've met a quite few people,' I replied, mentioning some of the girls with eating disorders.

'Do you think they're different to you?' asked Steve.

Easy question.

'Sure!' I said. 'Sure they're different from me. I don't have an eating disorder. I don't eat when I'm drunk or hungover because I feel too ill. But—'

'But their illness is exactly the same as yours,' Steve continued, 'except that their symptom is different from yours. And what about the heroin addicts? They different from you?'

Easy again.

'Well,' I said, 'I'm not a drug addict either, mate!'

'It's exactly the same,' Steve said. 'It's just that their drug of choice is heroin. Your drug of choice is alcohol.'

Oh.

I didn't know what else to say. This guy was talking bollocks. Not 'drug of choice', not 'drugs' ... a pint of beer! Or, in my case, a lot of whisky.

It was time for some straight talking with Steve.

'I've taken coke for the last couple of weeks,' I explained, 'and I used to take it years ago when I was a kid. Recently, life has become impossible for me. I've got in a terrible rut.'

Steve nodded and gave me some paper and told me to go away and write down all the damage I thought I'd done because of my drinking. Start at the beginning, they said, whenever you started having these problems.

So I went away and spent the entire afternoon writing.

Damage, damage and more damage. All this stuff that I'd done, the things I felt I'd messed up, situations I felt I'd played all wrong. It all spilled out on to the pages. Steve came back to me and had a look at what I'd written. He shook his head.

'No, no, no!' he said. 'That's not damage. Imagine the damage you've caused to other people. Imagine the damage you've caused to your Mum and Dad through worrying about you. Imagine the damage you've caused to other people like your sisters, your brothers and the people you work with, the people you've insulted.'

Phew!

So this time, I went away and wrote for a couple of days! I just wrote out heaps and heaps of all this stuff.

Then we had some group meetings, where there were six of us sitting around, just exactly how one could imagine it in an over-dramatised American film. It was just like in the movies, where you sit round and say, 'Hi my name's Jim and I'm an alcoholic,' and they answer back, 'Hi Jim.' It was like that. We'd just sit and talk. Someone would talk about the things that they'd done, and then my turn came to talk about things I'd done.

I didn't do much talking for the first couple of days. But that's what we did a lot of. We had group sessions where you would slag one another off. It was a bit like Big Brother *is now, I suppose. We'd all sit around and get on each other's tits. I don't know if they made you do that on purpose so you'd slag each other off. I think it was part of the training, teaching you not to be frightened of saying 'No', or sticking up for yourself.*

If people say to me, 'Will you come and do this for me at my charity night?' I'd always reply, 'Oh yes, OK. I'll be there' – instead of saying, 'No, I don't want to do that. It's not for me.'

We'd all sit around in the group session and for the first ten minutes, no-one would say anything.

Then I'd break the ice. I turned to Alan, this other alcoholic. 'Why don't you tell us what you told me in the tea room?'

Steve, the grinning counsellor objected to that. 'Stop trying to control people!'

'Oh, fucking hell. I'm only trying to help.'

We were all allocated various household tasks. I had to do the washing. The rota changed later and I had to do 'bins and bogs'. It turned out to be quite a tough regime really. I had, literally, to empty the bins and clean the bogs. That was my job for the week, what I was assigned to do.

Soon I was to meet Kinza, who would look after us in the night. She was a nice woman, who looked like she came from Malta. She was very posh, very scary, and very strict with the patients. But I liked her immensely. She came in, walked up to me and said, 'Here's a letter for you from Kenney Jones.'

That was great news. Kenney was a mate I used to drink with at the Windmill after I'd married Tracy. Kenney was the drummer with The Faces and then, of course, The Who. Over the years, he has done very well for himself and he used to come drinking with me. He used to keep a little more control of himself than I did. Just!

What I didn't realise was that, while I had been writing up notes of all my damage, details of what I'd done to people, Steve the counsellor had contacted Tracy.

'I want you to write down all the shit that Jim's caused you in your life,' he said to her. 'Please write it down for him. I want to read it to him.'

Tracy said she found it very difficult to do. But she did eventually. I found what she wrote very hurtful but in my state of mind, I thought she must be wrong. She didn't understand me at all, I reasoned. How could she say I was never there, how could she say I was always in the pub, always working? If I hadn't been working, she wouldn't have been in that nice house.

Steve asked someone else to write a letter. Kenney Jones. Kenney'd sat down, with the tears dropping down from his eyes on to the paper, and he'd written down what a complete arsehole he thought I was. He'd put it all in this letter, which was now delivered into my hand.

Well, I just sat there and I read. My heart sank. In utter despair, I thought to myself, 'Well, Jimbo, that's it! That is the end of my life!'

Kenney's letter was long. They had told him to be specific. So he gave me both barrels. He really let me have it. He'd written, 'Jim was rude to my wife. He told her to fuck off. You know, I like Jim but he's turned into an animal. He's someone I don't know any more. There's no need for this. He did this, he did that. He was rude. I've never seen anyone behave so badly. He was appalling ...'

And I thought to myself, 'Thanks mate, Kenney, you bastard! That's all I need right now!'

I couldn't believe I'd get this from my own mate, a mate I really loved. Now he'd turned on me.

Eight weeks later, I bumped into Kenney in the pub. And I put my arms around him and gave him a hug. 'Kenney mate,' I said, 'you probably saved my life ...'

Not only a great mate but also a great drummer!

'Kenney Jones is on drums. Who's the bass player?'

'Fuck knows ... pass the joint.'

The Oval was packed, heaving with 20,000 screaming fans. The crowd was swaying and chanting. The noise was deafening as Rod Stewart and The Faces made their entrance and began pounding through their fantastic, foot-stomping routine. The Oval in 1971 was really rocking. Other bands like The Who, Mott The Hoople and Frank Zappa had been booked to play the ground but when Rod and The Faces took to the stage, they thrilled the crowds, who were more used to seeing England being beaten by the West Indies at cricket.

Up there on the stage, the drummer who'd become my idol, the supreme professional who gave it his all. I looked up at Kenney Jones in awe and thought, 'Now *that* is what I want to do!'

At the time, I was playing drums in Woolwich at the Director General pub for my £4 a night, with £2 a night deducted to pay off the bloody drum kit. So seeing Kenney Jones, whacking this kit in front of massive crowds at The Oval, I thought, 'That's for me!'

That night I went back to the pub so fired up, you couldn't hear the singer for me whacking those drums. That was all I wanted to be.

And then of course, I saw Emerson Lake and Palmer three weeks later, also at The Oval. My God, they were superb. And that was when I became convinced, there and then, (a) that I wanted to be a pop star and (b) that I could never be in the same league as drummers like Carl Palmer. He was breathtaking.

So, not for the first time in my life, I was in a quandary. I'd finished working at Sun Air Holidays, finished with Rank Xerox and was now just slobbing around selling drugs. Including, I might not have mentioned, LSD. Although, I never *sold* LSD – I just *took* it. I didn't like that stuff very much. But everyone else in the world seemed to be taking it, so I did too.

Me and the boys were still living in Burridge Road but we had no money. But somehow, I knew I'd be famous doing *something*, even if it was going to be as a murderer or a gangster. I didn't know *what* I wanted to be. I wasn't really tough enough to be a gangster! But I was always the life and soul of the party.

When I sat round smoking dope, I would invent really weird stories and make everyone laugh. Some of my stories were pretty surreal. Of course, we were all into David Bowie and the book *Was God An Astronaut?*

I'd talk about these fantastic things, especially when I was taking speed. We'd sit up all night and have these ridiculous ideas, which we thought at the time were life-changing. I'm sure if we'd taped them and listened to them next day, we'd have thought we were all lunatics.

Larry was one of our other great mates. He was never really into drugs because he was into money. He worked bloody hard as a window cleaner and one day he offered me a job. I think he was paying me £4 a day to be a window cleaner – but it was so cold out, I'd have happily given him £5 a day to let me go home.

One day, however, he called me up and asked me a fateful question.

'D'you know that pub in Lewisham called the Black Bull?'

'Yes.'

'Well, there's a new governor there from north London who's looking for a comedian. I told him *you'd* do it.'

'Thanks, Larry. Why did you tell him *me*, you bloody fool?'

'Well,' said Larry, 'you know that day you got up in the pub pissed and told some jokes, well you ought to do it for real! I've told him you'll go down and audition for him.'

The following Saturday, me and Larry drove down to the pub and met a man called Jerry who was running it. Jerry didn't know the area at all but when he took one look at me, he seemed surprised.

'You're a bit young to be a comedian, aren't you?' he said.

'Yeah, well, I'm a young comedian,' I replied.

'What pubs have you done?'

I just made up a load of pubs – he didn't know any of them.

'OK, you start Sunday!'

Oh my God! Larry and the boys all started laughing and I was wetting myself for a week. Come Sunday lunchtime, I got down there and someone produced some amphetamine sulphate.

So I had some powder to get my Dutch courage going – nowadays I'd have a brandy. And off I went. Trouble was, there was no-one in the pub at all, apart from half a dozen black blokes and a beautiful white girl disc jockey.

Before long, I had the black blokes in hysterics with my Chalky accent routine, taking the mickey out of them. They were shouting at me and I was just shouting back in the same accent. They were rolling around.

Then a football crowd came in and I did quite well. My debut went OK, I guess, because I ended up doing every Sunday there. And then the governor of the pub asked how I'd feel about doing Saturday night and Sundays as well.

'I'll give you fifteen quid – but you have to work behind the bar as well,' he said.

Fine! So I started working behind the bar, taking my speed tablets and getting up and making everyone laugh. What a life! It was 1973 – I was just 20. And all of a sudden, I was having the time of my life.

The Truman Talent Trail was being advertised in *The Stage*. It involved going round various pubs and taking part in a talent contest. It seemed like a good idea, so I signed up.

First, I headed off to the Barge Pole in Thamesmead, where I did a routine and my brother Billy turned up to watch me. I was really proud when I won the heat and dead chuffed that my brother had joined the audience. He was with his mates at the bar and I could see he was proud of me. I could see him laughing at me as if I were a comedian, not just as his brother being funny. I genuinely made him laugh and I got a big kick out of that. Mind you, he was pissed.

When we went back to my sister's house afterwards, I told her I'd won. I said I was judged the funniest comic. She was thrilled too. We all sat round having drinks and I started telling jokes to my brother Billy, who was a policeman. I did this 'Nick-Nick' routine to him. 'Where did you get that from?' he asked me.

I said I'd heard a comic do it in the pub called the Howick, down in Woolwich.

'Christ, that's bloody good!' Billy said, 'except you want to change it round.'

So we adapted this 'Nick-Nick' joke to fit all my jokes about policemen. My brother said it was hysterical because he was a policeman at the time. So that was it! I had a little catch-phrase.

The second heat of the talent contest was at the Barge Pole as well. That was the all-winners heat – and I won that too. Next, we all trooped off to the Leather Bottle in Merton, in the middle of bloody nowhere, where posh people live! And, yes, I won that, too. There was no bloody stopping me!

The *final* heat was held at the Lyceum Theatre in London. I bought an awful white suit and thought I looked the business. My hair was like a fluffy David Bowie. I could never quite get it to go like his because mine was a bit curly. Nevertheless, I tried my best. I was thin and smoked loads of fags and drank whisky. I knew what it was like to be an underdog. I knew the Brits love an underdog. So you don't really need to win.

Someone said, 'Winning is not important.'

Fuck that! I reckoned. If winning is not important, why keep score?

When I turned up at the Lyceum, Mum and Dad and everyone had come. There was a fantastic atmosphere in the place and a huge crowd in. The place was heaving, boozy and smoky. But I could see clearly enough – this was my big chance – and I knew it. I wasn't so nervous that I couldn't control it. My adrenalin was pumping and I was really up for it. I *knew* I could win it. I couldn't wait to get on stage.

All the acts were to be judged by a panel, which had Jess Conrad and Arthur Mullard sitting on it. As I waited in the wings for my turn to go on, I felt the buzz in the place was perfect for my act. Then they announced me and my heart started pounding extra hard as I strode out to a cheer. I was really up for it and the audience loved it. They were a brilliant audience and I just paralysed them! I had them absolutely hooting with laughter …

When I got to the end of my act, a huge cheer went up as I left the stage. I was on cloud nine. I knew I'd done it. I'd clinched victory. I could sense it. They'd loved me.

And then, to general astonishment and amazement, it was announced that the winner of the comedy section was … a bloke called Joe Goodman.

When the result was read out, the audience went mad. They started booing and shouting. They were angry because they thought the judges had delivered the wrong result. I know Joe to this day – and I *still* remind him that he beat me.

So, I'd failed to win the contest. But when the crowd started booing at the result, I thought, 'Hey, this is great! These people love me! Never mind about winning. I'm happy to be the underdog, if everyone loves me as much as this.'

Doing so well didn't really come as a shock to me because I knew that, if I put my mind to it, I'd be sure to be the best at it.

Even though my performance at school was a slight failure, in my *mind*, it was a complete success because I was the *first* kid to get the cane, I was the *first* one to play for the football team, Susan Sargeant fell in love with *me*, she flashed her light at *me*, nobody *else* … and even when I went to work at Rank Xerox, I started as the junior office boy but ended up as the night supervisor.

When I went to Thomas Moore's, I started as a Rank Xerox bloke and ended up as the supervisor there, too.

Somehow, I always managed to get people to think I had the ability to do better. When they met me and got to know me, I got them to think, 'This bloke is a *leader* rather than a *follower*.'

When it came to comedy, I *knew* that everybody would like me – because I *knew* I'd be good at it. Or, if I *wasn't* good at it, I'd *make* them like me.

I'd *find* a way to make them like me. Like I'd find a way of *making* the teachers laugh at me rather than hate me. I'd find a way of making the kids like me, rather than bullying me.

I knew my way to survive. If you can run fast, you run. If you have the ability to make people like you, even though you're a bit naughty and you're a loveable rogue, then that's what you do.

That's what I had always played on. I still do it today. I don't really know where all my confidence comes from. I guess it comes from … and this was always a conflict in the clinic … the personality defects.

I learned that I am not the centre of the world. But I also always knew that I needed to use what I've got to the best of my ability. It was never a matter of confidence. It was the matter of having the ability to show off without getting embarrassed. If you can do that, then people will then notice you. As long as you don't get on their tits, you've cracked it!

Where did my showing off streak come from? Well, I was the youngest in my family. I had to show off to try to get attention. It sounds a cliché but in my case, it was absolutely true.

I think another factor in how things turned out in my life is that I never had the sort of Dad who would pat me on the back and say, 'Well done, son!'

I was always trying to show him what I'd done. Nowadays, I'm *still* always trying to get people to say, 'Well done, Jim.'

That's why I want an audience to stand up and cheer. *They* say, 'Well done!'

I'm sure that's why I used to play my little Tommy Steele guitar outside the gates of our house. As a young man, even as a tiny kid, I used to play so that people would say, 'Oh look, there's that Cameron. He's a clever little boy, isn't he? He's lovely.'

And, of course, Mum would encourage that, because I was her little soldier.

So, when I was a hit with audiences at the tender age of 20, it didn't really surprise me all that much. But what *was* difficult to judge then was how to progress from there.

How should I progress from coming second in the Truman Talent Trail, to making a career of it? One thing was certain, I'd now finally found what career I wanted to choose in life.

That was it. I wanted to be a comedian.

Within a month or two, I managed to get an audition in a pub called the Montague Arms in New Cross. The Montague Arms is a famous pub because that's where Mike Reid and the great Jimmy Jones had started out.

The governor, a great old guy called Peter Hoyle – who's still there – was being threatened with losing his licence because the gags there were too filthy. Honestly, these comedians ...

So off I went down there and the governor said to me, 'If you can keep it clean, I'll give you a job.'

I would be on £60 a week – £60!

The first night I performed at the Montague, I was a young comic. By my last gig, a few months later, I was an old comic. I'd had so much experience. For some reason, they had to finish with me at the pub. I think Pete worried about his licence. I found myself getting filthier and filthier. I couldn't resist it.

By the time I was 22, I was back living with Mum and Dad. Dad was doing some building and decorating work with my Mum's brothers at the time and I said I'd go with him.

I started work as a builder and decorator. It was quite good fun actually because we used to paint pubs – working at night.

One of the pubs we painted was the Crooked Billet, in Staines. We used to go in at 11 o'clock in the evening after the pub had shut and we'd come out with the job finished at 7 o'clock in the morning – half pissed, having painted about four square feet!

Dad used to drive us back and I would kip all day and spend what spare time I had trying to find out how I could become a comedian.

Mum would be phoning up people, making out she was my agent. She was phoning people up 'on spec', finding their listings in the Yellow Pages. She was probably ringing up the Chinese takeaway by mistake.

'I've got this young man. He's a comedian,' she'd say down the phone.

I sat there listening to her, cringing with embarrassment. Then, one day, in *The Stage* newspaper, I spotted the name of an agent called Derek Allen. I saw he was advertising 'Stags, Clubs, Hens etc.'. If this was what I thought it was, it could be something I loved.

I phoned him up. 'Hello, my name's Jim Davidson,' I said.

I'd changed my name from 'Cameron' to 'Jim' at the Black Bull because I thought I wouldn't have to pay tax on my six quid!

'I'm looking for a job.'

'Where have you worked?' he said.

'At the Montague Arms in New Cross for a month and a half, two months ...'

'What do you want to do?' he asked.

'Stag shows,' I said. 'Got any stags?'

Now stag shows were *great*! Really great value. I'd always gone to as many as I could – as a punter. They'd be held at somewhere like Roehampton Rugby Club on a Friday night. A real gentlemen's evening. Jugs full of beer would be flowing and on would come the compere.

'Good evening, gentlemen. We've got a great night for you tonight ...'

And he'd do a couple of minutes. Then he'd introduce a stripper, who'd come on and get her tits out. And then *another* stripper would get her tits out. And then he'd introduce the comic. The comic would come on and do twenty-five minutes. Hysterical stuff.

After the interval, the compere would come back on and tell some jokes. Then the stripper would go back on and show the cat's face – and then another comic. Finally, another stripper would strip at the end.

Well, I loved it!

Over the last couple of years, I'd been thinking 'How do I get into this?'

I'd been to the Welcome Inn once and seen a compere called Benny Palmer. Benny wasn't particularly funny but he'd told great jokes. The audience *howled* with laughter.

I'd once been to Catford and seen a bloke called Mike Felix. Not only was he very, very funny, he wasn't telling jokes. He was just telling anecdotes and stories. He ended up by playing 'Mocking Bird Hill' on the piano. He was the best and put me in my place somewhat. I thought, 'Christ, I've got some work to do.'

So when Derek Allen said to me, 'OK, do you know Blackheath?', I nearly bit his arm off.

'Do I …?'

He seemed convinced.

'Right,' he said, 'turn up there, Blackheath Rugby Club, and you'll be the compere.'

'Have you got your own PA system?' he asked me.

'Pardon?' I said, 'what's that?'

'You get an extra ten quid if you bring your own PA system.'

I said I hadn't got one.

'Anyway, you're compering,' he said. 'There's two girls and you – and a comic.'

Well! Off I went.

It was a typical stag night. There were about 150 blokes, a little dancer called Val and a comic. When I met Derek Allen – for the first time – I saw the instant horror in his face when he saw how old I was!

'Fucking hell!' he said to me, adding quickly as he pushed me on, 'Good luck then, son.'

And I bloody *paralysed* this room! I had them cheering the place down. Everything went really well and afterwards, I got chatting to Val, the dancer. She said she knew another agent who might help me.

'Oh,' she said, 'and I'm doing another job for Derek in Brighton next week. Can you help me out there too?'

I would get £18, spend a night in Brighton, tell jokes, have a drink, spend time with a stripper, and get paid for it. How did I fancy doing that?

The next week, Val and I were on our way to Brighton. I picked her up in my old car with a coat hanger aerial, drove down, did my comedy turn and blew them away. Then Val, who lived in Bermondsey, said, 'Do you want to stay the night at my place?'

Oh yeah!

So I stayed the night at her place – *on the sofa*, right. Mind you, we had a bit of a kiss and cuddle – and she made me a bacon sandwich, which I have never forgotten!

'*This* is the woman for me!' I thought.

Not only was she in show business, not only could we work together – but *also* she cooked great bacon sandwiches as well! Cor blimey, beat that if you can!

Before long, I had moved in with Val in Bermondsey. She was the dancer and I was the comic. And we would work and play together.

For a while, bookings dried up though, until one day I bumped into a comic called Monty Wells. When I wasn't working, I used to drive him round all over the place.

One day I'd been driving him down to Woking Football Club. He and three other comics were on and I watched them all die. Monty turned to Wally Dent, the promoter who was putting on the show, and said, 'Listen, young Jim's a comic, stick him on.'

'D'you wanna have a go?' Wally Dent said to me.

'Sure!' I said, jumping at the chance. 'I'm not scared of these bastards!'

'Go on then and do ten minutes.'

So I went on and did three-quarters of an hour. For my trouble, I got a standing ovation. I just destroyed them. Wally came over afterwards and gave me a tenner out of his own pocket.

'Are you managed by anyone?' he asked.

'No,' I said.

'Well, give me a call tomorrow, right?'

This was 1975 and I was 22. Things seemed to be going my way. But the next audition I was to try my hand at was for Hughie Green – *and I died on my arse.*

Wally Dent had fixed me up with an audition for TV's *Opportunity Knocks*. I went along to Nellor Hall, in Twickenham, went through my paces but I didn't do well.

'How long you been doing this for, son?' Hughie Green said to me.

'About three years,' I replied.

'Hmmm,' he said, 'well, go away and practise.'

OK, Hughie. Thanks for your assistance!

Then a couple of comedians I worked with phoned up their agents and said they ought to see this young lad Jim Davidson.

And the compere I'd seen at the Welcome Inn, Benny Palmer (apparently he was an agent, as well), phoned me up and said, 'I hear you're very funny.'

'I *try* to be,' I replied.

'Can you do a Sunday lunchtime for me?'

'Sure!' I said.

That weekend, I was heading up to some factory on the A10 in north London. I went on at lunchtime and paralysed them again.

'Are you earning £300 a week?' Benny asked me.

'No!' I said. Well, I had to be honest.

'Well,' he said, 'you sign with me, I'll pay you £300 a week, I'll put you on *New Faces* and if I don't make you a star, my name's not Benny Palmer!'

So what a pickle I was in! Now I had *two* people wanting to manage me. And I was doing stag shows all over the place, with another agent called Bill Gordon. Sometimes we'd do three shows a night. Wally Dent used to book me up for maybe two or three a week. And Benny Palmer would book me in for Mondays, Tuesdays and Wednesdays. Sometimes I'd do three a night and earn £15 a 25-minute spot.

There was a whole gang of us, all filthy comics. There was me, Jimmy Jones, Mike Kemp, the Mardell Brothers (who eventually wrote *Big Break* with Mike Kemp), and loads more comics, like the ventriloquist Roger de Courcey. We'd all work three shows a night and then meet up somewhere, maybe at the Adam and Eve pub in Peckham, where we'd go drinking.

One thing I can tell you is that Nookie Bear was *evil*! Roger was the *best* and Nookie Bear was disgusting! He used to call him 'Pooh Bear'.

'Why do they call you Pooh?' Roger would ask Nookie Bear.

'Because I fart,' the bear would answer.

Honestly, to hear that teddy bear swearing was absolutely hysterical. No-one wanted to follow him on stage.

I wanted to get to the stage where no-one wanted to follow *me*. It looked like I was going in the right direction, but first I'd have to sort out the fact that accidentally I seemed to have acquired three managers.

I spoke to Dad one night. 'Look Dad, I've got this Wally Dent guy, who wants to manage me and I've also attracted the interest of another agent, Benny Palmer.'

Dad looked at me and tried to clarify things.

'How much has Benny Palmer promised you?'

'Three hundred pounds a week,' I said.

'And how much has Wally Dent promised you?'

'Nothing,' I said. 'All *he* promises is that he'll work hard and do his best.'

Dad said, 'Sign with Wally Dent.'

I took the advice.

When Wally gave me my first gig, at Welwyn Garden City, I got forty quid. In the meantime, he had arranged for me to do an audition for *New Faces* and after my *Opportunity Knocks* experience for me it was a case of, 'Oh here we go! I can't stand the rejection. Why do I *need* this? I'm getting forty pounds a night. I can do three stag shows a night if I want to. I'm going down really well. I've got Val who likes me. We've got a little flat with Val's two kids. Everything's working out great. Why do I need to be rejected again?'

But I also realised that, if I didn't grab that chance, I was never going to think about making it on television. And once I'd got that exposure on TV, I *knew* I'd be able to crack it. I *knew* they'd like me.

The night before the audition, me and Val had an almighty row. Honestly, she could pack a punch like Freddie Mills! She tore my trousers off me and ripped them to bits! We were scrapping like cat and dog! It wasn't the ideal preparation for my big break.

I turned up the next day at the Victoria Palace Theatre in London to do my audition, wearing my brown tuxedo jacket, bought from Ken Furlow & Co. in Catford, and a pair of white stay-press trousers. I did feel out of place in the white trousers and I hoped they weren't going to earn me a black mark.

When I got there, I saw about 20 to 30 other people all waiting to go on. Finally, a voice called out, 'Jim Davidson' and I walked on. I looked out into the darkness of the theatre I now know so well – and there were four people sitting there. I could just make them out.

I did my first joke and it was a West Indian joke about a black policeman … and all of a sudden I heard a seat in the stalls go 'Ger-donk!' I soon found out that Les Cox, who was the producer of the television series, had fallen off his chair. He was sitting on it upright and he fell down, he was laughing so much!

As I continued my short routine, I could see a few of the cleaners in the theatre putting their mops down and coming over. They started listening to me. There were people in the wings, too. I did about four or five minutes and really got this place rocking. I walked off and the little gay floor manager walked up to me.

'Les Cox wants to know is *that* what you wear all the time?' he said, looking at my trousers.

'Oh fuck! Val's buried me, the trousers!'

That wasn't the reaction I was looking for. But nevertheless, I quickly walked round and shook Les Cox's hand.

'Can you do March the 9th?' he said.

Honestly! What a daft question! 'Can you do March the 9th?' What does he *expect* me to say – no?

So that was it. I went across to the pub and phoned my Mum, all excited.

'Mum,' I said. 'I've got it! I passed the audition!'

New Faces would be recorded on a Tuesday night. I went up to Birmingham with Val (who'd given me my trousers back by now) and the bloke from the local pub, Dominic, an Irishman who ran the Adam and Eve in Peckham, where I used to work doing the odd spot.

Wally came too and booked us into this bloody stupid hotel that didn't sell booze. So we managed to sneak a load of booze back in, and me and another contestant on the show, Rose-Marie, an Irish singer, got a bit pissed.

The next day I turned up, and *to my horror*, Les Cox was no longer the producer. His replacement, Albert Stephenson, was a nice guy though. He came up to me as I sat there watching this group called Canned Rock. They were playing 'Bohemian Rhapsody' – brilliantly.

'This band is very good,' I said to Albert.

He smiled at me. 'But I hear you're *better*.'

He then walked me through to the dressing room and asked to hear my routine. When I'd finished, he looked quite pleased.

'Fine, OK,' he said, 'that's OK. You *can* do this joke, you *can't* do that one. It's better if you do it like *that*,' and so on.

And so I went on. One member of the panel was Arthur Askey. When the time came to give the voting, I scored 10, 10, 10, 10, 10, 10, 10, 10, 10, 10, 10, 9.

When the group's scoring turn came, they got 10, 10, 10, 10, 10, 10, 10, 10, 10, 10 ... and then, finally, it was Arthur Askey's turn to mark them.

He looked up and for star quality he gave them 8. Arthur Askey had looked up at that scoreboard, worked out the maths, added up the scores – and decided to make *me* the winner.

'Jim Davidson is our new winner,' the show announced.

I couldn't believe it. I stood there as they applauded and I could feel my top lip curling up in fear. My heart was banging like I was going to die. Deep down, I knew that life would never be the same again. I would now be famous. I could be everything I wanted to be. Bollocks to the Navy, bollocks to having Jane's baby and bollocks to Sue. I was now famous. Everyone would get to know about me. I couldn't wait for that show to be transmitted on the telly, so I could go out and show off. I was ecstatic. I could hardly believe what I'd done. I thought, 'Right! That's it. I've cracked it.'

And I went down to the phone box in the corridor at ATV in Birmingham and I phoned Mum up. All excited, I said, 'Mum? It's Cameron.'

Before I could say any more, she cut in. 'Never mind, love,' she said.

'No!' I said, 'I won!'

We both had a good cry.

To celebrate, we invited some friends round to Val's flat in Naylor House. Some of my old mates from school came, like Ronny and Tommy.

We all sat there, got the drinks out and watched me on the telly win *New Faces*. It was on at a quarter past six. So there was some serious drinking to be done after that. What a night!

Later that evening, Wally Dent had booked me into a social club in Hayes in Middlesex. When I turned up, I strode in there like I was Elvis! They cheered the place down because they too had all watched *New Faces* and they knew that I'd be coming there. Obviously, Wally had told them what I'd done. The atmosphere was electric.

I don't think Dad watched the show but he was dead chuffed really, although he never particularly went out of his way to come and see any of my shows. I knew he was pleased.

He didn't come because he was either working or in the pub. I used to see him on Sunday lunchtimes. I'd get pissed and go round to Mum and Dad's house. My career success wasn't somehow that important to them then.

I was pleased for them because I knew I'd be getting rich soon, and that meant everyone would be getting richer as well. And what was *most* important was that I'd become famous.

Now everyone was talking about me. I had my picture in the *Sun* and the *South East London Press* ran lots of little articles describing me as the 'local boy done good'.

By then, 1976, I'd reached the ripe old age of 22 and my life was nothing short of fantastic.

One day, I strolled up to the Dun Cow on the Old Kent Road. It had a disco that was very popular with the birds. The manager there, Kenny Scott, asked me if I wanted to perform there on Sunday lunchtimes.

'How much?' I enquired.

'Seventy-five quid a spot,' he replied, quick as a flash.

I nearly passed out.

Within a couple of weeks, Kenny started saying, 'Oh, do Saturday night too, over at the other pub, the Green Man.'

Sure. I'd perform at one pub, then walk over to knock off the other pub on the Old Kent Road, get pissed, then walk home.

I met all these wonderful characters. I also bumped into Kevin Laming, who later became my friend and driver for twenty years.

By now I'd fully teamed up with Val. I was drinking gallons of whisky, getting up in the pub and making people laugh their heads off. All the time, I was becoming more and more inventive.

There was a great DJ in the Dun Cow and one day I was doing this joke about William Tell shagging and the DJ suddenly put the *William Tell Overture* on.

Immediately I started to do the joke to music, using the timing of the gag to match the music. Then he put other little bits on and I ended up thinking, 'Hang on, this is really good.'

One day, I bought one of those drum machines and every time I did Chalky's voice, with the West Indian walking down the road, I'd hit the foot switch and this drum beat would go off. Next, I bought an echo machine, so that when I did stories of people shouting, or when an echo was needed, even when I did my gag about the gynaecologist looking up the girl's bits, I'd switch this echo machine on.

It was all pretty revolutionary all this stuff I was doing. The crowds used to flock to the place. They loved me. In those days in the Dun Cow, everything I did turned to gold.

After I'd won *New Faces*, a nice man called Benny Hill (better known now, of course, as the late, great comedy entertainer), phoned up another nice man called Mark Stewart, who was a producer at Thames Television.

Mark was trying to put this show together called *What's On Next?* and they were looking for a comedian.

In the meantime, a guy called Alec Fine, one of the bosses at ATV Television, who put on *New Faces*, phoned an agent called Laurie Mansfield. Laurie was already a big agent who looked after top artists like Johnny Dankworth, Cleo Laine, Peters & Lee, and others. Alec said to him, 'Laurie, you really ought to come and have a look at this young lad.'

So Laurie Mansfield came and saw me do yet another Woking Football Club show for Wally Dent. He liked what he saw and Laurie and Wally did a deal between them. Wally would be my manager and Laurie would be my agent. It meant that my commission had now gone up to 25%, I might add, split between the two of them! But it meant I would get better and better gigs.

Laurie negotiated for me to appear on the TV show called *What's On Next?*, with Bill Franklin, Bob Todd, Hinge and Brackett, Barry Cryer and John Junkin.

But that July was the *New Faces Final*. And this was the big one.

My big rival on the programme was Roger de Courcey, the one I'd always feared working with, the one I'd always feared following – and now I'd got to follow him live on the television.

On the panel for that show was a man called Bernie Rothcoth, from America. He ran the MGM Grand. Another panelist was Tony Hatch, the Hatchet man. There were some other great contestants on the show, like the terrific comic Johnny Hammond.

When they came to the voting at the end and it fell to Tony Hatch to declare his score, he gave me quite a good mark which put me up into second place. The winner though was Roger de Courcey, who went off

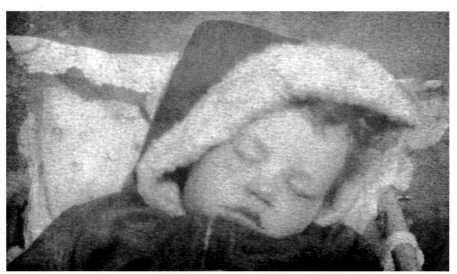

Sleeping Beauty aged two. I've not changed a lot, have I?

A card for my first birthday from Uncle Bill. I found out later that A-bu meant 'father'.

*Aged three, I chummed up with a baby lamb when Mum and
Dad took me to London Zoo in Regents Park in 1956.*

*I was two when this picture was taken at my sister
Eileen's wedding. The kilt looked good, didn't it?*

Mum and Dad. I miss them both.

Pretty impressive, eh?

P

LONDON COUNTY COUNCIL

KIDBROOKE PARK J.M. SCHOOL

REPORT FOR YEAR ENDING .... *July*. , 19 65

Name *Cameron Davidson* .... Number in Class *39*

Class *4a* .... Position in Class ....—....

SUBJECT	ASSESSMENT	REMARKS
ENGLISH	very good	Cameron uses his intelligence well, and writes interesting and thoughtful work
ARITHMETIC	very good	He is quick and bright
HISTORY	good	He has tried hard.
GEOGRAPHY	good	
SCIENCE		
ART		He uses his imagination well
WRITING		
HANDWORK		
OTHER SUBJECTS		

Religious Knowledge *very good* .... Attendance *good*

General Report

R Whitehead .... Class Master / Class Mistress

.... Head Master / Head Mistress

(P.2)

Can you spot the schoolboy heart-throb? (front row, second left).
I'm the only one of the lads whose tie is being used to hold up his trousers.

I was 13 on this trip to Southend — in 1966 with family friends.

(Opposite)
*Wife number one. Sue Walpole and I tied
the knot at Woolwich Town Hall.*

Skiving off work to go fishing was always great fun — here's proof!

Seventy-five quid a spot at the Dun Cow on the Old Kent Road was big money when I started performing there on Sunday lunchtimes. DAILY STAR

Fresh faced and raring to go.

Sally James admires Lenny the Lion with Terry Hall,
while Chris Tarrant and me could've won the
silly hat contest on Tizwas in 1976.

(Opposite)
May the Force Be With You. ROGER CRUMP

The crowd got an eyeful when I turned out for a charity match at Bournemouth — a few minutes after this shot, I lost my balance again and broke a bone in my foot! SUNDAY MIRROR

Even in the old days you would never catch
me on stage without a drink in my hand.

Time for a swift one in my dressing room before going on stage at the Winter Gardens, Bournemouth on my 1981 Summer Season. SUNDAY MIRROR

Being caught with my trousers down in the dressing room was a technique I perfected later at the London Palladium — to great effect! SUNDAY MIRROR

A turning point came in 1978 when Thames TV offered me my own series, The Jim Davidson Show. *The show ran until 1983.*

PETER BASDEN PHOTOGRAPHY

Dinner with my second wife, Julie. We jumped into bed on the first date, which I thought was tremendous.

to Las Vegas to do his act and become famous, or attempt to become famous anyway, with Nookie Bear.

OK. I hadn't won. But I'd had a great time. And I'd met some great people too.

The most distinctive of all the *New Faces* panellists was Danny La Rue. When it came to the marks, the great Danny La Rue triumphantly declared, 'Jim Davidson 100 points!'

I spoke to Danny afterwards and he told me what he'd said to the producer, Albert Stevenson, at rehearsal – 'This boy's fantastic, I'm going to give him 100.'

But the producer had replied, 'Danny, you can't give him 100, it's unheard of.'

Well, Danny La Rue, show business legend that he is, was incensed at this. Outraged. What an insult. He was infuriated by the cheek of it.

'How *dare* you!?' he demanded, indignantly. 'I'm Danny La Rue! I can give him one hundred and fucking *one* if I want to!'

Good old Danny!

Right. I was a star. Time to get drunk, or, as they say in 'show business', time to get 'out of it'.

4

Fun and frolics at the seaside

Day Three in the clinic

Frankly, I was pretty out of it all the time. I used to sit there and just drop off, whenever I wasn't writing, because I was really tired. When I eventually realised where I was and what was going on, it sunk in – this was fucking awful.

You worried a lot at night but, mostly, you slept OK. You got up at 7.30 in the morning and wandered downstairs. You got boiled eggs for breakfast and then, over breakfast, you'd look miserably around at everyone else. Some people obviously were in a better state of repair than others. For me, this was just Day Three. But some people had been in here for eight weeks.

I'd been busily writing out all my 'damage' notes. I'd been given a little book and, after breakfast, I would sit down with the others, open this book and start to read. Each page had a date. At the top it would say, 'God help me to realise my incompetence today by ...' and I'd have to fill that in and say my own bit out loud, helping me realise that I was not the centre of the Universe. People would say all sorts of things.

The routine would continue. I had something to eat at lunch and then, in the afternoon, I might go and listen to a tape, or there'd be lectures on what alcoholism is, explaining how we buggered our lives up. The talk was all about pride and fear, about anger and relationships, and issues like that. I'd sit and listen as best as I could. Then I'd write about it before having another one-to-one session with my own counsellor.

And then there'd be another group meeting. And then there'd be dinner. In the evening, I'd sit down and write out more 'damage' notes, before going to bed at 9 pm. There was no recreation. No down time. No nothing. That was all there was.

And I was frightened to death.

About a week into my stay, I still hadn't spoken to anyone on the telephone — but I knew that the following the day I was going to be allowed to call Tracy. I was missing her like mad. During that first week when I'd been admitted, everyone else had been celebrating New Year's Eve. I'd sat at the table and they'd made up a soft drinks punch.

They'd set a proper table and there were balloons and God knows what. I just sat there looking blank with this guy sat opposite me. I stared at the bowl of fruit punch with no booze in it. I didn't particularly want a drink. I just kept thinking about how much I wanted to be with my wife.

This guy looked over at me and piped up chirpily, 'You look pretty miserable.'

I could have killed him. I knew I felt miserable. I knew I felt sorry for myself. I didn't need this fucking dickhead telling me that.

But then I looked up and realised ... that he looked pretty miserable as well. But not quite as miserable as me. I think his name was Toby. He was a nice enough bloke, I suppose, but really, just then, I wanted to rip his fucking head off.

And it dawned on me at that moment that I felt the lowest I'd ever, ever felt in my life.

But tomorrow, the phone would ring ...

The phone rang. It was Laurie.

'How would you like to do a pantomime?' he said.

I didn't need to think for long. 'I'd love to do one,' I replied.

'Well,' said Laurie, 'it's *Dick Whittington* at the Alexandra Theatre in Birmingham and you'll be third on the bill.'

Top of the bill, as Dick, was Frank Ifield, the yodelling country singer from Australia. Playing Dame Trot was Patrick Cargill, who was in the TV series *Father, Dear Father*. It was Christmas Eve, 1976.

I would play the part of Idle Jim and, for my sins, I would be dressed in a white Bay City Rollers outfit that had a big 'I. J.' on the front of it. The show was directed by a very bossy but charming man called Alan Curtis, who played King Rat.

I was pottering around in my old Austin 1100, with Val and the kids in tow. We stayed at the Strathalyn Hotel, where my best mate Clive

Brandy visited us. Clive was married to Iris Williams, a Welsh, mixed-race singer, who had a hit with an old Cleo Laine record 'He Was Beautiful'.

Clive was a larger than life character, the one who made me laugh the most, and who was best at spending all my money. We'd go gambling, get up to mischief, go to bed at 4 am, get up late, just in time for the 2 pm matinée, spill out of the theatre about 11 pm, ready to start again. Bliss.

During the run, Alan Curtis decided he'd do a charity performance. He asked the cast from the Hippodrome panto to join us and some other stars turned up, like Eric Morecambe and Danny La Rue.

During this period I also knocked around with Chris Tarrant who at that time was in *Tiswas*. I used to go up there on a Saturday morning and join in. I was the first ever Phantom Flan Flinger, so there!

The charity performance of the panto turned out to be a wonderful night and Eric Morecambe was just fabulous. When he picked up that brown paper bag and threw an imaginary penny in it, everyone was hysterical. He was a very funny man and really down-to-earth with it. To be fair, those early days were tremendous for me because I was still only a kid, really. I'd only been in show business for two minutes and suddenly I found myself on stage with greats like Eric Morecambe. It was really weird and I had to keep pinching myself to believe it.

The following year, after the panto season had ended, I spent 1977 doing a round of the clubs again and having lots more fun. I was offered a summer season in Blackpool, on the North Pier and I thought, 'This is gonna be fantastic.'

Little and Large were top of the bill, then it was Frank Carson, Norman Collier and me. Plus a couple of 'spesh acts' and some dancers. It sounded like it would be fun.

So I called up my mate Kevin, whom I'd met in the Dun Cow and the Green Man, and various other great pubs in the Old Kent Road. Kevin was smaller than me and a bit older. He had a hairy chest, great legs and was good looking. He was the life and soul of the party and could drink and smoke for England. He was always laughing his head off and was really supportive and great fun. I would never have survived up in Blackpool without him. He was a great little guy and he had no fear at all. He was frightened of nothing.

'How d'you fancy coming up and being my roadie?' I asked him. 'You know how to plug my drum box machine in and put my echo chambers in and just generally be my mate.'

He was up for it.

We took a little house up there, round the corner from the theatre in Blackpool and started rehearsing. Then Val and the children turned up, and we were there as a little family. I must have been about nine and a half stone in weight then, with hair like David Bowie.

The day we drove into Blackpool will be forever etched on my memory. The first thing I noticed was how downmarket everybody was. I know I came from the Old Kent Road and from Kidbrooke but it really was a bit too much. I thought, 'Christ, this is gonna be hard work up here.'

I never saw any Londoners at all. Everyone there was the same – they were all a bit 'Northern'. And it was the first time I'd ever met Northern people, really.

I loved the Midlands to bits and I still do. But Blackpool's never really found a place in my heart. For a London lad, it was almost like a foreign country. The drinks hanging on the optics in the theatre bar were drinks I'd never even heard of before.

'Where's the Remy Martin and the Famous Grouse?' I wondered. 'And vodka does not really come from Wigan, it comes from Russia, doesn't it?'

I just couldn't get used to all the tacky things up there, the rubber hammers and all those holiday makers. In the end, I thought, 'Well, I'll just have to get used to this. This is probably what seaside holiday makers are like all over the world.'

But seeing as I'd never been to the seaside much before (I'd always gone on fishing holidays inland), I decided to grin and bear it.

I walked down the North Pier, which is about a quarter of a mile long, to the theatre. When I got to the end, I thought it stank. It was horrible.

The pier smelt really damp, horrible and nasty. I felt reassured though that, as far as the cast was concerned, I was among friends. I think I'd bumped into Little and Large once before – their agent was Norman Murray, now deceased – and I'd met Frank Carson a few times on the *Tiswas* show.

When these shows are put together, you can sit in the stalls waiting for your turn. The director goes on and the comics go on and they what they call 'top and tail.' So you'd walk on and say, 'Gag, gag, gag, song, another gag, song, another gag.'

And that's what Frank Carson did all through rehearsals. Norman Collier had us all in hysterics and Little and Large were very professional in what they did. Their act was fantastic, with Sid, very underestimated Sid, singing and playing his guitar, while Eddie interrupted him at every turn. When he came on as a punk Scotsman with a pin in his nose, I knew it would just bring the house down. They were unfollowable.

As for me, I didn't have to follow anyone, I had to follow *the interval*. The worst damn slot possible. Although, thinking back, the interval was actually quite good fun because our company manager, who had a terrible stutter, used to announce that there would be an interval of 15 minutes. Some nights, by the time he'd spluttered it out, the interval would be over. I used to love that bit. And then there'd be me.

Frank Carson took me aside during rehearsals and said, 'You've got to finish on a very strong gag, Jimbo, because you don't have a song to end on. When you finish, you can't walk off the stage to the sound of your own footsteps.'

I was quite aware of that. After me, there'd be a dance routine and then Little and Large would go on. So I'd have to be excellent if I was going to get anywhere in this set up.

We had three or four days of rehearsals. The director sorted what little lights were on it. I mean the production in those days was such crap. They thought that a couple of bits of scenery were more important than lighting. The band weren't really 'miked up' and the sound system was unbelievably awful.

The trouble was that, in those early days, I didn't know that it could all be done so much better. You just relied on these directors some of whom, I have to say, were appalling and useless. Maurice Fornier, our director, was one of the few good ones. He made the best of what was there. And I made the best of what I could do too.

One day I was pulled aside by Maurice for a quick word.

'Norman Murray's very upset,' he said. 'He's upset about you doing these black jokes.'

'*What* black jokes?' I said.

'That black voice you do in your jokes,' said Maurice.

Now, I didn't do jokes *about* black people, I used to put a black person's voice in any ordinary joke. So, instead of these two Irishmen walking down the road, it would be these two West Indians walking down the road. This was 1977, and political correctness hadn't been born at that stage.

Perhaps it was because my routine was so strong and funny, or perhaps because it was so offensive to black people in Blackpool (of whom I never saw any in twenty weeks, by the way), that Norman Murray took it upon himself to tell Maurice, our director, that I'd got to drop that whole routine. I got a bit annoyed about it and I phoned up Laurie Mansfield, who said he'd come up. Maurice and Laurie took me to lunch at an unspeakably awful hotel, and we tried to work out a way round the problem.

'Can you personalise the characters?' they asked me.

'Well,' I replied, 'why don't I just call this bloke Chalky?'

I'd used that voice earlier in my career but I hadn't previously referred to the character by name as 'Chalky'.

'What a good idea,' they said.

'And you can make Chalky a bit stupid,' I said, 'so that black people can relate to a silly black person within their community. So it obviously doesn't refer to all black people.'

'Fine,' they said. 'Nobody can have any problems with that.'

So we personalised my black man, and Chalky was truly born. So really, the fact that the character Chalky became firmly established in my routine wasn't down to me at all, it was down to Norman Murray not wanting me to do it in the first place. I'd tried out a few early Chalky gags before, in the Dun Cow down the Old Kent Road. But from now on, Chalky would become a fixture.

I went on stage on the opening night and everything went OK. I did alright but after a couple of weeks I wasn't really enjoying doing the show much. The old audiences were a bit Northern for my liking. Now I love everybody from England. I think we are a great bunch. But I do feel there is a North–South divide. Our pubs are different, the people are different and I always felt Northerners didn't quite like us. I know we're all in the same boat but down here it's just a bit different. I used to think that the North set itself low standards and then failed to live up to them.

The people in this seaside town didn't particularly like Cockneys. They used to love Frank Carson and everybody else but I wasn't going down all that well. I suppose they didn't really understand me, and I was thinking I wasn't very good.

In the end, I just got so hacked off, I decided to become mates with the band – they always seemed to be enjoying themselves. Me and the band used to go out at night, after the show. We'd just get blind drunk all the time. They were one of those old-fashioned 'pit bands,' as they were called. The guys that played in the pit are famous for craftily running to the pub.

This lot were like Olympic sprinters – because if they had a fifteen-minute break while the comedian was on … woooff … they'd be gone.

I also decided that I missed London so much that, with my £600 a week wages, I'd spend £250 of it chartering a plane to fly me back to London every Sunday. That way, I could do Sunday lunchtimes in the Dun Cow and pick up my seventy-five quid too.

It was crazy, I know, but without that chance to get away, Blackpool would have driven me mad. I ended up just hating everything about the place.

One Saturday, we were invited to a charity showbusiness football game. Because I had really thin dodgy legs, I thought I couldn't be running round the park with my spindly pins, so I bought some of that tan stuff you put on to get instant tan.

I rubbed it all on and when I'd finished the rub-down, I looked like Pele running down the wing. Some idiot, dressed as a clown, came out and threw a bucket of water over me and my legs went *streaky*.

And the commentator piped up, '... and Jim Davidson's legs have started running for the first time in the match.'

I thought that was quite a good line.

But it was at this match that I met another important person in my life – a really beautiful girl. She came up to me and said 'Hello' with this *fantastic* Northern accent. She really was the most beautiful thing I'd seen. She said that her name was Jane Beaumont and she was in a band called January, who were playing along with the Black Abbots at the South Pier. That famous band was, of course, the launch pad for Russ Abbot.

Jane and I got chatting and she said to me, 'Why don't you come down and see the show?'

So, we started seeing one another, in secret really, while Val and the two kids were still up at the other end of Blackpool, up the North Pier. I was spending all my time down the *South Pier*.

I decided, as the season drew on, that I'd fallen in love with Jane. And she decided she'd fallen in love with me. I had to break the news to Val and the two kids and I just couldn't do it. I mean I can't stand confrontation to this day. I don't know if anyone can, really. I suppose that streak in me is in some way connected to alcoholism.

I had to tell Val that I wanted her to go back to London and that I'd see them there. It really was a sad thing to do, and I can still see those little kids' faces. They probably hate me to this day.

I was really in a quandary because, as much as I adored Val, there really was no future for us. Her two boys were great lads but I wasn't their father. They needed their proper father. I had my career to think of and I'd met this beautiful woman Jane. Then it was back to the old alcoholism line again: 'I want it, I want it now. I must have this woman.'

It was a fucking horrible thing to do really. I just couldn't help it. I'd fallen in love – again.

Val and the kids went back to their flat in London and I stayed there with Jane and the season started to feel a lot better.

As my luck would have it, Little and Large fell sick. Eddie had terrible peritonitis and Frank Carson moved up to top of the bill.

That meant that I got to close the first half, a much better slot. With Little and Large off, I opened a bar in their dressing room and called it 'JD's Bar'. The company manager went *mental* but it saved the band running all the way to the pub in the interval, so things worked out quite well in the end really.

In addition to the party we had in the dressing room most evenings, there were other parties going on around town. One I went to was down the South Pier. Jane took me to her theatre, where I met the great Les Dawson. What a memorable meeting *that* was.

Jane and I were mingling and I saw him across the room. I was obviously aware that he was a big name in the business and so my throat went slightly dry as we walked over to say hello.

'Hello Les,' I said shaking hands. ' I'm Jim Davidson.'

'Who?' he said.

'Um, Jim Davidson.'

'Oh,' he said.

And I thought, well, this is really going well. I told Les I was playing the North Pier. He didn't seem very impressed.

'Right, look here, son. Mike Reid died on his fucking arse up here, so *you've* got no chance.'

Hmmmm. It obviously was very tough for London comics up here.

'Oh,' I said. 'Oh, OK.'

So then I, sort of, staggered off. I felt dejected and I wondered how Les could have been so awful and insensitive to me. But there again, he was a Northerner, you see. He fitted in with the rest of the scene up there. I didn't.

A couple a days later, I bumped in to him again. To my surprise, he came up to me and apologised.

'I'm sorry about the other night,' he said. 'I was pissed.'

'That's alright,' I said.

Then he added, 'But I fucking meant it.'

As I wandered off, I thought to myself, 'Hey, thanks, Les. You've really done my ego some good!'

But then it occurred to me what a complex man he was. He apologised to me one minute and then, the next, told me that he meant it.

Hmmmm ... I wasn't sure what to make of Mr Dawson and decided to keep out of his way in future.

Towards the end of the season, Wally Dent decided I needed a rest. He knew how hacked off I was with Blackpool and I'd vowed never to go again. I'd spent twenty weeks there. We were doing the summer season in November, walking up and down that pier in the rain and going to these awful clubs after the show and getting drunk. So Wally decided to fix me and Kevin up with a holiday in Guernsey. He booked us in to stay at a hotel run by a mate of his.

Kevin and I flew over there and got smashed in the hotel. We took in a film, *The Greatest* with Mohammed Ali. The movie's a terrific story, all about how he falls in love with his wife ... and suddenly I started missing my Jane like mad. Back in Blackpool, Kevin had this bird that he'd pulled and he was missing her like mad, too, especially her cowboy boots. So we decided, 'Sod the holiday, we'll sneak back to Blackpool.'

So only one day into our holiday in beautiful Guernsey, we got back on a plane and flew back to Blackpool, which we 'hated'. I smuggled back an engagement ring in a fag packet, and when I sneaked into Jane's theatre, Jane still thought I was in Guernsey.

As she came off stage, not only was she amazed to see me, I also placed a ring on her finger and asked her to marry me.

'Yes,' she said.

I think Jane was relieved to see me. Ours was a match made in heaven. We were both at the start of our careers, two young people drawn to each other. I thought she was the best looking woman I'd ever seen and she loved me and I loved her. Well, she came a close second to me!

Jane and I were fabulous together and her Mum and Dad were fabulous too. At first, I thought she'd be with me for ever. She was everything I wanted. But with so many things going on in our hectic lives, it turned out that our big romance was not to last. Jane and I were together for about eighteen months. We took a small house in Twickenham but I was increasingly busy chasing about all over the place, and so was she.

While I was away, I also started pursuing other girls and before long, we inevitably started drifting apart. We decided, in the end, we each had our own lives to lead. After she'd gone, I felt pretty 'down' for a while but my work schedule was soon to provide a timely distraction.

The following year, 1978, I headed down to summer season in Margate with Bernie Flint and Roger de Courcey. I stole all the limelight, this time, and was doing really well. Then, producer Mark Stewart got in touch with my agent Laurie and I was offered *The Jim Davidson Show*. It was just fantastic. I couldn't believe it. I'd been offered my own TV show by a producer whom I loved so much.

After Mark had spoken to Laurie, Laurie phoned me up. 'Are you still planning to go to Montreal to see Emerson Lake and Palmer in concert?' he asked me.

'Yes I am,' I replied.

'Well, you can't go,' he said.

I wasn't having that. 'There's not a fucking thing in this world,' I said, 'that would stop me going to see ELP.'

'You've been offered your own show on the television,' said Laurie.

'Well,' I thought, 'I'd started to like Pink Floyd a bit more anyway ...'

We recorded in 1978 and ran into '79 when the new TV series was being screened. I was down in Torquay playing summer season at the time. Torquay is just a million times nicer than anywhere else in this country. It has that beautiful bay, and for me that means speed boats. So I immediately bought one. A little Fletcher.

We used to go out every day and soon bumped into other people who had boats as well. Of course, speed boats led to drinking, lots of it.

One day we came out of the pub in Babbacombe, crossed over to Brixham, had some more to drink, and as we motored out of the bay, we started playing a game we used to play, quite a dangerous game. You'd steer your boat straight towards another boat and, at the last minute, you'd pull a hard left hand turn, thus sweeping the arse of your boat towards the other boat, sending your wake splashing all over them. Well, on this occasion, two of us had the same idea and we banged together. My boat ripped open and started to sink – and the impact broke my collar bone. Even as this nightmare was going on, as we were sinking, I saw my sax player Tony Harper sat in the front of my boat, pissed as a fart. With a typically trad-jazz-cum-Muppet expression on his face, he said, 'Hey man, the seats are floatin'.'

I had to do the show that evening in a figure of eight bandage round my shoulder. I looked like Frankenstein when I walked on.

The great Peters and Lee were top of the bill. I was second on the bill and there was no threat. I'd do two shows a night, a six o'clock show and an eight o'clock show, finish at 10.30 pm and hit the pub. From the pub, I'd go to Doodles night club, stay there until two. From two o'clock till four in the morning, Kevin and I would head back to the house with as many birds as we could find. Then we'd get up in the morning, go to the pub and get in our speed boats. We'd mess around all day until it was time to come back, take off our wet suits, and do the show.

We kept up that routine for 16 weeks without fail. Relentless, it was. We drank a lot, I guess, because the excitement of the boating was intense – and if we couldn't go boating, there was nothing else to do and the boredom was horrific. So we used to get drunk.

One day though I got my first serious warning that life can suddenly go 'tits up'.

A bloke called Danny Read, who was a mate of Kevin's, decided to come down and spend some time with us in Torquay. We were convinced he was on the run from something or other. He was a very quiet, funny south-east Londoner and he used to come out on the speed boats with us.

One day, we arrived down at the harbour to pick up our speed boats, ready to start touring the various pubs around Brixham and Babbacombe, only to find that the sea was really choppy that day. So we thought, 'Oh, to hell with it, the day's ruined. What are we going to do?'

We wandered over to a little pub on the quayside. It was just an ordinary funny little pub, where, after a few drinks (and this is at 11 o'clock in the morning), we decided that because we were all a bit bored, we would play a game of Jacks.

We got out a pack of cards and dealt them out between the three of us. The rules we played by were these, the first Jack meant 'order a mixture of three spirits, or three different drinks mixed together.'

If you were dealt the second Jack, that meant you had to pay for the round. And the person who got the third Jack had to drink it.

When we got round to about two o'clock in the afternoon, there was a big pile left of real dregs that no-one would drink. One cocktail was Advocaat, Guinness and Creme de Menthe. Another was brandy, vodka and whisky, mixed together.

Hanging around in the bar while this daft game was going on were two birds. One of them was lovely and she wore a nice summer frock. The other girl had a pair of jeans on and plimsolls and had short hair. We thought they must be lesbians. With her short hair, she didn't look like a girl, didn't act like a girl. But they happily joined in our company and drank all the dregs.

At four o'clock, when we staggered out of the pub to catch a cab back to our place, the girls came with us. When we got back to the little house I'd rented, they were so pissed that Kevin took the girl's dress off and danced around naked with her in the front room. Dirty little sod. The rest of us couldn't stop laughing. Except that her mate in the plimsolls and jeans didn't see the funny side.

'Look at her, the little scrubber,' she started shouting. 'She's pissed.'

After the girl had finished dancing, she went to lie down in the back garden because she was a bit drunk. She put her little summer frock back on but I think her knickers had now been removed, courtesy of Kevin.

As she lay there, her mate went out and threw a bucket of freezing cold water over her, to try and sober her up.

The poor woman was now drunk, shivering and soaked with the cold water. Kevin, the idiot, raced upstairs and ran a hot bath for her. Then he carried the girl up and plonked her in it. Complete with her dress on.

I wasn't aware that he'd done this at first, but ten minutes later, when I went up to the bathroom for a wee, lying in the bath next to me, right next to the toilet, was the body of the girl, completely under water. With her eyes open, staring up at me.

Aaaaagh! Panic stations! What the fuck had happened? Was she dead? Christ.

I immediately ripped down the shower curtain and jumped in the bath to rescue her, while at the same time, hurriedly trying to put my willy away after taking a leak. I grabbed her body and dragged her out the bath. I started giving her mouth-to-mouth and artificial respiration and suddenly, to my huge relief, she bucked into life and spewed water and beer out all over me.

It was messy and smelly but I didn't mind. It was a complete relief. I was in bliss because I had already seen the newspaper headlines flashing through my mind, 'JIM AND THE DEAD BODY IN THE BATH'.

I didn't think about the poor girl, or her family. All I was thinking about was what trouble I was going to land myself in – all because Kevin wanted to shag her. The fucking idiot!

So, we helped the poor girl downstairs and tried to give her a cup of tea. Her mate was still pissed so I said to Kevin, 'Sod this. We don't want any of this mess, Kev.'

We fetched her a football shirt and a pair of shorts to wear.

'I wanna go home now,' she said.

And as I pushed off back down the pier to do some work back on stage, the two girls were last seen weaving down the high street shouting abuse at us as they walked home.

'We know where you live, you bastard. You'll hear more about this.' We never did though.

That was just about the first time I'd ever really *nearly* been in serious trouble. When I stopped for a moment to think about it seriously, a dead body in my bath was a pretty bloody scary thought. Normally, I was fairly skilled at talking myself out of tight corners but how would I explain that?

The fact that I'd come so close to disaster was a seriously sobering thought – and a depressing one too. My drinking and the girls' drinking had landed me in a situation that had *nearly* ended in tragedy. I'd lost control of that situation and that unnerved me slightly. The demon drink had cost me my collar bone – and now, nearly, a girl's life. This was threatening to go beyond a joke …

5

Wine, women and ... war

I kept thinking about Frank Carson's wise words when he said to me, 'You can't just walk off to your last joke. You have got to finish on a song.'

The logical next step was to take a band on the road with me and that's just what I did in the autumn of 1979 (by this time I was 26). I wanted to include some music in my routine bearing in mind what Frank had said.

'Well, I might as well finish on something rock 'n' rolly,' I thought to myself, ever the wannabe rockstar!

So I gathered a small band and a bit of a lighting and P.A. equipment, and off we went. Well, OK, in fact it was a 40-foot truckload of equipment ... Don't forget my favourite group was ELP – and they never did things by halves – so I thought I'd do the same.

I ended up appearing at a club in Leicester, called Bailey's. It was there that I met a girl named Julie Gullick. She was working for Rothmans at the time. They were staging a promotional event that night and the popular radio DJ David Hamilton was doing something for them as well, presenting some awards on behalf of Rothmans.

When I turned up early for the show, Julie was sat in the front row watching what was going on. She looked fabulous in her party frock. She really did look the part, 'up for grabs' as they say. She was the cigarette promotions girl for Rothmans, so I knew she was well spoilt, so I decided to turn it on and win her affections.

I was up on the balcony and so, for a laugh, I grabbed the spotlight and moved it across, away from David Hamilton, to shine on *her*!

David already had another spotlight on him, so it didn't matter that much. But it caused a bit of a stir.

Julie and I got chatting afterwards, and I thought I'd go for it.

'Would you like to come back to the hotel for a drink?' I asked her.

She did. And for once, my mind wasn't on the drink. Off we crept up to my room where we 'cemented our relationship'. Julie was quite sexy. We did jump into bed on the first date, which I thought was tremendous.

A lot of girls say, 'I'm not that type of girl. I'm not doing this on the first date.'

Julie didn't give a toss. She was out to have a good time. She was the one for me. But, funnily enough, I didn't see her again for a while. We said our goodbyes and that was it – for the time being.

One small detail I forgot to mention, of course, is that, throughout all this time, I was still married to my first wife Sue. I was married to Sue when I got engaged to Jane. I hadn't got divorced yet. But quite honestly, I didn't think that mattered!

It *didn't* matter, did it?

Well, I was really fed up when my relationship with Sue had gone wrong. Then suddenly, I'd met this gorgeous Jane and I was knocked out by how beautiful she was.

'Well, let's get engaged!' I thought.

I thought I'd do it just to make sure she didn't run off with someone else. I thought I'd sort the divorce out with Sue a bit later on.

In fact, I had started to speak to someone about getting divorced. Sue and I had been going through the process of trying to sort it out but it was taking forever. To make matters even more complicated, I was still engaged to Jane when I met Julie at the club in Leicester. Er, as well as still being married to Sue. Can you keep up with this?

Marriage still appealed to me though. I'm not married now but I reckon I've taken longer to learn my lessons on that front than most people.

My Mum and Dad were in a stable marriage, you could say, except that they argued all the time. I didn't really want to change my life. I didn't really want to get rid of Sue. In fact, she got rid of me eventually.

I think when I meet women, they sort of quite like me. I'm really good at chatting them up ... But when you get to that levelling out period in a relationship, that time when you're not in love or in lust all the time any more, they go off me and I go off them – and then that's the end of it.

A few months later, Julie called me out of the blue. She was working at the Motor Show in London and I was appearing at the London Palladium. I asked if she'd like to come along and see me, so she turned up in her white fur coat, looking very grand.

We started dating quite a lot after that. By now, Jane and I had split up and gone our separate ways and Julie and I were a couple.

Not that I remained exactly faithful to Julie either. In fact, I have to admit now, looking back, that in that Palladium dressing room of mine, I had more women than you could shake a stick at! Honestly, we wore the carpet out in there. I scored some absolute beauties at the Palladium! I even met George Best's sister-in-law, Lindy James. What a beautiful girl she was, absolutely stunning! I still don't know what she saw in me. I wonder what's become of her since. I went out with Lindy for about three weeks.

Julie was never one of my Palladium 'carpet conquests' though. She was a bit above that. The star dressing room floor was just for 'quickies'. They used to file in, get their passports stamped, and then leave again.

I guess I was a bit of a 'Dear Diary,' if you get my drift. You know, as in, 'Dear Diary, I had Jim Davidson in the star dressing room at the Palladium last night.'

All of which, I should add, was absolutely fine by me. People always moan, 'Oh, they're only in it for what they can get out of him.'

Well, fine by me. I knew what I wanted and so did they.

After a while, Julie and I decided that we were going to see each other quite a lot. But before the end of the run at the Palladium, she had to go to Scotland for three weeks. She was involved in a skiing exhibition, up north in Aviemore. This left me with a little time on my hands, and as a result, I got involved with what is now known as the Ronnie Biggs Incident.

One night, Lionel Blair introduced me to a bloke called Johnny Miller. He'd actually been to see the show and Lionel brought him into the dressing room. He was an instantly likeable type of guy, a great big Scotsman. He said he used to be in the Scots Guards and seemed a very charismatic type. I think Lionel was very impressed with him.

Lionel, Johnny and I chatted for a while about this and that, and then we went out for dinner with Windsor Davis, who was also in the show. We headed down to a club in Chelsea called Stocks, run by Dai Llewellyn, who is now my great mate. He's also now Lord Dai Llewellyn who could drink for England. Everyone adored him, including me – until he dropped me in the shit that night.

We were all at the bar having drinks when this Johnny Miller character started telling everyone that he'd got an amazing plan. He said he was intending to kidnap Ronnie Biggs. I refer to Ronnie Biggs the train robber, who'd escaped from Wandsworth Prison and had fled the country in 1965 after completing 15 months of a 30-year jail term. He'd ended up in Rio de Janeiro.

So I listened to this guy with great glee, lapping up all his tales of derring- do. Apparently, Biggs was about to be extradited to Australia for non-payment of maintenance, and then from Australia he could be extradited back here. But it just seemed so far-fetched that this man, an ex-British soldier, could walk into my dressing room, then meet me and tell me later on that he was going to kidnap Ronnie Biggs. It was a bizarre thing to think of. And the way he liked to be the centre of attention and hold court well, it made me think that he was making it up. But I didn't want to say to him, 'You're a fucking liar' because he was too big!

Yet when Lionel said to me, 'Of course, he was in the SAS, you know,' I found him fascinating and I listened intently to his story.

'What are you doing now?' I asked him.

'I'm looking after a man called Alex Harvey,' he replied.

Alex Harvey was a great Scot, a heavy drinking man, front man to the sensational Alex Harvey Band.

In two weeks' time, he said, they would be appearing at the Marquee, in London.

'Why don't you give us a call?' said Johnny. Intrigued, I said I probably would.

A week later, we were at the Palladium and Stucky, my mate from Leicester, was now working with me because my friend and driver Kevin had gone off to work for Michael Barrymore.

So Stucky had taken Kevin's place helping me out. He was a great lad from Billingham, and another great 'Malaprop,' who'd always get words wrong.

'What's the matter with you?' he'd say to me. 'Get yourself together. You're transvestited' ... meaning 'transfixed'.

Or he'd say to me, 'Ere Jim, there's a great bird in the audience – she's got *jet blonde hair*!'

He was great at malaprops. But useless at everything else! Apart from being my mate – and that counts for a lot.

One night, a week later, Stucky came back to me from the stage door telephone and said, in his Geordie accent, 'I've just phoned up Johnny Miller at the Marquee because Alex Harvey's on tonight. I've spoken to Alex Harvey's roadie and he says Johnny Miller's not there – he's in Brazil!'

Well stone me! It was true then! He was actually going through with his plan. I sat there in my dressing room, dumbfounded and with a week to go before I was due to leave the Palladium – and then Julie would be back from Scotland.

I phoned up John Ashby. 'John, I want to go away on holiday,' I said. 'I've met this bird and if I can persuade her to go away on holiday with me, I'll have cracked it. Where should I go?'

'You should go to the Sandy Lane Hotel in Barbados,' John immediately replied. That sounded just the ticket. My office booked me two first-class flights from London to Barbados, staying at the Sandy Lane Hotel.

The Saturday night before I was due to fly to Barbados, I was in my dressing room watching *News At Ten* when I saw Johnny Miller being interviewed on the TV. Apparently, he'd kidnapped Ronnie Biggs and they'd all been arrested and taken to Barbados, where Biggs had been thrown in jail.

'Blimey,' I thought, 'they're actually in Barbados!'

It was pure coincidence that I was flying there as well next day.

Now, I had overlooked one small problem – Julie was at that moment stuck out in the middle of Scotland somewhere. So I asked my brilliant tour manager Rick Price to track her down for me.

'Will you do me a favour? Will you take a couple of days off, go up to Scotland and get Julie Gullick here? Now! Just find her. Get her in a car and bring her here.'

He found her, they flew down, I met Julie at Heathrow, we got on the plane, got high on champagne, I proposed, she accepted and we flew out to Barbados.

Job done.

When we arrived in Barbados, a nice black man in a cab picked us up. I was wearing a white suit and as we drove past all these dreadful shanty towns before you get to the Parish of St James where the great Sandy Lane Hotel is based, I stopped at every other pub. Our driver kept warning me, 'Man, don't go in there.'

There was me, dressed up to the nines, dripping in gold watches and diamonds as well, and we just walked into these ramshackle old buildings. I wanted to get in with the locals, have a laugh, share a jar. I didn't really want to shack up with all the posh people at the hotel. I was an outrageous guy. I wanted to go in and smoke some dope and drink beer and say, 'Listen, I love you guys. I'm from England and I'm mad.'

Of course, people's eyes were popping out at Julie and she was quite liking all the attention.

When we eventually got to Sandy Lane, we were quite pissed and feeling no pain. I walked right past reception, straight down onto the beach and waded into the sea up to my waist. Julie and I were both fully clothed. I didn't mind making a spectacle of myself – after all those drinks on the journey there, *I was desperate for a wee.*

Sandy Lane Hotel was fine and we drank lots, spent loads of time at the bar, generally lazed around, had dinner, relaxed a bit. We bumped into Michael Parkinson, who was also there on holiday.

Then, one day, a mysterious note was slipped under my door. It read, 'I'm getting married at the Hilton Hotel tomorrow. Would like you to be Best Man' and was signed 'John Miller'.

'Well, hang on,' I thought. 'Why does he want *me* to be Best Man?' I'd only met him once!

I was curious to find out what the hell was going on though. Did he have Ronnie Biggs with him? Was he really getting married? Now, suddenly, all the bullshit about Biggs that Johnny had been telling me was coming true.

'You coming?' I said to Michael Parkinson.

'No fear!' he said. 'And you be careful!'

And as I rushed off, I thought, 'Huh? What is there to be careful about?'

When I got down to the Hilton, I found Johnny Miller with a team of camera crews. It was all happening. He'd only gone and done it. He'd kidnapped Ronnie Biggs! I wasn't his Best Man in the end but I did go over and shake hands with him afterwards and I had my picture taken.

Suddenly I was on *News At Ten*! It looked like I was part of the team that had kidnapped Ronnie Biggs. And Julie was also on the TV.

Remember, she was supposed to still be skiing in Scotland. Back home, her Mum and Dad turned on *News At Ten* and saw their daughter looking like she was some kidnapper.

Oh dear.

I phoned up Laurie to tell him about the wedding and when he came on the blower, he just said, 'What – have – you – done?'

'What do you mean?'

'Our switchboards are jamming here,' said Laurie. 'Half of London's gangland want you dead!'

I couldn't believe my ears. 'Hang on,' I said, 'what's it got to do with *me*?'

'The newspapers here are full of the Ronnie Biggs kidnap,' said Laurie, 'and the headline, "I HEARD THEM PLOTTING IT IN MY CLUB".'

Dai Llewellyn had told a story to get publicity for his club.

Shit!

I flew home and had to go into hiding. People kept coming up to me and saying, 'You're that arsehole who kidnapped Ronnie Biggs.'

'No, I'm bloody *not*!' I said. 'Not at all.'

This went on and on for *years*, until, one day, I finally bumped into a guy called Brian Wright. He seemed to be 'in the know' about what was what.

I gave him the whole story straight and when I'd finished, he went away and smoothed a lot of people's ruffled feathers. There's very few people now in London's underworld who still actually believe that I was involved in that episode. But it took me years to 'clear my name.' It drove me mad because I wasn't involved in that business at all.

Much later on, I rang up Dai Llewellyn and accused him of getting me into trouble.

'Well,' he said, half apologetically, 'I was just trying to get some publicity for the club. I didn't think it would hurt.'

And that's the way it was. And if there's anyone out there who *still* doesn't believe me … well, ask Ronnie Biggs! At the time of writing,

Ronnie is back in the UK. He's been arrested, handcuffed on a plane, and padlocked to a bed with detectives. It's ridiculous, absolutely ridiculous the way this man has been treated.

In those days, we used to visit my best friend Clive Brandy a lot and spend time at his house in Sunningdale. He'd decided to convert his beautiful former pop star's house into a farm. He wanted to do things the other way round! He'd *been* a pop star, now he wanted to be a farmer.

But, instead of setting up a farm, he had 900 chickens in his back garden, some rabbits and a pig called Dopey, that used to waddle into the house. His poor housekeeper was always getting told off.

One day, Clive said to me and Julie, 'Look, if you two ever planned to get hitched, why don't you come and buy a house round the corner from us here?'

Good idea, I thought. 'Well,' I said, 'first, Clive, I've got to do my summer season down in Bournemouth. *Then*, we'll have a look at a house.' As far as I could plan things in my life, that was the plan.

As events turned out, the running order changed slightly. First, Julie and I got married at Poole Registry Office. It was a great day. All my showbizzy pals turned up. Dad got very drunk, as normal. I wore my Scotland rosette. Roger Kitter and Lionel Blair got thrown out for laughing. Clive was my Best Man, of course. Then that was it, we were married.

Julie and I went to live in Wentworth, just round the corner from Clive, as arranged. We were happy for a while, then, as the fifth Thames TV series of *The Jim Davidson Show* started, 1982 turned into a difficult year for me, a year that really got to me.

In January, Julie announced to me that she was pregnant. My heart skipped a beat.

'Oh, that's great!' I said. And I meant it.

We had a fabulous new house and things were starting to happen. I'd been given *The Jim Davidson Show*, I had a house in Wentworth, a beautiful, outrageous wife who was pregnant and my best mate Clive down the road. Things just could not have been happier.

Julie said she was due to have the baby around August.

'Well, that'll be great, we'll be in Torquay.'

But Julie wasn't happy with that. 'No, we're not doing summer season this year,' she said.

Julie wanted to stay at Wentworth and have the child locally.

'We've *got* to do the summer season,' I insisted. 'It pays for everything.'

We had quite a few rows, including some pretty hairy ones. They were just rows that husbands and wives have. They were bitter but we never got really violent.

I did want to settle down but settling down to me was having your wife with you when you did the summer season, or having her wait at the house for you. I still wanted to go away and do my summers but I wanted to be a married man as well. I wanted to have my cake and eat it too, really.

During April, I was on tour all over the place. I'd bought myself a yacht while I was down in Bournemouth, a 31-footer, a Sunseeker called *Dish Bee Doo*, named after the Swedish chef. I also became a director of Bournemouth Football Club, only because my great mate the ex-Chelsea footballer David Webb, who was now the manager, asked me to.

'Come up and see the team,' he'd said. 'You know, you could be a director here. We'd have a great time.'

So I did. I became a director. I didn't have to do much. Just turned up and had free drinks.

Julie was now becoming quite heavily pregnant as we were preparing for our summer season. We were doing quite well then. I had a little red Ferrari, the same one that Magnum drives – you know the little 308 GTSi; Julie had a Mercedes. We had a lovely house, complete with tropical fish tanks, our best mate Clive nearby and our favourite restaurant down the road.

Then, just as everything seemed to be going so swimmingly, we were hit by a calamity. When I say 'we', I mean, of course, the whole nation. Somehow it took us all by surprise, with little warning, but this turn of events was going to change all our lives. The Falklands War started.

Suddenly the news bulletins on TV were filled with footage showing our Armed Forces preparing to respond. A huge surge of patriotism gripped the nation as our troops sailed for the South Atlantic. It was a dramatic, highly charged and emotional time for everyone, whether you had friends or relatives in the Forces or not. Everyone felt involved. Everyone rallied round to the cause.

Over the past few years in the business, since I had started becoming a more popular name in the industry, I had made it my business to do what I could to support the troops. I had received various invitations to go abroad and had fitted the trips around my other stage and TV work whenever I could. In 1975, when I started, I used to go and do these CSE shows in Northern Ireland. I'd get paid seventy-five quid, meet all the troops, do five shows a day, get pissed, go on stage, get pissed, go on stage ...

I'd meet all these hard playing and hard fighting young men. I'd also been to Cyprus, Gibraltar and Belize. And now these young men were off to war and I wanted to get involved. I wanted to be with my contemporaries, if you like, and I wanted to be their hero. I knew they'd all be off now to the Falklands. It hit me incredibly hard.

While the Falklands campaign got underway, I found myself getting quite involved in being a director of Bournemouth FC. I enjoyed it. I even drove up to Wigan to watch a match – that's how involved I was! I remember the date, it was 4 May 1982, two days after the *Belgrano* had been sunk by HMS *Conqueror*.

It seemed like the whole country was behind the Task Force and everyone seemed to be worrying about what was going to happen next. All except for the football fans, that is! Their main worry was the promotion battle between Bournemouth and Wigan.

I sat watching this match on 4 May. I was in the boardroom and I met a man that day who's since become a friend. His name was Ken Bates and back then he was the chairman of Wigan. He's now, of course, the chairman of Chelsea.

That day he was very pleasant and we were chatting away happily. I think the score was 1–1 as we went in at half-time and made our way to the boardroom for our whiskies, cups of tea and a pie. Somewhere the telly was on – and then came the newsflash.

I remember it as if in slow-motion now. It was a hugely dramatic moment. In that room that had been bustling and buzzing with an excited football crowd, suddenly everyone stopped dead in their tracks and stared at the screen. You could have heard a pin drop.

It was the Ministry of Defence spokesman Ian McDonald who delivered the famous bulletin.

'HMS *Sheffield*, the Type 42 destroyer,' he announced, 'has been hit late this afternoon by an Argentine missile.'

And in that directors' gallery, we all looked at each other in utter disbelief that one of our ships had been hit by a missile. We just couldn't believe it. That wasn't supposed to happen.

After the newsflash, everyone just started quietly talking again, and carrying on nattering about football. And that really churned me up inside, so I left.

I left because I couldn't believe that they had just pushed the news to one side. I suppose normal people have the ability to do that, to carry on with their lives, to accept the things they can't change. But to me, it was devastating. I wanted the whole country to stop. I wanted everyone to just stop and say, 'Look, we're not having this!'

So, instead, I didn't watch the second half of the match – I got pissed and drove home. I knew then that this bloody Falklands War was going to affect me – more than a lot. I was outraged by what was happening in the Falklands. I was just torn apart by the fact that all these people whom I knew, and all these guys I'd been drinking with in Cyprus, were now going down there and might be killed.

The bombing of HMS *Sheffield* starkly brought it home to me. The same day HMS *Sheffield* was sunk, Tuesday, 4 May 1982, Lieutenant Nick

Taylor was shot down in a Harrier over Goose Green.

I just couldn't *wait* to get down there. I wanted to be with them. I could hardly believe what was going on. I've always been a bit jingoistic but this affected me *so much*.

I even idolised Mrs Thatcher because of that bloody war. Every day, I couldn't wait to watch the news. Every five minutes, I'd be glued to the news to try to find out what was happening. I'd read all the newspapers. I'd read everything I could.

If you look at my library at home now, there are many shelves full of books chronicling exactly what happened in the Falklands War. I became an expert at it. I became *'Nobby Know-It-All'*.

I couldn't wait to get down to the Falklands. I even asked if I could go down on the *QE2*, which sailed down there slightly later on. I was going to jack the summer season in, and say, 'I'm sorry, I've been requisitioned, you know, by Royal Appointment, or by Maggie Appointment.'

I just felt *so helpless* that our blokes were being killed. It drove me mad in the end. It just drove me mad.

Somehow, and for some reason, I felt pain at every bloody battle we lost. I also felt the pride and the hurt. It really got to me. I couldn't comprehend anyone who didn't get into it. I couldn't understand why there were people walking round the streets, going about their jobs and going in the pubs – and not actually queuing up down at Southampton to go away and bash up the Argentinians. I suppose it is a bit unusual but it's like sticking up for something that you feel is right, while everyone else just sits on the sidelines and says, limply, 'Oh, good luck lads.'

I wasn't like that. I was far more intense.

The Falklands War plodded on, and, of course, ended – around about the same time as Julie and I packed and went down to Torquay. I'd got my way. By now, Julie was quite pregnant and we had rented a little house up in the aptly named Thatcher Avenue.

I had the 31-foot *Sunseeker* moored in the bay, with the theatre close by. It was fabulous. I was top of the bill in Torquay, a place I loved.

Then, one night, we heard that our troop ship the *Canberra* was coming home along the coast. So I did the show and told them at the theatre, 'I'm just going out to the *Canberra*. Put the singer on!'

We raced out and me and Kevin jumped in the boat, still in our dinner suits, and we sped off and got right alongside *Canberra*. She was about six miles out, coming up the Channel. When we pulled alongside, I called her on the radio and wished her God's speed. It was a memorable moment. I felt intensely patriotic.

Then I came back and told the audience what we'd done. I pointed out where the ship was and made everyone in the theatre stand up and wave through the wall. At least I'd got someone interested ...

Throughout the summer season we had lots more fun and enjoyed many more boating excursions. Julie didn't really join in that much – she was heavily pregnant.

The rest of the family were staying down in Torquay and my sister Jean flew over from America to visit my other sister, Eileen.

Two weeks before Julie was due, I rang the house and asked Jean, 'Where's Julie?'

There was a pause on the line.

'Don't panic,' she said, 'but Julie's in hospital.'

I felt incredibly nervous as I anxiously paced the corridors outside the delivery room. After the blind panic of the dash down, fearing that I might miss the birth altogether, I'd arrived in a terrible fluster. Now I stood outside, powerless to help, while Julie gave birth to our son. I'd made the mistake of watching Sarah's birth – and had nearly passed out for my trouble. However supportive I felt, I wasn't doing that again!

We returned to the house after the birth and immediately took on a nanny to look after the baby. We hired some poor girl who didn't quite know what to do. She quit after three or four days, leaving us the job of finding another nanny. It must have been difficult for Julie, coming from the Jet Set, as she did, where she'd been used to running around as the glamorous promotions girl, going out with racing drivers and skiers and God knows who. Then, to go from that to suddenly having a baby with me, a south London comic, who loved doing summer season and had become a military nut.

For me though, it was wonderful. My heart swelled with pride – I had a son at last.

I would call him Cameron.

6

'To the South Atlantic …
quick march'

'Don't you think that's a bit self-obsessive?'

'Well, I guess I wanted my son to take the name that I should have had,' I replied.

Steve, my counsellor, looked puzzled. 'How do you mean?'

'Well,' I explained, 'when I was born, I was supposed to be called Cameron James Davidson. But my Dad went down to Woolwich Register Office and christened me James Cameron Davidson.'

Steve still look puzzled.

'Why did he do that? Was it because your Dad was drinking at the time? Was he drunk?'

That wasn't really it.

'No,' I said, 'he probably didn't like the idea of my first name being the same as his brother's regiment.'

Steve looked confused again. 'And so you think your Dad was jealous of your brother, do you?'

I shook my head. 'No,' I tried to explain, 'I'm not saying that. I'm just saying that my name on my passport and birth certificate is James Cameron Davidson.'

'So then why did they call you Cameron?' said Steve.

He was beginning to nark me now.

'Well, because that is what my name should have been,' I said.

Steve carried on relentlessly. 'So, you think your father doesn't like you? Is that it?'

'For Gawd's sake, Steve, don't complicate matters,' I said. 'I just wanted to call my son Cameron. Why do you always look into things so deeply?'

Steve started explaining to me that he looked into things because I was in the clinic, because I was sick.

'You're an alcoholic and this might be part of your self-obsession,' he said.

I flipped.

'Look. I've come in here because I drink too much — and I'm quite happy drinking too much. I just can't stand bloody hangovers. Just cure me of hangovers and I'll be fine.'

That would shut the bloke up, I reckoned. Silly little so-and-so...

Wrong!

It was week two of my time in Farm Place drinks clinic. Steve gave me a stiff talking to.

'Listen, Jim. You've got to get this straight. You are an alcoholic. You have terrible co-dependency problems. You are a drug addict. You are a sex addict——'

'Christ,' I butted in, 'where did you get all this from?'

'It's all the same thing as I told you before,' Steve replied. 'Now, there's only one way to save your life. You've got to get on the Twelve Step Programme. And the first step is to acknowledge that you are powerless over alcohol. At the moment, you are totally in denial.'

'If I am in denial, what am I doing here?'

Steve stayed calm. 'You are here because you have nowhere else to go and your life is unmanageable.'

I stared into space. I sat there motionless. Then he snapped me out of my daydream — and his words threatened to turn into a nightmare. He spoke to me slowly. 'If you do not get on this programme, you will die.'

Well, that came like a smack in the mouth really. I couldn't understand what the hell he was on about. To me, it was all a little bit American. You know, the great alcoholic, the Twelve Step Programme that was devised by 'Bill W,' as he's known in alcoholic circles, who decided that if you're a drunk, the only way to cure yourself is with other drunks.

You should practise this Twelve Step Programme all the time.

We were told in the Farm Place clinic that we would only practise five of the steps at first and then carry on throughout one's life getting more and more sober. It just seemed a load of bunkum to me. All I seemed to be doing was putting up with these drug addicts who were in there with me and thinking to myself,

'What has heroin got to do with Famous Grouse whisky?'

I couldn't see it at all. Just couldn't see it. And now I had Steve telling me that if I didn't get on The Programme, this and that would happen to me. He bombarded me with those clichés they used all the time there, like 'I was sick and tired of feeling sick and tired.'

The place was driving me bloody mad.

So, if I didn't get on the programme, if I didn't get it, I was gonna die... Well, I couldn't get it, so I was gonna die.

The Twelve Steps are taken from Alcoholics Anonymous, published by AA Services in New York (I'm reading from a little book I have in front of me now). Of course, it's American:

Step 1   We admitted we were powerless over alcohol, that our lives had become unmanageable.

Step 2   Came to believe that a power greater than ourselves could restore us to sanity.

Step 3   Made a decision to turn our will and our lives over to the care of God, as we understood him.

Step 4   Made a searching and fearless moral inventory of ourselves.

Step 5   Admitted to God, to ourselves, and to another human being, the exact nature of our wrong doings.

Step 6   Were entirely ready to have God remove all those defects of character.

Step 7   Humbly asked Him to remove our shortcomings.

Step 8   Made a list of all the persons we have harmed and became willing to make amends to all of them.

Step 9   Made direct amends to such people, except where to do so would injure them, or others.

Step 10   Continued to take personal inventory, and when we were wrong, properly admitted it.

Step 11   Sought, through prayer and meditation, to improve our conscious contact with God, as we understood him, praying only for knowledge of His will for us and the power to carry that out.

Step 12   **Having had a spiritual awakening as a result of these**
            Steps, we try to carry this message to alcoholics and to
            practise those principles in our affairs.

Now, that was what we had to do. There was all this talk about God and all this stuff about the Higher Power. When I'd heard about these steps, I turned to Steve.

'You know, Steve,' I said, 'it's all very well handing your problems over to God, but what if, deep down in your heart, you don't know if God really exists?'

Steve wasn't phased. He'd obviously heard this one before. 'Then you should pick what we call the Higher Power.'

'Is that like in Freemasonry,' I asked, 'where, instead of God, you call him "The Great Architect of the Universe"?'

Steve didn't really understand what I meant. I'd been a Mason for four years and I tried to explain to him that in Freemasonry, you believe in a supreme being. So, a Muslim and a Hindu, an Arab and a Christian can all be together in believing that their deity, their 'something or other', created the Universe. And then created Man and Woman, and then divorce lawyers!

I don't think Steve did accept my 'Great Architect of the Universe' idea because it was my idea. Their idea at the clinic was to strip away all the things that you had in your mind – and get you to think along the lines of the Twelve Steps. Because the 'Great Architect' was a grey area, he drowned it. It pissed me off a bit. I thought I had him there.

Steve didn't laugh at this. 'You could make the group your Higher Power,' he suggested.

'I don't understand.'

'Well, think of all the people that you sit round with in your group,' Steve continued. 'There are eighteen of you in the clinic at the moment. You're in three groups of six. If the collective thoughts of the group you're in are better on a subject than yours are, maybe you should take them as your Higher Power.'

'Oh great,' I said. 'So now, not only can I not give my problems to God, but you're telling me I've got to give my problems to two alcoholics, two anorexics, a guy who can't speak English and a heroin addict.'

'Yup.'

I was not happy. 'Well why? What has that got to do with me?' I demanded.

'What do they understand about me?'

And that was the way it was left. I was in total confusion.

One day, another letter arrived at the clinic from Tracy. She was telling me what an arsehole I'd been and how rotten and unhappy she'd felt.

I sat there, then I started to feel sorry for myself, thinking, 'Well, Tracy's off in that nice big, bloody house that we've got, The Old Forge, which I'm still paying for ... and I don't know if I'll ever be able to go back to work again.'

I hadn't spoken to Tracy for a while. I'd spoken to her on the phone twice but I was still not allowed to see her for another week. But even when we did speak, she didn't seem that pleased to talk to me.

It was now January and well into the NewYear. Over NewYear it was awful and someone kept telling me that if I didn't get on this Programme I was gonna die...

That was the routine. Up at 7.30 in the morning, breakfast, boiled eggs at 8 am, sit round and do some prayer, do some writing, do the group, have lunch, more lectures, more this, more that. And although I was feeling better, I was still on the Heminevrin and I was still feeling a bit woozy.

I couldn't help thinking that maybe, after a couple of weeks off the booze, I'd just push off, because I couldn't get the idea of the place at all. I continued joining in the group sessions, and I started to stick up for myself. There was this feeling of jealousy, you see ... because I was famous? That's what it was. Must have been because I was famous.

We sat round and everyone talked about their friends.

'I was out with my friend Ron and we went for something to eat,' one girl named Camilla said. 'Then he dropped me off and I felt so upset that I thought I'd go to the off licence and get a bottle of vodka and drink it. But when I got to the off licence, it was shut. And I knew it was my "Higher Power" taking care of me.'

'How you can be so fucking stupid,' I said, 'as to believe that your Higher Power has got his eye on you and so he shuts the fucking off licence? Oh dear. Is that what a "Higher Power" is? This thing that goes around in front of you, locking up off licences up and taking the alcohol out of vodka ...? This is absolute cack. I can't get this at all.'

So, then we'd argue and I'd eventually just give up. I'd think, 'Oh, bollocks to this.'

One day, I was telling them a story of how I'd been out with a few people, and I mentioned a few famous names. I mentioned Eric Clapton, who lived round the corner from my pub, because I thought where I used to go drinking was relevant. And I mentioned Elton John, of whom I was an admirer but had never met.

And then some posh guy called John piped up. He was a heroin addict. 'Yeah, I'm a smack addict,' he used to say and I felt he'd always phrase it as if he were in the Premier Division and I was in the Conference League because I was just a poor alcoholic. Fucking pissed me off.

'I don't like the way Jim namedrops all the time.'

What a stupid thing to say.

'What are you on about?' I said to him.

'Well, I just don't like the way you namedrop.'

'Well, I'm not namedropping,' I said. 'You're talking about your friends. I'm talking about my friends, that's all.'

He continued his whinging. 'Yeah, well how do you think the rest of us feel? You're trying to make us feel this way.'

And then someone else chipped in, 'Yeah, we think Jim's being very grandiose. Why does he wear that silly watch, the Rolex watch, with diamonds on it? Why doesn't he put it in a Trust Fund for his kids?'

At this point I really saw red. 'What's it bloody well got to do with you?' I said.

Then an argument broke out and the counsellor had to interrupt us. 'Well look, Jim,' he said, 'perhaps we can compromise here. You don't have to mention your friends' names completely, just mention their first names … How about that? Will that do?'

Everyone round the group nodded begrudgingly in agreement. That was settled then.

'OK,' I said, 'I was at the House of Commons the other day and Margaret said to me …'

'How would you like to go to Beirut, Jim?' said Margaret Thatcher.

I was inside the House of Commons. I'd been taken along in my capacity as Patron of the Sharon Allan Leukaemia Trust, by a lovely man called Humphrey Berkeley, who was our Director. He knew the Prime

Minister by first name. Wow! And he took me along to meet her.

When I was presented to her, she promptly led me into a back stage room at the Commons and showed me the table where they had planned the invasion of the Falklands.

'Jim is hoping to go down to the Falklands later to entertain the troops,' Humphrey said.

'Oh, what a *marvellous* thing you're doing, Jim,' Mrs Thatcher replied. Then, with a twinkle in her eye, she added, 'But first, how would you like to go to Beirut?'

I didn't feel as if I was in a position to argue. I said I'd be delighted and thought no more about it.

Then the Prime Minister's office or the people from CSE, Combined Services Entertainment, started saying that the Prime Minister had asked Jim Davidson if he would go to Beirut with a team and entertain the troops.

'When he comes back safe,' they said, 'we'll announce it to the Press.'

Now, little did I realise at the time, but what *actually* brought all this on was the then Leader of the Opposition, a scruffy little man called Michael Foot, who used to do his duffel coat up with the wrong buttons and wore his shoes on the wrong feet. He walked along like Doctor Who's great, great grandfather and he looked remarkably like Zippy from *Rainbow*.

One day, Zippy leapt up at Prime Minister's Question Time. 'Can the Prime Minister confirm that the British troops in Beirut are under deadly danger, and can she tell us why they are there?'

And I believe Mrs Thatcher stood up and replied something along the lines of, 'Our troops are in no danger at all. They're professional soldiers and they're doing a great peace keeping job for the UN.' Well, that told him.

Beirut in 1983, of course, was a real battleground. Once the jewel of the Mediterranean, a sort of Rio de Janeiro, a Las Vegas, with its fantastic people, the city had been turned into a ghost town – all due to the fighting between the Lebanese Army, the Israelis, the Syrian-backed Hezbollah fighters, and the Palestinians.

In an excellent piece of foreign policy, Mrs Thatcher's Office then decided to send Jim Davidson out there to entertain the troops.

When I was asked to go to Beirut, I knew that I'd be taking Terry, my new minder, with me. The rest of the show was laid on for me in typical government style. Instead of sending some dolly birds or some striptease artists, or some Page Three girls, or some glamorous female singer, I was given 'JJ' Steward, a nice bloke ... *but a trumpet player.* A male trumpet player, I ask you. To go out to a war zone and entertain the company of the 16/5th Lancers and their accompanying engineers – all blokes.

Also on the trip, funnily enough, was Andy Beaumont, my ex-fiancée's brother, who had a band with two girls.

'Well,' I thought, 'that'll be OK. He sings a bit, plays guitar and the two girls dance around. But they're hardly "bum and titty", which is what the people out there will really want.'

And the other disappointment was ... there was no-one for me to shag – very badly organised indeed. And one of the girls was married to Jane's brother so this looked like it was going to be a disaster. Plus, no-one was supposed to know that we were bound for Beirut. *No-one.*

Except me and my minder, Terry.

So we drove down to RAF Lynham, where the C130s live. Off Junction 16 of the M4, you'll see these fabulous C130s, the Hercules, or as they're known in the trade, 'Fat Alberts', their little noses and their big tails, whizzing away, churning out huge great exhaust fumes from their four turbo prop engines.

At Lynham we partook in several whiskies with the team. It was about 9 o'clock in the evening. It was a drizzly and horrible April and we were off to *Germany* – that was the 'official' plan. We were off to ... Germany (wink, wink).

On the plane, I was invited up onto the flight deck, where I met Peter Forshore, a full colonel.

'You sit with me, old boy,' he said, 'and we'll watch the take-off together.'

Terry got in the back.

Now, the back of a C130 is nothing like you ever see in the films. It is just like an empty Pickfords van, really. You sit on boxes, held up by straps. They're supremely uncomfortable and the noise is *horrendous*.

We'd totally fooled the Press and anyone else who thought they knew where we were going. Actually, we were bound for Cyprus, and then on to Beirut. We'd totally fooled ourselves, too – because we'd only got 400 yards down the runway when we had a hydraulic system overheating on the aircraft – and we had to stop, turn round and taxi back to the terminal.

Disembarking was tough on poor Terry, who'd taken two sleeping pills, was totally unconscious and now woke up, bleary-eyed, convinced we were in Cyprus – when, of course, we were still in Lynham.

As we shuffled off, he was heard to mutter, 'Bloody cold in Cyprus, innit?'

Back inside the mess again, we waited while they repaired the aircraft. At the bar, Peter Forshore told me he was a bomb disposal expert, and that he was Deputy Chief of Staff in Cyprus, where we'd put on a warm-up show for the Scots Guards, who I knew all about from the Falklands War.

Arriving in Cyprus six hours later than scheduled, we had a bit of scoff, got to the little cinema in Akrotiri, the air base on the coast, and in came the Scots Guards. The show we did for them went down a storm.

We stayed up drinking in the mess afterwards until about 2.30 am. Then at 5.30 am we got back on our Chinook. It was *then* I told the team.

'We're going in to *Beirut* to do a show,' I said.

They all thought we were going to do a show on a ship, just offshore. But I said, 'No. We're going into Beirut, and if anyone doesn't want to go, say so now.'

'Right, come on, we're up for it,' everyone said. 'Let's bloody *do it*.'

The Chinook's codename was 'ET'. I sat down on a great big box of Point 0.50 Browning ammunition. I sat on my tin hat and the flak jacket they gave me, and we took off ... only to smack straight back down on the runway again from about ten foot up. Everyone jolted – and I put my hands over my nuts in case there was an explosion. Old 'ET' had gone 'tits up'. This safe little trip Maggie had promised me wasn't going too smoothly at all.

So, now we had to get off that bloody aircraft and wait for another one. Once airborne, we pretty soon ran up against the problem of where to refuel. To my dismay, it dawned on me that the pilot had a moving target in mind!

To land a Chinook, a twin-bladed, stonking great helicopter on a ship, takes some doing. It was amazing how that pilot got us on it. We were all huddled inside the helicopter, bracing ourselves against the deafening noise, when into our sights came the Royal Fleet Auxiliary Ship, *Reliant*. She was steaming at 18 knots through – what seemed to me – were choppy seas. What happened next was nothing short of a miracle.

The Chinook pilot flew us in over the ship, attempting to hover over the landing area. It was a feat of incredible skill to increase the helicopter's speed steadily to bring us perfectly in line with the course being steered by *Reliant*. Somehow he managed it. The guy had nerves of steel. I was terrified, of course, but acutely aware at the same time that I was in the hands of consummate professionals. The drama was intense as we slowly descended on to the deck and touched down. When I realised we were down, a huge sense of relief washed over me. Only the laundryman knew how I felt …

We re-fuelled and took off again, which was only marginally less scary. And then we headed towards the Beirut coast.

I sat in between the two pilots, looking over their shoulders, as we sped along, 30 feet above the sea. Then we flew up the wadi, with skyscrapers on either side of us, about ten-storey buildings. The bad guys had strung up huge, big, thick two-inch metal cables from one building to another to try and trip the helicopters over. So we were leaping over them, diving up and down, pulling a lot of 'G' as we climbed over them, and negative 'G', as we flew down. Everyone was throwing up in the back. It was absolutely terrifying. My knuckles went white.

There was a guy on the chaff launcher, ready to fire chaff off. Chaff is little bits of silver paper, hundreds of little bits, used to try to deflect radar-guided missiles. The guy would also fire flares to try to distract heat-seeking missiles, the popular shoulder-launched *Sam Seven* – a fashion item in Beirut at the time!

Finally, we landed, jumped in some trucks and drove to Hadath, a base in between West Beirut and East Beirut, Christian Beirut and Muslim Beirut.

They were firing at one another, right across our heads. We arrived at an old school house, where we were to be based. The 16/5th Lancers were there and I was met by an engineering officer, a major. I was shown in, still shaking, and told the show was to be in two hours' time.

The name 'The 16/5th Lancers' sounds really posh, like a cavalry regiment – but they're all from Birmingham. They recruit from the Midlands, so all the blokes had these great Midland accents. One soldier came up and said, in a thick Brummie accent, 'Fuckin' great to see you Jim, it really is. You're a sight for sore eyes,' he said.

'We've had all sorts of fuckin' shit thrown at us here. We've been fuckin' mortared, we've been fuckin' shot at, there've been suicide fuckin' bombers, the fuckin' Yanks have been blown up. We've had the lot here, guns and fuckin' rabid dogs. The food's fuckin' crap and I fuckin' hope you've brought some fuckin' crumpet with you because we're *gagging* here. It's going to be great to see you, you funny cunt.'

'Thank you, Colonel,' I said, 'I can't wait either.' (That's a joke, by the way – colonels don't really talk like that!)

Next, a brigadier came up to me. 'Hello,' he said, 'I'm Brigadier So-and-So.'

I was confused. 'Oh,' I said, pointing to the colonel, 'I thought *he* was in charge.'

The brigadier corrected me. 'No, no, I'm not actually in charge. I'm just here to make sure that everything goes smoothly with the Press.'

'We want to invite some of the photographers and some of the world's TV camera crews to show that, er, we Brits are doing a good job ... and that you're here to entertain them and that we're not in any danger.'

'Hello,' I thought, 'this is all now beginning to make a bit of sense. That bit of what Zippy was saying to Mrs Thatcher, and what Mrs Thatcher was saying back ...'

The brigadier turned to me. 'Now look Jim, tonight, you *will* keep it clean, won't you?'

'Oh no,' I thought, 'this is getting worse.'

'Well, we only want ten minutes nice and clean for the TV newsreels – and then you can go for broke,' the brigadier emphasised. 'We want to make this a good PR exercise for the British Army, you see.'

I took another swig of my Red Label whisky. 'If you want to make it a good exercise,' I said, 'why don't we invite the Americans up from the airport?'

'What a bloody good idea,' said the brigadier.

A month before, 280 of them were killed in a suicide bomb attack at Beirut airport, and these guys were living underground like rats.

Half an hour before the show, up came sixty US Marines. Now, these were the biggest blokes you've *ever* seen in your life. Their arms, with bulging muscles, gripped M16 rifles, grenades hanging off them. They looked like *proper* soldiers – whereas ours looked like cadets, little skinny blokes, with funny Brummie accents.

When I saw the size of these Yanks, I thought, 'Oh my God, if I go on stage and take the mick out the Yanks, they're going to get hacked off with me, because they don't understand my humour – and there's going to be a fight. And they'll *massacre* our lads.'

The Brits must have been frightened to death of these Yanks. Suddenly, it looked like I wasn't going to die from a passing bullet, that I'd die from a brawl with our huge American cousins.

Slowly, the penny dropped. It suddenly dawned on me – almost every one of the American soldiers was black ... the biggest black men you've ever seen in your life.

And the brigadier turned to me with a smirk and said, 'Well, that's Chalky out the fucking window for starters.'

So, now I'd got no Chalky and I'd got to keep it clean. All this on top of all the other problems with the trip.

As the show started, I introduced the trumpet player who, by now, had terrible piles. The Americans were sitting on one side and the Brits were on the other – and there was an icy divide down the middle.

As I was about to go up on stage, I thought, 'This is going to be *horrible*.'

Outside, all I could see was tracer bullets whizzing across the sky, a real firefight. And not very far away.

Then the battle got closer until someone started firing at <u>us</u> and the rounds were cracking over our heads. I could *hear* them buzzing over our heads – then you could hear the bang.

'Brigadier,' I said, ducking into my shirt, 'hang on, this is all a bit arse upwards. In the films, you hear the bang go off … and *then* you hear the bullet.'

'I'm afraid, Jim, it doesn't work like that,' replied the brigadier, 'because bullets travel faster than the speed of sound.'

'Well, in that case,' I said, 'how do you duck?'

The brigadier looked rather apologetic. Then he said something *really* frightening.

'You never hear the one that kills you.'

'Oh my God,' I thought, 'I am going to die …'

After the girls finished their spot, I stood in the wings, adrenalin holding me together. I mustn't tell anti-American stuff; gags that people could complain were racist were out; no blue gags; and I'd got to say Margaret Thatcher was wonderful and that we were doing a great job …

'Ladies and Gentlemen, CSE are proud to present, live in Hadath, in Beirut, on behalf of the UN Peace Keeping Force, Jim Davidson.'

The lights of the various TV cameras flashed on – BBC, ITV, CBS News, ITN. At least fifty reporters took note as I walked on stage. I saw the huge American troops in the front row and knew, if I mentioned Chalky, there'd be a riot – and I would be killed.

So I reached the microphone. I knew that what happened next – the very next words that were uttered – could detonate the charge in that room. Beads of hot sweat on my brow scorched my skin. The dry dust of every Beirut alleyway seemed to grate in the back of my parched throat. My nerves jangled. I'd never been brilliant with words but now, in this moment of truth, I prayed my sense of tact and diplomacy would not fail me. I had to exercise extreme caution. Everyone in the room was watching me – to say nothing of the millions of television viewers around the world who would be tuning in.

Finally, I found the courage to begin. Just as I opened my mouth to speak, I swear to God, one of our corporals stood up, a British black guy. My heart stopped. He shouted out at the top of his voice, 'Hey Jim, don't forget to take the piss out of them fucking niggers.'

A blinding flash ripped through my brain. This squaddie's words had surely triggered the end. I prepared to meet my Maker. No time for a last cigarette. No time for a blindfold. The firing squad had already taken aim and were ready to complete the execution. I braced myself, almost in a crouch, waiting, any split second, for the machine gun bullets to explode my way and rip into me and then him – but, to my amazement and relief, all these huge black guys, these Americans, just burst out roaring with laughter at the tops of their voices. They cheered and the Brits all cheered as well. A few beer cans were thrown at the bloke – and the atmosphere switched *just like that*.

So, I carried on with the show. And I learnt something that day. If you are yourself and there's no malice in the way you treat people, there's a good chance that your words or actions will be received in the way those black guys received the humour from that English guy. They laughed at his bravado and at the fact that a skinny little Englishman would *dare* to say that to some big black American guys. In fact, they loved it.

With the show over, next day, we did another show and then we left. We had to go quickly because we were being shelled. The landing zone was under fire too. Although I didn't see any explosions, I *did* hear some guns and shells whizzing overhead. Then 'ET' flew us back up the wadi. The Chinook picked us up and off we went, back to Blighty for tea and medals!

When I returned safe, the following week on Prime Minister's Question Time, Zippy jumped up to the Despatch Box again.

'Can the Prime Minister confirm that the British troops in Beirut are in mortal danger, that they were mortared the other week ...' and so on.

Mrs Thatcher rose to her feet and said – and apparently this is all recorded in *Hansard*: 'The troops are in *no* danger. In fact, they've just had a concert there from Jim Davidson and his team. And they were all in fine spirits.'

And with that, Zippy sat down.

As time went by and 4 May 1983 came along, I was asked to get involved in an HMS *Sheffield* reunion. She was sunk on that 4 May 1982, and as those sailors were dying, it grieved me to think that there I was, knocking back the drinks with Ken Bates in Wigan, listening to that announcement on the TV.

I shared those sailors' sense of loss, so I turned up in Portsmouth for the reunion 'do'. Most of the people who were killed on the ship were the chefs because the Exocet hit the ship's galley.

Sailors say, 'I spy with my little eye something beginning with E. You have six seconds to answer. Once you've seen it, you've got six seconds to hit the deck.'

When the missile hit *Sheffield*, some said it didn't explode but that it was the kinetic energy of it hitting that ship at nearly the speed of sound that caused the damage.

They say the fuel left over in the Exocet started the fires. The explosion, which blew up the galley, made all the chip pans catch fire. Terrible.

Now I was faced with some of the crew a year later. I didn't quite know how this evening would turn out. I'd already met some of the veterans, people like Sergeant Hatton, from the Scots Guards, also Simon Weston, the Welsh Guardsman, who was on the *Sir Galahad*.

The do was at RAF Chessington and I went with Iris Williams and Clive. One brave Welsh Guardsman told us, 'We were trying to put the flames out with our hands. Afterwards, they put our hands, smothered in Flamazine Cream, inside plastic bags. I could hear some rattling in the bottom of my plastic bag,' he said, 'so, I looked down and it was my little finger in the bag.'

I gulped.

'Bloody funny, actually,' he said.

And that was the first time that I'd met people with such terrible injuries who could still really laugh about it. I learnt something from that as well.

I faced crew from the *Sheffield*. Some were drunk, some were crying. Some wives were bitter. I did my straight cabaret performance. Some people heckled. It was pretty awful, actually.

At the end, I went to the bar and this girl came up to me and asked me which hotel I was staying in.

'Thank God,' I muttered to myself under my breath, 'a bird. That'll do me.'

'I'm staying in the Marriott,' I said.

'What's your room number, then?' she joked.

'Hang on,' I said, 'your big hairy-arsed husband isn't going to come up and punch me in a minute, is he?'

'Oh, I doubt it,' she said, 'he was killed on the *Sheffield* ...'

Ever since the war had begun, I had wanted to go to the Falklands. My whole life now revolved around just getting there. I just don't know what made me feel that strongly about it all. Maybe it was wanting to be a soldier, wanting to be a sailor or just not being part of it. I just thought, 'My life is so *easy*. And *their* life is so hard. And although they couldn't do my job, I *certainly* couldn't do theirs.'

I wanted to be part of it all. I think, probably for the first time in my life, it dawned on me that there were other things in life apart from Jim Davidson.

Anything that *wasn't* part of the Falklands, anyone who *didn't* want to know about it, I just pushed to one side. Even Julie. She'd say to me, 'Oh, I don't know why you're bothered.'

'*Don't know why I'm bloody bothered?* Are you mad? These blokes died for our country,' I said to her, in utter disbelief.

There were 256 British blokes still in the ground in the Falklands and it just drove me mad. So, I put this little show together and off we went to entertain the troops that were still there.

The flight to the Falklands was just amazing. We flew by VC10 to Dakar, on the east coast of Africa via Senegal. We got off the plane to refuel, then flew down to Ascension Island. We did a couple of shows on Ascension and I remember the funniest thing about the place. There weren't any proper toilets there.

You used to sit in a long bench at the American base. You'd just sit there for your crap and there'd be another bloke sat right next to you.

'Hello,' he'd look up and smile. 'You Jim Davidson?'

'D'you mind?' I'd say.

Then we got on the old C130 again for our thirteen-hour flight. The mid-air refuelling was fantastic. They invited me up to the cockpit to watch the refuelling from a VC10 tanker. It was refuelling our aircraft and the amazing thing was that the VC10's *slowest* speed is still *faster* than our *fastest* speed. So, I wondered, how could we catch up and get fuel off it?

'Watch this,' they said.

We were all at 28,000 ft and both aircraft then went into a dive, a shallow dive. She was screaming with the air brakes on, and we were going flat out in a dive and we eventually caught up and took the fuel out of her. I'd never seen anything like it. I mean I couldn't *believe* I was sat in a cockpit, and barely twenty feet away was the tail of this other aircraft. We were flying flat out, taking this fuel on board. These blokes who were doing it were something else, I thought.

'You guys are *fantastic*.'

And here's little *me*. What the fuck do *I* do for a living? A few jokes, and I get girls and booze … and God I envy you, you men of derring-do…Brits!

We had the most wonderful time doing shows in the Falklands. Dear Richard Digance was my supporting act.

One day, he did a show for four people in a dug-out. *Four people.* Two of them got up and left halfway through his act. … That's not to disparage

Richard's act, because he's brilliant. But two of them had to report for guard duty.

Despite this, I *still* enjoy telling everyone that fifty per cent of Digance's audience walked out one night. Sorry Richard.

So, we flew back to Ascension, then home to England. I'd collected every piece of memorabilia I could find, including a Colt 45 automatic. Guns lay everywhere. I cleaned it up as it was all rusty and stuck it in my bag. Bit naughty, I suppose, but I didn't tell anyone and I brought it home.

When we eventually got back to Brize Norton, we all hugged each other. We felt we had done the most fulfilling thing in our lives. We'd worked our butts off. We'd done five shows a day sometimes, living on chicken curry. The troops had loved us and cheered us. I'd never felt so much appreciation in my life ...

Terry drove me from the base back to Wentworth. I'd been away now for two weeks but Julie was *not* thrilled to see me back. She didn't ask how it went; she didn't ask how emotionally involved I'd been caught up with the whole thing.

Now I was faced with leaving my family of entertainers. We'd worked our balls off down there, given everything we had, just as those troops had. I missed the troops, the adulation and the gut-wrenching sadness I'd witnessed, of people missing their loved ones. Yet now I was back with *my* loved one and all I could think about was getting back to the Falklands.

It had been such a high in the Falklands. Now, back home, I got the whisky bottle out and sat there. I took out every bit of memorabilia I'd brought back, and laid it all out over the kitchen and the front room — flags, maps, bayonets, bullets and shells. I also got out the little plaque that I'd found that some Argentinian soldier had made to stick over his trench.

I'd planned to take that to Tramp night club and give it to the Argentinian waiter there as a gift. I didn't know how he'd take it, but I wanted him to have it. When I did give it to him, he cried — and then I did too.

Julie came downstairs, looked at me sitting on the floor and said, 'Is *this* a man in his right mind? Is *this* what people do?'

Not for the last time in my life, I sat there drunk and sobbing.
I never really got over that first Falklands trip. I went again in June 1984 and this time I took my little video camera with me. I videoed all the shows that were going on. We had a great time and when I came back, I played it to Philip Jones, at Thames Television.

'Let's go down and do a Christmas show there,' I said to him. 'We can film it and you can screen it on Christmas Day. It'd be great.'

Little did I know that he had *another* show lined up to get me on TV ... and that the name of that other programme was *This Is Your Life*.

I didn't smell a rat at all when Eamonn Andrews came knocking.

'I think I'll pop down to the pub,' I said to Julie one night.

'Oh, *don't* go,' she said quickly.

'What do you mean?' I said, 'going to the pub is what I *do*.'

She back-tracked. 'Well, don't get too drunk, then.'

'What are you talking about – don't get too drunk?' I said, 'that's what I *do*.'

So, I came home drunk, took a sleeping tablet, then headed up to bed. I was in a bit of pain because the Christmas before, I'd dropped a bloody paving slab on my foot, nearly chopped my toe off and had had to cancel my show. It was a nightmare. They'd sewn my big toe back on and, even to this day, it's grown back like a monster's toe.

I'd woken up the following morning, a bit hungover, a bit groggy, and my toe was killing me. Suddenly I heard bagpipes in my driveway. 'What the fuck is this?'

I was listening to the hi-fi at the time. I turned up the volume, thinking it was interference. The bagpipe noises didn't go away.

Suddenly, a knock at the door. With my poorly toe, I limped to the door, opened it, looking like a dog's breakfast, and there in front of me was the sergeant major I'd met on my first trip to the Falklands, with a company of the Royal Irish Rangers, who were the battalion down there at the time.

And Eamonn Andrews popped up with his Big Red Book and said, 'Jim, This Is Your Life.'

'Oh,' I thought, 'this is it. Fantastic. I've cracked it. About bloody time.'

Then I thought they'd push off. But I had to get straight in the car and go with them. They don't hang about on that show, you know. I hurriedly grabbed a fresh shirt, yanked some trousers on, combed my hair, and jumped in the car with Eamonn.

As we drove past the Crooked Billet pub in Staines, I said to him, 'I painted that pub once, you know.'

And there I was, heading off to the greatest accolade in British show business. Eamonn looked at the pub and replied, 'Good for you.'

And, with that, he opened a bottle of champagne and we drank it in the back of the car.

'All your family are there, you know,' he said to me.

I panicked. 'It's the afternoon now,' I said, 'what time's the show?'

Eamonn replied, 'Seven thirty tonight, why?'

Oh, oh.

'How long has my father been there?'...

'Ah,' said Eamonn, 'your Dad's a bit of character, isn't he?'

I shuddered. Dad would be as pissed as a fart by now.

Eamonn must have read my thoughts.

'He's been there since midday.'

That was it.

'Oh noooo.'

When we arrived at the studio, I was locked away in a little room, trying to work out who was going to be on the show. I suspected my sister would be there from America because I know the way television works. And I knew that all my family were going to be there. It was going to be great.

But I was dead worried about Dad.

So I walked on to the set, down the ramp and I limped on with my bad foot. I sat there and on came Julie, my wife. Then on came Mum – without Dad – and I thought, 'Oh no, they've sent Dad home and they're going to have to say he's passed away or something because he's so drunk.'

Then Eamonn asked me his famous question, 'Do you recognise *this* voice?'

And I heard some indecipherable man, spouting this Glaswegian gibberish over the PA system.

It was Dad.

The doors opened and my little old Dad stood there with his walking stick. Seeing my Dad, old Jock from Glasgow on the telly was bloody marvellous. One of the great moments in my life.

Mum and Dad were sat there, and Eamonn asked them, 'What's it like having a famous son?'

'Well, Eamonn,' Mum replied, 'when Jim cracked it in show business he said to me, "Mum, you'll never have to work again as long as you live." And I never have.'

She never *did* work again. I paid for her *not* to work. And Dad was then too ill and too old to work.

But that was a great *This Is Your Life* and a great night.

After the party, we all jumped in cars and took the limousines to my Dad's pub in Woolwich, where he used to drink. We got drunk as skunks and I got Keith Emerson playing the piano while I played drums. It was a night to remember forever.

These days, I can't bring myself to watch the video of my *This Is Your Life*. It's just too sad for me, especially now that my Mum and Dad and sister Eileen have all died. Looking back at the past is always a bit scary for me. I tend not to ever look back, if I can avoid it.

If I do look back, instead of saying, 'Weren't those great times?' I'll always tend to get terribly nostalgic.

But I think the real reason that I don't like to look back is that deep down I know I could have done it so much better and hurt less people.

7

'How *dare* you phone me when I'm out having affairs?'

The mid-1980s were the boom days of the cabaret club and I was really busy. I'd just turned 31, and I was living down in Wentworth with Julie.

I found myself playing lots of clubs. One of my regular haunts was Blazers of Windsor, run by the brilliant George Savva. Sometimes, I'd go there and work for three weeks solid, seven nights a week. I'd go on stage at 11 o'clock and come off at 1 am. It was great fun – and dead easy, too.

Sometimes, Julie would come with me. Julie was much more of a party animal than the other wives.

I bought a Ferrari Boxer. Bloody awful it was, but I thought we just *had* to have one to go with the house. The thing kept breaking down. It would conk out as I was pulling out of my drive. So, I spoke to those nice people at Marinellos, who look after the franchise for Ferrari, but I was landed with some idiot there who said to me, 'Perhaps you're not driving it correctly, Mr Davidson.'

'What *are* you talking about?' I said. 'The bloody car keeps breaking down. It's had three clutches in the last year at £2,000 a time.'

'Well, I'm going to have to ask you to take me out in your car,' he said, 'and show me how you change gear.'

Pompous dick!

So I flogged it. Funnily enough, I sold it to my mate Dave Franks for £14,000 – and then he did it up and sold it again for £20,000! And *then*, I believe, the new owner sold it *again* the following week for £125,000! Typical of me! If only I'd kept hold of it.

I started recording a new series called *Up the Elephant and Round the Castle*. I played a bloke called Jim London, who lived in his old Auntie's railway-side terraced house in London.

It was a great show, a little dated now when you see it on UK Gold. But it was the first sitcom I'd been in. I never really feel quite at home with sitcoms because I feel it's difficult to draw that line between reality and fantasy. *Only Fools and Horses* oversteps that line. It's brilliant but not real. Whereas *Minder* is more real but doesn't have so many laughs. Sitcoms are always a dodgy area for me. I don't like them, to be quite frank with you.

Come September, we flew back to the Falklands to do a TV show, much to Julie's displeasure – not that I was bothered that much because, by then, I'd started to have a little bit of a thing with Suzanne Dando.

Suzanne was lovely! I'd met her at the Palladium in 1980. She was only a kid then and she was beautiful. And I had now began to realise that my marriage with Julie wasn't working. We were just drifting further and further apart. The only times we ever went out together was when we were with lots of friends and my old best pal Clive. Julie and I just had one of those entertaining 'smiley-at-each-other' marriages, really.

Once I took Suzanne off to Paris and the boys down the pub told Julie, rotten sods! She phoned up the George V Hotel. She guessed where I'd be because I'm a creature of habit. The room we were staying in was a sumptuous suite, the most romantic, lavish and luxurious bedroom in the world – but it had a telephone ...

It rang, I picked it up and heard Julie's voice on the other end.

'Are you enjoying yourself?' she said.

'How *dare* you phone me when I'm out having affairs!' I replied.

And that was the end of that. We ended up fighting and arguing.

Julie and I just drifted further and further apart and eventually I left. I was just moving on. I knew my marriage wasn't working. I thought I might see less of my son. The house would probably have to be sold. There'd be a divorce coming up.

'It's all going to be shit,' I thought to myself, 'but who gives a fuck? Let's go down the pub with Suzanne.'

So, one day I decided I'd had enough of all the pretence. It was time to take the bull by the horns and have a grown-up conversation with Julie. We'd reached the end of the road. Honesty seemed to me to be the best way forward, however much I disliked confrontation.

'Look, you know, it's the end of our marriage really,' I said.

Then Julie decided she would move out because I had quite a big mortgage on the house and a tax bill to pay. I rented her a house round the corner where she moved in with young Cameron and immediately acquired a new boyfriend called Gary Farrow. He used to be the record plugger for Elton John.

Of course, this was all OK as long as I had Suzanne, but I couldn't even hold that together. Suzanne left me when she found me on the bathroom floor one morning, throwing up with a hangover and sweating like a pig. She probably thought, 'Stuff this for a laugh,' made her excuses and left.

All of a sudden, from having everything, I had nothing.

I always thought Julie was a bit flash, I must admit. However wrongly I always thought she was a snob. They were crazy times. We just moved from party to party. I wasn't really in a fit state to be a parent. Julie, though, has been a really good mother to our son, Cameron. In fact, she doted on him so much, I had to 'rough him up a bit' when he came to live with me. Otherwise Julie would have had him too prim and proper.

Julie ended up with the house in Wentworth, which we then had to sell to pay off the mortgage. I also had to pay her considerable maintenance. Cameron had gone to a private school, of course. I didn't see him but I was paying. I was going through so much hurt after the split up, I didn't see him. I actually chose not to see him to punish *her*. Figure that out!

'Bugger it!' I thought. 'Well, in a way that will punish her as well. Get rid of me and you lose your son's father.'

This is something I do. I always cut off my nose to spite my face. I always tend to run away from confrontation and I always want to punish people I think are being horrible to me, even if, in fact, it's my own fault. I'm suffering and I suppose it's easier for me, in my own little mind, to punish someone else rather than get myself together. So, I decided I wouldn't see my son.

'That'll teach her,' I thought.

Not seeing Cameron didn't bother me because I was so pissed off with Julie, blaming her for us drifting apart. And I just thought, 'Well, there's nothing I can do. If I start seeing Cameron, or trying to get access to Cameron, then he's going to be brought up in one of these social climbing lifestyles.'

I knew there was no way I could get custody of him, so it was best for him to be with his Mum. I just kept out of the bloody way.

What am I going to do with a three-year-old anyhow? I thought. I can't take him anywhere, can't do things with him.

I just resigned myself. I haven't got a child now, I thought, I'll see him later, like Sarah.

Anyway, my lifestyle would have been terribly wrong for him. I couldn't have gone round in show business and dragged a little boy with me. He needed stability, not hanging round with this nutcase.

And it seems to have worked. Cameron's grown up a lovely boy. I wonder what he'd have been like if he'd been dragged round the theatres and bars with me. He probably would have ended up like one of those country and western songs. Yuk! Today, at nineteen years of age, he's living with me. A wonderful young man. Julie's up a mountain in the Himalayas. Really.

My eldest kid is Sarah. Her Mum Sue decided she didn't want me when Sarah was five months old. There was nothing I could do much there, so I buggered off. I suppose if I'd been older, I would have come back and said, 'I want to see my daughter once a week.'

But instead, I thought, 'Oh bollocks. That chapter's shut now.'

I used to drive round and look for Sarah when she was 12 or 13 years of age. I saw her when she was seven and eight – and then didn't again for ages.

When the kids all grow up, I suppose I would like them to think of me as someone who did his best, tried to the best of his ability and that I cared a lot.

I wasn't there a great deal of the time because I didn't have the *ability* to be there a great deal. I've had to go and work, not so much for Sarah, but I've always had to 'be there' for the others, for Cameron and the three little ones round the corner, Charlie, Freddie and Elsie.

I mean, I *could* go and spend more time with them but it would mean that I wouldn't be able to work. I wouldn't be doing a summer season; I wouldn't be going away doing a pantomime.

I think the kids understood but I don't know if they realised why I was away so often. I remember Charlie saying to his mother, Tracy, 'I know why Daddy's away a lot. He goes and sees his other families, doesn't he?'

And that was quite upsetting for me. But then what am I supposed to do? What am I to do now when I'm away all the time, to earn money for things I don't have?

By now, you would have thought, because of all the women I'd been with, that I would have learnt enough about women not to keep repeating all the same old mistakes. But no. They are just different creatures. I mean I love them, but I haven't got a clue about them. They take total control over me. I'm a real co-dependent. If I've not got a woman I'm in love with, then I'm fucking useless.

I started going out with a lovely singer called Tricia Duskey. Tricia was Irish and was with me for a couple of months, I guess.

It was in September 1984 that I headed back to the Falklands after Thames Television had considered my little home video was quite good. They wanted to take everyone down there to make a film.

I begged for Tricia to be on this show. She wasn't the greatest of singers but she looked quite tasty and I loved her to death. She had that wonderful great charm that only the Irish have.

So I bought her an engagement ring, slung it at her so she couldn't leave – you know, as normal – take them hostage!

And off we went.

I'd been out to the Falklands three times. First, in June 1983, then again in June of the following year, when I'd taken my little camcorder with me and shot that demo recording. Then came this trip that autumn, with Tricia and the Thames TV team. The show we made went out on ITV that

Christmas – and the whole nation cried. Perfect.

Tricia came back to my house in Wentworth and suddenly I found myself completely surrounded by an Irish family. First Tricia's sister turned up, then her sister, then another sister, then a cousin, then her Mum and then her brother … everyone turned up and my house became like a little piece of Ireland.

Keith Emerson, my favourite rock star, came to the house one day.

'Your house is full of people,' he said.

'Yup!' I said. 'It's great. I love it.'

But Keith had a point. When you are rich and famous, or the centre of attention, it's nice to be surrounded by everybody. But, although it certainly wasn't the case in this instance, you get that nagging worry that you're paying them all to be your mates, or that they're taking advantage. It's a question a lot of famous people never really ask themselves because they probably wouldn't like the answer.

Tricia even bought me a pool table to make the house a bit more like an Irish pub. But things slowly deteriorated. It all went from bad to worse and the last time I saw Tricia, I was leaving for some charity event.

'I'm going to do a parachute jump with the Paras,' I said. And off I went.

As I landed, I phoned Tricia up.

'Have I got big news for you!' I said.

I was *going* to tell her all about the parachute jump but she got in first.

'And have *I* got big news for *you* – I'm fucking off!'

And that was it. The last I heard, she was happily married with lots of children. She was lovely. I was madly in love with her.

Before she met me, Tricia was going out with an agent friend of mine called Brian Shaw, a nice guy. He looked after Freddie Starr at the time.

He used to manage Freddie and put on his tours. Brian was going out with Tricia and I did everything I could to persuade her to stop seeing him. I begged and I cried and she went back and told him … and *he* begged and cried. We were both begging for this woman.

Eventually, she went out with me and I hated Brian, in a funny way, because he was my rival. But since those days, Brian and I have become great mates.

In this business, 'great mates' means when you see each other, you strike up a conversation, you get on well and you have respect for one another.

A while ago, after my production company went a bit funny this year, he wrote to me and said, 'If I can help, don't hesitate to give me a call.'

After all the things I'd said about him, after I'd nicked his girlfriend from him, he was still man enough to write to me and offer me his help. Now *that's* a sign of a *real* man, isn't it?

I learnt something from Brian that day.

Tricia was a lovely girl but she was very Irish. In fact, when I took her to the Falklands that September and she sang that wonderful song, 'Hello' by Lionel Ritchie, on a ship called *The Fort Grange*, she said to me afterwards, typically innocently, 'Tell me Jim, was this the ship that was sunk in the war?'

She also said to me once – and this is all true, 'I went home to Ireland and put £10 worth of petrol in the car ... and you wouldn't believe how much it fucking cost me.'

That was Tricia. But what I think Tricia really wanted was to be successful in her career. She came from a famous showbiz family and she wanted to be a great singer.

Tricia had gone now. I had a bloody great tax bill to pay and nowhere to live. By December 1985, I was living back at Mum's. I was 32 years old and things had all going horribly wrong.

Julie moved back into the Wentworth house and was preparing to sell it, so I buggered off to do pantomime in Oxford with Liz Fraser. Just when I thought life was getting better, I met Liz Fraser!

Liz Fraser was part of the *Carry On* team and she is the most bonkers woman I've ever worked with in my entire life! Everyone warned me, 'You watch her, she'll be great fun but a bit strange!'

She was playing the Fairy in *Cinderella*, which was being produced by my great friend Peter Elliott. I was a bit late in on the first morning but a mate Roger Kitter, who was playing the Dame, tells me that just before I walked into the room, Liz Fraser had apparently announced that she'd rewritten her part *in rhyme*! I mean, does a fairy talk in rhyme?

'No dear,' said Alan Blackburn, the director, 'you don't change the script. I want it as it is.'

Liz was furious. 'But I've been up *all night* writing all this.'

And with that, Roger said, she burst into tears! She started striding towards the door to leave – just as I walked in, never having ever met her in my life.

That morning, I had a terrible hangover and as Liz passed me she wailed, 'I can't *do* this show …'

And my first words to her were, 'Well, fuck off then!'

We got Liz to do it in the end. We compromised a bit. She could be a bit eccentric though. The ponies in the show that pulled Cinderella's carriage used to come down some old stone stairs. One day Liz stormed, 'The horses *cannot go on* – they're lame. I'm not allowing these horses on.'

So I phoned up Peter the producer.

'She's refusing to let the ponies go on!' I said. 'In fact, she has sacked the ponies!'

'Well thanks for letting me know, love,' replied Peter. 'I've got to work out their holiday money!'

After the panto, which was, you might be surprised to hear, a success, I didn't know where to live. I didn't have any clothes. I didn't have a sense of fashion. I was still a Seventies bloke, really. I had stage clothes but nothing else. I was a bit of a mess really. And I was drinking heavily.

Terry was driving me around at the time. I'd go down to Tramp nightclub in Jermyn Street and talk to the owner Johnny Gold. I'd be slumped in a heap until three o'clock in the morning. I'd just sit in Tramp and get drunk every night.

One night, the most beautiful girl in the world wandered in. Her name was Janine Andrews, a great big tall girl with a Birmingham accent. Bill Wyman's girlfriend at the time, Mandy Smith, whom he later married, said to me, 'Oh, Janine's a friend of mine.'

So, she helped introduce us and Janine and I started talking and then started going out together. I was only madly in love with her because she was so fantastic looking. I thought, 'What a beauty to have on your arm!'

I even bought shoes with bigger heels so I wouldn't look such a titch next to her!

Another girl I met and ended up going out with was Lesley Ash. Lesley was great fun but she used to get up at five o'clock in the morning to go filming and get to bed at two o'clock in the morning after nightclubbing. It was all too much for me so I pushed off to Great Yarmouth for a summer season. I had a feeling it wouldn't last though, and I was right.

Lesley's done very well for herself now. Got a nice footballer and owns a wine bar. She's great.

The following year, I headed off to Germany to film a show with the troops. That's when I met my great friend from the SAS. He wrote a book called *Freefall*, under the name of Tom Reid.

I needed someone to drive me around and Kevin was still working with Michael Barrymore. On one of my many visits to the SAS camp in Hereford, someone said to me, 'Tom's just left the regiment, why don't you offer him a job?'

And so, a great friendship with Tom started.

We got on fabulously. I had a couple of SAS mates. Tom's pal, whom I also got to meet, was called Paul Hill, who was in 'B' Squadron. Paul used to be in the Paras, which he joined quite late after being a croupier aboard a ship. He was big man who looked a bit like the martial arts film star Chuck Norris – and he was just as tough. Me and Tom went out to Germany where I did a few shows. In Germany, Richard Digance taught him to play the guitar.

Afterwards, Richard said, 'Christ! I've never seen *anyone* pick up something so quickly.'

Tom was a great parachute jumper and was in the air troop at the SAS. We had fantastic fun together.

Then we came back to England and put on a little tour. I didn't have a house at the time, so we'd go up to Hereford and stay at Paul's.

We used to drink as much as we could. Tom was about 6ft 1in, lean but with a brilliantly muscular body. He had a big nose and looked like a wolf, with his light blue eyes. He was always picking his nose and farting, and he used to drink too much, live on junk food and wear plimsolls. He was a bit scruffy – yet the girls adored him. Tom was not what you think of as a typical Special Forces soldier.

One Christmas party we had at Paul Hill's house was dubbed an 'Orphans' party.' We called it that because, at that time, none of us had girlfriends, or families, or anywhere to live.

And what did this say about us all? Well, I was with a bunch of people who weren't in one place for very long, similar to me. They worked hard, played hard, they were the elite – and, to an extent, I was the elite in my little job. They were wary of people being round them whom they didn't trust – and so was I. So an unspoken bond developed between me and half a dozen guys from the Regiment.

The parties were great, lots of girls who didn't have boyfriends turned up, and it was time to let your hair down and say, 'Let's have no responsibilities, for tomorrow we die ... them perhaps on the battlefield, and me at the Circus Tavern, Purfleet.'

Around that time, I met a reporter named Alison Holloway, who came to interview me on HTV. I thought she was wonderful. We met up again. Then one thing led to another and we started having an affair ... and then, we fell out.

Our relationship was quite volatile.

On reflection, it was, of course, more than an affair. We got married, I forgot that bit! I always seem to forget Alison because I feel that marriage didn't really count. We had a sort of a passionate affair, and then we decided, 'Bollocks to this – we'll get married!'

And so we did. To the wedding we invited Tom, my minder, the best minder in the world, Mick Gould, who used to teach the SAS boys at Hereford to fight and who went on to work for me when he left the Regiment (he later worked with Robert de Niro and is now Robert de Niro's right hand man who puts all his films together for him), and the famous 'Goose', who later won the Military Cross in Sarajevo for looking after General Rose.

*'How **dare** you phone me when I'm out having affairs?'*

Also at the ceremony was the strongest SAS soldier in the world, a man called 'JB', who is now looking after some rich Greek family.

Alison and I were going great guns … and then we fell to bits. By the summer season, it was all over. It was a very, very volatile marriage. I'm reluctant to talk very much about it for two reasons really.

First, because it was such a short-lived episode in my life, and I feel it was not fair to lay the blame on anybody. And second, because I'm terrified of her new husband.

So Alison and I split up. But in the meantime, me, Tom and the boys from Hereford were having a great time. We were at Paul Hill's house having a party one evening, and Paul had nipped into the bedroom with some girl while Tom Reid kept lookout outside the door. Then Paul's *proper* girlfriend walked up the stairs and asked, 'Where's Paul?'

Tom had a 'code knock'. He knocked at the bathroom door and the bedroom door at the same time and called out, 'Are you in there Paul?'

As his girlfriend stood waiting on the landing, like a true SAS soldier, Paul immediately leapt out of the first-floor window – and the bird he was knocking off, talk about Special Forces floozy, she climbed out the window as well, edged along the drainpipe and climbed back in through the bathroom window.

Then she came out the bathroom just as Paul walked up the stairs – with two pints of milk in his hand, which he'd nicked off the neighbour's doorstep.

'I just popped down the garage to get some milk, dear,' he told her.

My great friendship with Paul, very sadly, came to an end when Paul tragically died. Paul was apparently working abroad somewhere when it happened. I'll never forget the awful day when I received a phone call to say that he had died of a heart attack.

We all buried him in the church in Hereford. All the Regiment turned out, not in uniform, for some unknown reason. I spoke to 'Gonzo', who was the Squadron Sergeant Major and asked him, 'What happened?'

'Don't fucking ask,' he replied.

When you're told that by a 'B' Squadron Sergeant Major, you don't fucking ask!

Another mate of mine in the Regiment was Andy. After the funeral, we sat there eating a curry. I'll never forget his words.

'Paul tastes nice, doesn't he?' Andy said. 'Regimental tradition, you know, to eat the body.'

Friendships are very important to me. I like men's company but if I was in a room of an evening with men and there were no women there, I'd be bored. I'd have to try and flirt with someone!

I used to enjoy the company of the SAS boys, and the Paras, and the Marines – not just because they'd all have wonderful war stories but because they had that way about them. They're all just so confident and so fit and they really go for it! They don't give a shit and they're all pretty tough.

'JB' was going to teach me to abseil.

Well, what the SAS used to do before it was popularly known and everybody started doing it – is what's called 'fast-roping'. The rope is knotted up and you throw it down. As the knot unravels, you're sliding down behind it.

'JB' and his friends taught me in a gym in Hereford. I'm scared of heights and as I slid down on this rope at about one inch at a time, screaming and kacking myself, all I could see below me were people crying with laughter.

Tom Reid was splitting his sides laughing.

'JB' greeted me at the bottom. 'Fucking crap!' he said. 'Grab on to the rope and I'll pull you back up.'

I held on and he pulled me up, *hand over hand* – he just pulled me up to the top again.

I'm telling you – never argue with those bastards!...

So my position in life, my relationships and responsibilities had changed. I didn't have a house. I didn't have a girlfriend. I didn't have a wife. I was very thin. I was drinking for England and I wasn't eating very much at all. I filled my life up with my new friends in Hereford.

After the summer season in 1987, I had bought a boat, a little 31-footer.

Kevin had come back to work for me again and we lived together on the boat.

Alison Holloway was now distant and in the past. I was 34 and I'd been through three divorces. What did I think about that? Did I ask myself, 'Hang on a minute, there's something wrong there?'

Well, I looked at it like this. I'd been divorced three times but I reasoned with myself as follows.

'The *first* marriage didn't count because I was only seventeen at the time; then I had a *proper* second marriage with Julie, who left me, but I didn't feel it was really just my fault that one ended. And the *third* marriage didn't really count because it only lasted three months, including the divorce.'

So really, I'd only been married *once* – with two hiccups. I'd just married the wrong women. I told myself if they'd *really* liked me and let me shag their mates, it would have been perfect. It was just the way my luck was running.

But my luck was set to change.

At any rate, one thing was for certain. I'd decided now that was fucking hat! As far as re-marrying was concerned, I was *not* doing that again.

No way I was ever going to go through all that shit again … and all that heartbreak again. I did *try* when I got into relationships. I phoned them ten times a day, I bought them presents, I loved them. But I wanted to be myself. It wasn't all about the shagging. That was more of a joke, really. But I wanted to be the centre of attention, to be with the lads and occasionally glance over and spot the wife smiling at me, saying, 'Oh look at my Jim.'

I have always wanted to be a 'fly on the wall' and hear two women talking about me. One, my wife, would be saying, 'Oh, he's great, my husband. He's a bit of a card. But look at him. I love him even though he is what he is …'

But all these bloody women I'd married and been out with wanted me to be what *they* wanted me to be. I couldn't have that. I still can't cope with that. It drives me mad…

And they say I'll end up a lonely old man … Well, they might be right. But what can I do?

Find myself a lonely old woman, I guess.

8

Snakes and ladders

The first thing that struck me about her was her eyes.

She had the eyes of a cat, glowing amber in colour, and when she looked at me, I looked straight back at her and thought, 'Wow. I've *got to have that*.'

And she looked back at me and she thought, 'Urrrgh.'

I was mesmerised by those cats' eyes as I handed her the money for my pints of Guinness.

'You're going to be my fourth wife, you are,' I said to her.

'Urrrgh,' she replied again.

Her name was Tracy and she was a Guinness girl at the Southampton Boat Show.

The sun had been shining every day down in Torquay, where I had enjoyed a great summer season. My boat *Dish Bee Doo* was feeling a bit of wear. Every time you threw her in forward gear, the 'props' leapt out of the water to say hello to you.

I was driving around with my 'Roadie' Kevin, who'd had a bit of an accident – not in the car but with his tooth. Kevin had a false tooth at the front but he'd got pissed one night, thrown up down the toilet and lost the tooth in the bowl. He hadn't had the courage to stick his hand in the loo and fish it out – so instead, he was now minus a front tooth altogether and looked like he'd got a cat flap in the front of his mouth.

We decided the best thing to do was to say, 'Bollocks to women and relationships. Let's just have loads of women on boats … and drink our way through life.'

I had decided to become amphibious. I was going to buy myself a boat and live on it all the time. Boats are much better for pulling girls than apartments or houses in the country. There's something *about* boats and women. As soon as a woman walks up the gangplank, the old knickers become a bit loose. Fabulous. And, of course, the first thing you do when you climb aboard a boat is …

'Welcome aboard. Have a drink.'

We decided that we should have a 'ship's drink'. Ours should be made of 100 per cent vodka, or as near as we could possibly get it, soaked in green peppers for a couple of months. Peppers make it like firewater and the idea was that whoever came on board, we'd offer them a tot of this extremely firey drink. Then we would write down in our Visitors' Book precisely what their first words were after they'd drunk it. This wasn't my idea. I actually nicked it from the RAF, who ran this system in the Falklands.

It proved a great icebreaker when people came aboard and it worked well for us – until, one day, when I invited on board a Norwegian bloke and his son who had built a Viking ship. They'd left Norway and were sailing round the world.

This proud seagoing father and son from Norway visited us and I gave them a glass of our firewater each. They whacked their drinks down in one … and I waited for the response, which normally would be along the lines of 'Oh fuck…', 'Oh Jesus…', 'Oh shit…' or 'What the fuck is *that?*'

But these two seafarers just stood there with their proud eyes shining and slightly watering. I waited poised with my pen in hand, hovering over the book.

'Excuse me, I have to write down your reaction to that drink,' I said.

To which the Dad replied in his calm Norwegian accent, 'That is undoubtedly the strongest drink I have ever tasted in my life.'

And in measured tones, the son added, 'That's for sure.'

The 1987 Southampton Boat Show was looming and two weeks before the summer season finished, Kevin and I took *Dish Bee Doo* across Lime Bay, round Anvill Point, up the Channel, down Southampton Water and anchored her just by the Boat Show. Off we went to look around for what would eventually end up as my new home.

I saw a beautiful 55-foot long boat called a *Princess 55*. It was a little more expensive than I'd wanted to pay, so I trotted off to the Lombard finance people, who offered marine loans. That was what I wanted. Of course, I wanted it *right away*.

The deal was done and we went off to the Guinness stand, the traditional bar where you enjoy a celebratory pint of the black stuff.

As we stood in the queue to buy our drinks, I said to Kevin, 'Right. Forget women – we are now *sailors*.' Then, I turned round to the bar and said, 'Four pints of Guinness, please.'

'No problem,' the most beautiful girl in the world replied.

Her name was Tracy Hilton and she was all dressed up in her little black Guinness jumpsuit, one of eight girls, all beauties. She had these incredible eyes.

Well, that was it. I'd been hit by the bombshell. So, after about eight pints of Guinness, and then a couple of bottles of champagne, and then some oysters, I took Tracy and her friends down to the boat to show off. We were bobbing around on it and I said, 'I've just bought one of these,' thinking it would impress her.

I didn't know if it did or not but she went back to the Guinness stand. We leapt back aboard *Dish Bee Doo* and I whizzed back to Torquay to continue with the summer season – armed with Tracy's phone number.

When the season ended, I said goodbye to Torquay and made my way back to London.

The year was 1990 and I had just got the sack from Thames Television, a turning point that was to prove a major milestone in my career.

It all came as a bit of surprise, really, because I had done quite a few successful shows for Thames, like *Up the Elephant and Round the Castle* and *Home James*, which was already into its fourth series. *Up the Elephant* was being produced by a man named Tony Parker. Tony was quite a nice bloke but I found him a bit bombastic. I thought he was a bit like a prep school teacher and I didn't quite like his way of directing. Already I'd decided that I knew better than him.

I always hated sitcoms where you see people walking down the stairs with a blinking great shadow following them like a monster. I mean, you don't see shadows in *real* houses, do you? Light comes from everywhere.

I couldn't work out why films look great and videos always look like *Crossroads*. And then he'd make us all stand in a line behind the sofa and talk to each other.

Frankly, it was beginning to get on my tits.

Anyway, a different director joined the programme – a guy called David Askey. He sometimes used to get a bit angry and shout at people. He didn't shout at *me* though – he was a bit scared of me.

My co-star was the great George Sewell, the big gangster-looking bloke. He was ever so kind to me. In series four of *Home James*, which I thought was the best ever, we had a new director who I felt was just great. He let me have some input into the writing.

It was also tremendous working with the wonderful Irish actor Harry Towb, who was playing the part of the butler. After all these changes and a lot of hard work, the show was just how I wanted it.

Laurie had also arranged for me to perform a *Jim Davidson Stand Up* series. I was to be the first one to do a sort of rudish, stand-up show on TV. Naturally, we received one or two complaints but not that many. We did six shows and received only about half a dozen complaints (which was disappointing!).

Philip Jones, the then Head of Thames Television's Light Entertainment division had moved on and along came John Howard Davis. He became the boss. He was the original Oliver. He was also in *Tom Brown's Schooldays*.

Under John Howard Davis Thames came to the conclusion that not only was Benny Hill 'old hat' but also there was no place for Jim Davidson. (Boo!)

Political correctness was taking over. People like Mister Bean and Ben Elton. Ben's got a lot funnier nowadays, I think. He's now got the ability to talk, whereas before, I thought his timing was just rubbish. I couldn't understand what people were laughing at because he was technically so bad. I mean, forget what he talks *about* – I don't like that much.

But over at Thames TV, at the end of the summer of 1990, I was given my marching orders and I felt terrible. I actually thought that that was the end of the line for my type of comedy, that this John Howard Davis had decided in one fell swoop to alter the way comedy was portrayed to people. But what he didn't take into consideration was the public, who still flocked to see me in the theatres and still paid good money for me to play in their clubs.

But, at the time, I thought, 'Christ, that's it! That's the end!'

I'd got no house, no kids, no nothing. It was bloody horrible and there were those moments when I was in the pub, when I'd whack down a few drinks and think, 'Oh, Christ. It's all over!'

It was really frightening – but luckily, I still had support from my people, the public.

Me.

Benny Hill.

Gone.

I loved everyone there at Thames. Bob Louis, the second in command, Stuart Hall, the director.

I knew so many friends, so many great characters. I'd enjoyed all those good times in the pub with Bob Todd. And where was Mark Stewart now? My producer, whom I loved so much, like a father. I loved Teddington Studios. I loved every bit of the scene there.

Plus, I thought I was becoming quite good at what I was doing. They wanted me to do a show that was *on the edge* a bit, pushing it. So I did. Great. And then they seemed to lose interest in me. I was a bit bitter. But luckily enough, I knew I could still fill theatres and the clubs ...

One day, Laurie said to me, 'Take a look at this video.'

He showed me a pilot show called *Big Break*. Mike Reid, the comedian, was hosting this pilot show – and he didn't seem at home with it. There was no John Virgo, just the normal snooker referee, Len Ganley. So, I said I'd have a go.

I met the producer, John Burrowes, who was a very nice man, and I suggested John Virgo. John's was a relatively unknown name, so the BBC dug out some old tapes of him being very funny. Then Virgo and I got together. We made a fresh pilot show of *Big Break* and it was sensational.

And the show is still going *to this day*.

At the time though, I thought, 'God, I've become a *game show host*.' I panicked. 'I'm going to turn into Les Dennis in a minute. This is awful.'

(Mind you, looking at Amanda Holden now, I'd quite happily swap places with Les Dennis. Any day you want, Les.)

But really, it was *a bit much* doing a game show.

Christ.

But I had a new lease of life at the BBC and I would make the best of it.

The thing I always wanted to create at the BBC was a really fun atmosphere, similar to the buzz we'd enjoyed at Thames. When I was at Thames, we'd had the great *Rainbow* there. Remember *Rainbow*? With Zippy and George? Well, the highlight of our day was when we discovered that Zippy and George were recording in a next door studio. We'd go down and watch their rehearsals. And Zippy and George were just *filthy*. I laughed until I cried.

The fun would start when we did *Big Break* run-throughs. In rehearsals, we'd use real contestants and I was *filthy*. We recorded loads of these rehearsals on tape. To this day, I've always thought that if the BBC would give me permission to release those outtakes of *Big Break*, I would never have to work again because everyone would want a copy of what went on there. They were just so funny.

I'm not really a snooker fan myself. I can't play snooker so I have never become a fan of it. But the snooker players became quite famous in their own right, and when they turned up to do the shows, I realised how nice they all were.

When the first series was filmed at Elstree Studios, we all had a bit of a buzz when Alex 'Hurricane' Higgins turned up. We all wondered how he was going to behave. Well, I drink a bit myself, so I wasn't too worried.

When Alex breezed into the Green Room hospitality suite, I asked him, 'Would you like a drink, Alex?'

He shook his head. 'No,' he said, 'I'm not drinking.'

'Oh go on,' I said.

'Alright, fuck it,' he said. 'Give us two bottles of champagne.'

John Virgo and I were worlds apart, really. We had great respect for one another and still do, to this day. But John is from 'Up North' and I'm from 'Down South'. I'm a staunch Conservative and John is a stalwart Labour supporter. I'm a Charlton fan, he's a Manchester United man – but we *both* like to play golf and we *both* like a little drink.

We used to stand backstage behind the scenery. We'd stand back there and the moment we heard the theme song of *Big Break*, John would knock back a nip of Scotch and I'd have a nip of brandy.

He'd have his hip flask and he'd say, 'This is 14-year old Glenfiddich.'

'And *this* is 14-pounds worth of Remy Martin,' I'd say.

And we'd have a little sip. Then we'd always shake hands before we walked on. It's a routine we still run through today.

I think the chemistry really works well between us. John and I just have the ability to bounce off one another.

It's obvious that JV and I like one another. *John* is the star of *Big Break* because really I should know how to ad lib and I should know how to talk to people. And I can manage that OK normally. But when I run out of things to say, I just hand it over to John and ask him, 'What do *you* think, John?' and he always has something interesting to contribute. He's quite a genius is old John.

As time went on, I began to realise that John's personal life was in just as much of a mess as mine, so we were able to share a little smile between us. We created an atmosphere in the *Big Break* studio which worked really well.

We don't really socialise together a great deal. We always seem to be working. But we do play golf together occasionally. If I were to say to him, 'I've got some time off, let's go down to Spain and play some golf,' John would reply, 'I can't. I've got to be up in Sheffield. I've got to go and do a commentary on the snooker.'

When we *do* get together, however, we get on extremely well and we have great respect for one another. We argue about politics like mad, of course, but we're always slightly tongue-in-cheek with each other and I love to wind him up rotten, often to the extent that he gets quite angry.

John would say, 'Margaret Thatcher's ruined this bloody country' and I'd say, 'How can you get coal out of a mine when there's no fucking coal left in it, John?'

He'd get annoyed then. 'That's not the point,' he'd say.

Then, I'd always have a go at him. 'So you're a *socialist*, are you then John?'

'Quite right,' he'd reply. 'I'm from the North and proud of it.'

'So, where do you live now?'

'Weybridge, actually,' he'd say in a posh voice.

I love him to bits.

When John started in TV, I didn't really give him any advice on how to develop his television career. He was just a naturally funny bloke. When *Big Break* started being such a big success as a format, I suppose I was surprised that it had gone down so well.

I had been hoping, of course, that the BBC would like *me* as a presenter – but what really took everyone by surprise was that the viewers loved *the game*. The game on the show actually worked.

Rehearsals were always great fun. There was one marvellous 'off screen' moment, which we filmed. It was when *Star Trek – The Next Generation* was on. We started the *Big Break* rehearsal, or 'run through,' as it's called, at 20 minutes to five. Now, I knew *Star Trek* was on at 5 o'clock on Sky One … and, as you know, I am a huge *Star Trek* fan. So we raced through the forty minutes that it normally takes to do the show – in *eleven* minutes flat. We did it by speeding up all the dialogue and movements. Whizzing through a 40-minute show in eleven minutes was hysterical – plus, of course it was peppered with loads of swearwords.

The other funny part of *Big Break* is John Virgo's famous trick shots. John gets them right *all the time* in rehearsals but as soon as that camera goes on …

I think to be fair to John, once people come into the studio to watch, the heat of the audience and the lights make a big difference. The cloth on the table changes a bit, so it's difficult for him … there you are John, I'm getting you out of the shit now.

We had a sweepstake on the series once. We recorded forty of John's trick shots over the series and the crew and I bet on *how many* attempts John would make to achieve them all.

I think he managed 40 trick shots in 75 attempts – which is not bad. Of course, I can't play the game at all. I can't hit a ball. We also have bets sometimes when we're doing the run-through, when we're playing 'Red Hot'.

They put up the eight balls to pot and off we go. Then they have bets with me and I think the best I've ever got is about two.

Then, one night, I said to John, 'Come on, let's see you do it.'

This is when we were recording it. And John had a go – and he only got *one*, I think. So I got my own back on him a bit.

Once, John and I *nearly* went over the top. I was on tour in Scotland at the time. I was in Aberdeen and had had to fly back to record *Big Break*.

I used to be frightened of flying – I think it was just an excuse so I could drink more, actually. To get down to London in time, I had to catch the 7 am flight. So, I got up at about half past five and started to down a few large vodkas.

I boarded the plane and eventually arrived at the studios. I was still pissed by the time I got to rehearsals at one o'clock. We had a spot of lunch and then John saw what a state I was in – and so immediately tried to catch up with me. He drank the best part of his hip flask of whisky and we did two shows that afternoon – pissed. I couldn't talk and I didn't know *how* I got through it.

The producer, who I thought was going to sack me on the spot, was quite understanding and said, 'Jim, look, just try to be as sober as you can. It's just one of those things.'

I must say, he acted in a very mature way about it all. But never again. I have never been pissed doing a TV show since that day. It was a nightmare.

Everyone looks back at it now as a laugh. We just about – *just about* – got away with it. But when we were doing it, I thought, 'Oh please, just let this be over. Let me go home and hide my head in shame!'

Generally though, I quite liked it at the BBC. I didn't mind the place because I only turned up and did *Big Break*. I wasn't asked to do anything else and I was working with my own little team, the same camera people who did it all the time. They liked me and they laughed in all the right places. That made me feel important. If this was going to be my new home, then that was fine by me.

By now, the lovely Tracy and I had firmly established our relationship and had settled down together, living happily in our house, the Old Forge, down in Surrey.

Our first child, Charlie, had arrived and Tracy and I were absolutely thrilled to bits. I headed off, as happy as Larry, down to Great Yarmouth for the summer season.

But soon, Fate was to deal me a terrible blow. My Dad's health started to deteriorate rapidly. He'd never really enjoyed good health but now it looked as if he was nearing the end of the road. He'd never looked well, or acted well, and at home we could hear him coughing and spluttering. I'd never seen him kick a football or run around. He used to smoke and drink quite a lot and had a touch of asthma. He used one of those inhalers.

He'd taken to keeping a supply of oxygen next to his chair. He'd stick a mask on and puff away. Strangely enough, he seemed to feel better when he'd had a few whiskies. I had an extension built to the side of our house, a small bedroom downstairs for Dad. He'd been spending more and more time in bed and when I visited him, I felt he'd turned into a little old alien. I was frightened, really. I didn't know what to say to him. I'd never known what to say to Dad over the years. We never shared a touchy-feely-cuddly sort of relationship. Great respect and love, of course.

Now he was dying and I didn't know what to say to him. Eventually he stopped drinking as well. He'd just sit there with his oxygen mask on.

One day, Mum walked into his room. 'You don't look very well, Jock,' she said.

'Oh, don't worry about me,' he replied. 'Go and make a cup of tea.'

So she went to the kitchen to make him a cup of tea and when she came back he was dead. That was that.

I was in Great Yarmouth doing the summer season when I got a call from my brother, Billy.

'Cam,' he said, 'Dad's dead.'

And as he said that, I could hear all the girls crying and wailing in the background, shouting out, 'How *dare* you give him the news like that.'

Billy asked me if I was still going to go through with my performance of the show in Great Yarmouth that evening. I said I thought I would.

There's normally a slot in my act where I sit down on stage for ten minutes and ask the audience if they have any questions for me. People ask things like, 'Who are you shagging this week?' or 'When do you get your licence back?' or 'Have you been in any fights lately?' and so on.

That night, I sat down on stage, on the day my father had died, and asked for questions from the audience. And a bloke shouted out, 'How's your Dad?'

'He died this morning at 8.30,' I said.

And it got a bit of a stifled laugh. This bloke, it turned out was an old friend of Dad's from years ago, when we used to visit Great Yarmouth on holiday. Dad used to drink in his pub. This chance remark was pure coincidence … or was it old Jock 'up there' having fun. Something was going on …

The funeral was a week later. I got some time off work. Me and the boys had to carry the coffin out. It was bloody awful and I'd had a fair bit to drink. I went to the crematorium and said some ridiculous words and then they scattered my father's ashes to I know not where. Now, there's nowhere to go and say, 'Hi, Dad. Is it cold down there in that coffin?'

Afterwards, I got pissed as a fart and ended up slapping my brother John round the face. I can remember putting myself in a fantasy. It was almost like being in an episode of *Star Trek*. It was just so unreal. Eventually, Tracy and Kevin put me in a car and drove me home. I slept for 24 hours.

Bye Dad.

Tracy and I decided to try and have another baby – but somehow we couldn't seem to make it happen. We kept 'doing it' but nothing was happening.

So Tracy went to see her gynaecologist, Percy Coates. He told her, 'Look, you've got to make love and then run down here quick and I'll take a look at it all going on.'

'Oh Gawd,' I thought. I could think of nothing worse.

In desperation, I said to Tracy, 'Why don't you come and see my Dr Frederick Lim?'

Tracy had never heard of him.

'Actually,' I said, 'he is the best doctor of sexually transmitted diseases in the world.'

Freddie is a Chinese Malay and I've visited him a few times in my life when I've picked up various things at various Army bases all round the world. In fact, that doctor knows my willy better than *I* know it.

I spoke to Dr Lim and I explained, 'My missus is trying to have a kid and we've tried everything.'

'Bring her up to see me,' he said. 'If there's a bug in there, I'll find it.'

Apparently, he said, when women have had babies in hospital, sometimes the wards can be a bit dodgy. There are lots of little bugs living there. They can infect a woman but sometimes the doctors there can't pinpoint the infection.

'They don't know bugs like I do,' said Dr Lim. 'They know about babies.'

Tracy consulted with her doctor friend Christine and they smelt a rat.

'Hello,' they thought, 'why are we going to see Jim's doctor from his dreaded past?'

I won through though. I took Tracy up to see Freddie. Of course, he was charming to her. He's a lovely man and a great friend. He offered Tracy an explanation. He did the little scrapey bit that gynaecologists do and then prescribed these tablets for her. Tracy took the tablets back and showed them to her doctor friend, Christine. They didn't impress her.

'These'll do nothing,' Christine said. 'This is the smallest dose of penicillin, or whatever it was, possible.'

And within one month, Tracy was pregnant.

When our son was born, on 20 February 1991, we called him Freddie.

That day, I went down to Guildford Hospital, where Tracy had been admitted a bit early. She was waiting to go into labour and I stayed there, by the bedside, until 11.10; by that time I couldn't get to the Windmill pub before closing time.

'You go home, love,' Tracy said.

Ah, but I had a Plan 'B' up my sleeve. I'd booked into the hotel across the road and so when I left the hospital, I popped over and into the hotel bar. I walked in and announced to everyone there, 'I'm about to be a Dad.'

And, naturally, everyone bought me drinks. I got totally pissed, fell asleep and woke up in the morning with the phone ringing.

'You'd better come over quickly,' Tracy said. 'I'm having our baby.'

'OK,' I replied. 'Who's calling?'

That didn't go down very well. So, I raced over – and I *didn't* watch Fred being born ... because I fainted. The doctors invited me to go into theatre to watch but, instead, I went and bought Tracy some fruit.

While I was about it, I got myself a couple of tins of Guinness, as well.

I had my feet up in the bed as they wheeled Tracy in and Percy Coates, her gynaecologist came in and said, 'Come on Jim, your wife's fully dilated.'

And I just looked at him, a bit blurry eyed, and said, 'So am I.'

'Come on,' said Percy, 'be a man.'

'I've *been* a man, Percy,' I said, 'that's why you're here.'

Then the Irish midwife woman started shouting at me.

'How *dare* you get this woman in terrible trouble?'

And then, two pushes and a shove later, that was it ... and apparently, I went as white as a sheet. *Tracy* had to hold *my* hand. She kept telling the nurses, 'Quick, help Jim, he's fainting.'

So, in the end, I waited outside and went back in when I heard little Freddie's voice. I'd gone all dizzy and seen stars. Actually, I was told I'd gone green. It was awful. But when baby Freddie was born, Tracy and I were, for a while, truly, truly happy.

Everything started to look up. I was a snooker game show presenter, I'd got two kids and a house and I found myself thinking that everything was OK. I felt that having another baby might somehow give us another lease of life. And Tracy's friend Jackie was there to look after the children. Despite the lure of all this apparent domestic bliss, pretty soon, duty called once again and I flew out to entertain the troops in Saudi Arabia. This was towards the end of 1991 and the Gulf War had just ended. Under Saudi Arabian law, any public entertaining was frowned upon, so, I got my hair cut quite short and entered Saudi Arabia pretending to be a member of the Armed Forces.

I phoned up my mate 'Minky', who was a sergeant in the SAS. He was just leaving the Regiment after having served in the Gulf.

'How would you like to come back to the Gulf?' I said.

What I needed was a nice, sensible 'both feet on the ground' former SAS sergeant to look after me.

'OK,' he said. 'Great!'

We'd been mates for years. Minky was one of the original boys on the Iranian Embassy Siege. He's a great bloke and although he has an English cockney accent, he comes from Scotland and on famous New Year's Eve nights in Hereford, if ever you bumped into him, and Minky was wearing his kilt, God help you! He's a real tough guy, a great boxer and when he works, he doesn't drink at all. But when he *finishes* work – well! It's not unusual to walk into a pub and to have this pair of starey eyes grip hold of you and he'll say, 'Come on, let's have a drink!'

I've had some great times out drinking with Minky. Once, he came to a golf tournament. We played for Mike Osmon down in Southampton and by the eighteenth hole, Minky had drunk something like 16 bottles of champagne, 35 pints of Guinness and was now on the red wine and white wine.

After the golf match, we all sat in the Jacuzzi to get rid of our aches and pains, and a bleary-eyed Minky came in – how he was still standing I've no idea – and with great derring-do, known only by the SAS, he did a perfect ten-point swallow dive, straight into a two-foot deep Jacuzzi. I can see him now with his little legs sticking out at the top.

The Mink used to get up next day, look like hell and have another couple of pints of Guinness for breakfast.

'Bloody hell, Mink,' I'd say, 'you drink a lot.'

That didn't phase him.

'Ah,' he'd say, 'but I never drink spirits, so I don't have a drink problem.'

I tell you this, if ever Minky stopped drinking Guinness, Ireland would go into a recession.

So Mink and I met at the airport bar, where I had my half of lager and Minky had his two barrels of Guinness. He decided that, as there was no drink in Saudi Arabia and as I was posing as a member of the Armed Forces, I'd better screw the nut a bit.

'We're there for three days,' he said, 'so we'll have three days' worth of drinks on the aeroplane.'

So, we jumped on board and we drank the plane dry. We got to Saudi Arabia and I was stood in the line with various soldiers and The Mink, waiting to check through customs.

Then a man with a Kalashnikov rifle, accompanied by a British officer, walked up to me and started talking to me.

'Oh God,' I thought, 'I'm going to be in trouble here,' because we were both pissed.

Then the man with the rifle looked me straight in the eye. 'This way please, Colonel,' he said.

'I'd better act the part,' I thought.

'Get my bag, will you?' I said to the soldier, and off we went to entertain the troops.

It was great fun and hard work. It's the hardest thing when one meets troops. You do a 'grip and grin', where you go around and meet as many people as you can, sign autographs, have some photographs taken, and so on. After a while, you run out of things to say and your grin is stuck on you permanently. And then your hangover starts to kick in. And I knew mine was going to last three days and there was no way of curing it.

Mink called me up one night. I'd actually gone to bed. I'd walked back to the hotel to find there was no bar open, so I'd taken two sleeping tablets, sat up in bed watching camel racing on the television, then dropped off to sleep. Then Minky rang.

'I've found some booze,' he said, 'and I'm sending a corporal to get you.'

So, we jumped in a car and went off to drink all this awful stuff into the middle of the night. Next day, with an even *worse* hangover, I was out on my rounds again. We were in the desert at 38 degrees, visiting troops and gripping and grinning these guys. It was wonderful.

When we came back to England, we patted ourselves on the backs and I told myself, 'I'm too old to go to war again.'

'And, by the way,' I added, turning to Minky, 'so are *you*!'

He laughed. 'Bollocks to that!' he said. 'I'm going to the pub.'

Out of the blue, early in 1992, I got a phone call from Jeffrey Archer – whom I didn't know from Adam. Jeffrey was then Deputy Chairman of the Conservative Party. There was a General Election coming up and he asked me to go and do some campaigning for the Conservatives.

I'd never met Jeffrey Archer before. The party was on a celebrity hunt, I guess. They wanted as many celebrities as they could get to help the party during the Election campaign. I ended up walking up and down Putney High Street with David Mellor, getting shouted at by people.

One bloke started heckling about the working class. I don't think you need to vote Labour just because you think yourself working class – especially nowadays. The reason I vote Conservative is because they're the party that makes me feel proud of my country. They're the ones that want to make Britain *great*, rather than give it away to Europe. But try telling people and you're flogging a dead horse.

I always say for a laugh, 'I've been working class once and I hated it – having to drink Blue Nun and shag ugly women.'

It's only a joke. I think you stop drinking Blue Nun once you start to earn a few bob. I *did* come from a working class background but we always thought we were a bit better and I don't think Mum was *ever* working class. She had great style, my mother – and we didn't class Dad as working-class because he was Scottish – he was a soldier.

He did, mind you. Dad classed *himself* as working class but we just thought he was, like, from another planet. To be 'working class' was something for dockers, wasn't it. Dockers, lorry drivers, people like that. My Dad was a *soldier*.

My brother-in-law Ted, my late sister Eileen's first husband, was a docker. He used to think, 'What do the bosses do? They don't do any fucking work, do they?'

That's the working class mentality that means if you pick up a box and move it from A to B, you're doing the work, while the boss does bugger all.

There are people that *take* and there are people that *give*. It's sad to think that because you're a working man who works hard that all you're going to do is vote Labour because you have this great jealousy of bosses. You know there have to be people who *lead* and there have to be people who *follow*.

I don't really know for sure what class I am today. I suppose I'm a working class lad, living beyond his means, like I always have. I have to go out and do a job for my living, so I am still working class. If I won the Pools, or the Lottery, I'd *still* be working class though. But I've always taken a leaf out of my mother's book and said, 'Just because you're born in the gutter doesn't mean you have to *stay* there.'

And when I go to entertain the Beaufort Hunt, and I meet the folks in their Barbours and wellies, I look at them and think, 'Christ. I wish the rest of the working class boys could see this lot. They're just the same.'

You know, working class people say, 'Oh, they're stuck up bastards.'

But they're *not*. They're all the same. No matter how you go through life, it's all the same. All the blokes want to have a drink, be successful, have a shag. And that's all.

My mate Paul Hill, the SAS guy who died, said to me once, 'Everything that we do is for *women*. You wash for women; you wear clothes to attract women; you go to the gym for women; you get a job so you can spend money on women; you have a big house to attract women.'

In the autumn of '92, I still had the boat. Everything was going great guns for me and I was doing *Big Break* at the BBC. I brought the boat up to Southampton on the way to bringing her up to London for the winter.

I spent some time on the boat having a few drinks with Kevin and finally returned home.

I walked into my front room at the Old Forge to find the children were in bed and Tracy and her friend Jackie were sitting there pissed. Tracy had declared that she wanted a nose job, and we'd already had terrible rows about it. We'd argued and argued and then, she'd gone and got it done behind my back anyway. She'd come back with a little plaster stuck over her nose and she looked like a boxer.

I found Jackie and Tracy sat there with two empty bottles of wine on the floor. They were talking about going out for something to eat, or doing something. It felt like they didn't want me there at all. I felt like I was an intruder in my own home.

So with that, I decided I wanted to take her car up the pub. I'd bought her a white Mercedes and my taking her car keys to stop her going out drunk proved too much for her. A scuffle broke out and as I went to grab her car keys and walk out, the two of them grabbed me by the front door. I thought, 'I've had enough of this.'

So, I pushed Jackie on her arse and went to phone Tracy's father, Burt.

'Burt, will you come down because I've just had enough,' I said. 'I can't take any more of this. The two of them are pissed and they're picking on me. I've pushed Jackie on her arse and I've told them both to fuck off.'

With that, Tracy came bounding in the room screaming at me.

I was still on the phone. 'Hang on, Burt,' I said.

Then Tracy snatched the phone out of my hand.

She then went out to the kitchen and phoned the police. She was pissed. I went out to the kitchen and took the phone off her and carried on the conversation with this police officer on the phone.

'Look,' I said, 'you'd better send someone round here because these women are irate and there's been a bit of a scuffle. I've been accused of this and, quite frankly, I'm not having it. So, you get round here and fucking sort it out because *I'm* not doing it.'

And with that, I went back to the Forge and poured myself a nice large brandy.

Soon two policemen turned up, came into my room and said, 'Excuse me, you will have to leave.'

'I *beg* your pardon?' I said.

'Is there somewhere you can go?'

'Yeah, *to bed* in a minute,' I replied.

That didn't seem to do the trick.

'No, no, no. You've been violent,' they insisted.

'Forget all this, I haven't been,' I said.

Then I persuaded these policemen that it was not worth arguing and shouting about and that it was best for them to bugger off. So, they buggered off. As they left, they said to me, 'Do you promise to stay down here?' I replied.

'I'm going to stay down here. Goodnight.'

I grabbed my bottle of brandy. Jackie and Tracy went to bed and I was locked in the room downstairs. Then I started thinking to myself – because now, as you might have realised, I was pissed – that I'd do something in the kitchen. I went along to the kitchen and got all those little teapots that Tracy collected and I start smashing them. One by one, by one.

I was thinking, 'If you don't want me, and you don't want me in the house, then you can do without your teapots.'

So I started smashing things up – and Tracy and Jackie then came down. Tracy phoned the police again. I was arguing with Tracy as the police walked through the door for the second time. I wasn't *raging* pissed but I knew I was in a terrible state and I was *so* fed up with the world, fed up with these two, and I knew the police were going to cart me off to a cell. So, I said to them, 'Will you excuse me, I've just got to go upstairs and get my heart pills?'

One of the policeman walked into the bathroom with me. I opened the bathroom cabinet and took out two enormous sleeping tablets. They were Valium. I took two of them, drank some water ... and then I knew that *wherever* they took me, I was not going to give a fuck. If they put me in a cell, I could still sleep.

They took me down to the police station and started questioning me.

I was being a bit shitty to them when the phone rang and it was my lawyer, Henry Brandman.

'Would you like me to come down?' Henry asked me.

'I don't need a lawyer,' I said. 'I haven't done anything. Henry, I'm just going to tell them the truth.'

So they put me in a little cell for the night and I got myself off to sleep. They told me they would question me in the morning.

The reason I took my sleeping tablets was because I knew they'd put me in a cell. I knew I'd be lippy and I knew I'd be feeling frustrated because I felt I hadn't done anything wrong.

As I slowly woke up the next morning feeling like shit, the events of the night before came flooding back. It wasn't as if I hadn't been in control of what I'd done. I was in control ... until I had that bottle of brandy. I whacked down some sleeping tablets to avoid that awful nightmare of pacing up and down in a cell not knowing what's going to happen. I knew that, in the morning, they were going to come and speak to me and that I would have to give a statement and possibly appear in court.

No-one had brought me a cup of tea, or anything. And I figured in my silly little head, after having talked to my SAS mates, that I was now facing 'interrogation'. So I wanted to get myself together. I washed my face in the bowl of the toilet and dried myself on my shirt. I just tried to get myself together.

Then they took me into their interrogation room. My overnight cell hadn't exactly been a suite at the George V in Paris – and the interrogation room was almost as grim. It seemed to be full of shadows, dark and dank. I still felt pretty rough, even after a splash of cold water on my cheeks. And the grim decor of the room matched my mood. Frankly, I just wanted to get it over with, explain to the police I felt I'd done nothing bloody wrong, and bugger off home. My sense of frustration was growing and they kept me waiting and waiting ...

Then a man, straight out of *The Sweeney* came in and started to interrogate me.

'Did you hit the nanny?'

I told him the exact story, and he said, 'Well, you're going to be taken to court and charged with assault.'

Oh charming. Bloody great. I could see the headlines then and there.

'No-one knows you're here, it doesn't matter,' the detective said.

In time they decided not to press charges. I was eventually released ... to walk straight into a mass of Press who '*didn't know I was there*'.

Finally, I escaped and went home. Tracy and I were still pretty much at loggerheads with each other about the whole saga. And the episode had made the television news, the papers, the lot.

Thames Television were also getting shitty with me. I was doing my stand-up show and Laurie suggested that we should have a nice picture of me and Tracy together, as well as a press conference, to say that we were all fine.

I agreed and eventually Tracy did too. We were worried that it could just escalate into 'Jim Davidson the wife beater' and 'We don't really want to have him working for us do we now?'

But that's not how it was. The truth was, it was just a very pissed argument between a man and a wife.

I went to speak to the Press. I told everyone, 'We're fine now and I *didn't* hit the nanny. I didn't mean to. Tracy ducked.' I tried to make a joke out of it.

Then we had a nice picture taken of us together. And the photocall made big banner headlines, which read, 'JIM AND TRACY PATCH UP THEIR DIFFERENCES AFTER PUNCH-UP'.

And, of course, what was the picture? Tracy with her nose job, a plaster slapped over it – and two black eyes.

I never minded the world's Press being there on these occasions. But I just wish their camera lenses could sometimes tell the truth.

9

Life begins at 40 – does it, fuck

Back in 1976, when I appeared in my first pantomime at the Alexandra Theatre, Birmingham, our director Alan Curtis staged a midnight matinée with various stars and celebrities turning up.

They 'sent up' the pantomime a bit and I thought it was the *best* night of entertainment ever. So it then became a tradition for me to do one every year. I put on these midnight matinées where I'd invite various people along – and the cast would 'blue it up' a little bit.

We were playing *Cinderella* at London's Dominion Theatre with me, Carl Wayne, Charlie Drake and the others. I asked them all if they'd do the midnight matinée, and 'blue it up' – just take the script and make it filthy.

The cast were fantastic. They just ad libbed their way through it. We laid on just about the best two hours' entertainment any audience had ever had. After that, I decided that we'd have a *proper* go at writing a blue pantomime.

Me and my writer Bryan Blackburn sat down and wrote the script for *Sinderella*, beginning with an 'S', with me playing Buttons and the great Charlie Drake as Baron Hard-On, as opposed to Baron Hard-*'Up.'* We opened in Ipswich and put a little tour together.

The first night was about three hours long, so I had to trim it to make it work. But it turned out to be a fantastic show. When Prince Charming Jess Conrad made his entrance in the guise of the Las Vegas Elvis, it was just brilliant.

I really enjoyed doing the tour, which ran for about three months. We played *everywhere* and the show went down fabulously. I was still drinking, still enjoying myself, chasing after one of the dancers on the show, whom I managed to 'get' *once* on the whole tour. And that was my lot.

But I had witnessed the birth of the great *Sinderella*. It went on to become *Sinderella 2* and *Sinderella Comes Again* and we also made a highly successful video.

One of the reasons for *Sinderella*'s success is maybe that I think it's funnier putting swearwords in people's mouths who *don't normally swear*. If you see Zippy and George put on a rather filthy rehearsal, it's hysterical. We all know how people normally behave in pantomimes. This audience all booed and hissed like crazy. Fabulous.

While I was beginning to enjoy this new-found success with *Sinderella*, sadly, Mum started to get a bit unwell. Eventually, she was diagnosed as having cancer. I don't know how I really felt. It was like it wasn't really happening. I knew that she would probably die and I still missed Dad but I used to put it to the back of my mind. I never let my feelings out. I kept them in and just switched off. It's a terrible thing to say.

I arranged for my sister Eileen to pack up work and look after Mum. I took care of Eileen's expenses and she looked after Mum pretty much full-time. Mum was getting more and more ill and we were all putting off the inevitable moment when we felt that Mum was going to snuff it. That would be it, we thought, we'd all be orphans.

I was in my old haunt, Morton's in Berkeley Square in London, where I'd been to a rock 'n' roll lunch, where they raise lots of money for children's charities. I did the auctioneering, which went down extremely well. I had a good old drink and ended up with, would you believe it, Samantha Fox on my arm. Sam Fox, the ex-Page Three girl-now-popstar. She's really cute and I like Sam a lot.

So, I thought, 'This is brilliant. I've had a great afternoon and now I'm sitting here drinking champagne and I've got Sam Fox with me.'

Just then, John Virgo's manager wandered over. He tapped me on the shoulder and said, 'Your brother's been on the phone and he says you'd better go home.'

I drank as much brandy as I could, then fell asleep in a black cab which took me home. I went into the house and saw my brothers Billy and John – and Eileen, of course. My other sister Jean was still in America. We decided that we'd better phone her and ask her to come over immediately.

The atmosphere was pretty rotten and then I went in to see Mum, who was sitting on the sofa. The doctor was in the kitchen, just about to go in and see her. When I walked in, she placed her hands on my head, looked into my eyes and said, 'I'm *so* sorry.'

And I didn't quite know what to say to her. She was sorry because she was going to leave us. It was a woman saying, 'Look, I have no control over this. I'm going to have to leave you, children, for the first time in my life.'

And the little old Indian doctor came out with tears in his eyes and said to us, 'I'm sorry, there's nothing I can do.'

Uncle George turned up and Mum lay on the sofa stuffed full of morphine and I went off to the pub with Billy and John and pretty pissed. I came back and slept in the kitchen all night, on the floor. I was drunk again and feeling awful and I just wanted to run away and vanish. So, I was in my little drunken rosy glow while Mum was in the front room dying. I don't think I was being selfish – I was being frightened. I was frightened to face up to it, to the confrontation of seeing my mother being so upset at dying. I think she was upset at the thought of dying and leaving us. And I couldn't face that. So I got myself pissed and lay on the kitchen floor waiting for the inevitable.

She left us a couple of little poems. I think she'd tried to write a version of, '*Do not stand by my grave and weep, for I am not here, I do not sleep…*'. She kind of made up her own version of that. She also left a message for me not to be drunk at the funeral. I suppose she had seen the state I'd been in at Dad's funeral and so she left me a message not to be drunk at hers.

My sister Jean got here from America just in time for the funeral. She didn't have time to say goodbye to Mum. We went to the church, the crematorium where Dad had been cremated, and listened to Debussy's 'Clair de Lune' again – and that was Goodbye Mum.

Mum was a great. She was the one who made up for Dad being like Dad. Mum was kind and cuddly. She use to get a bit annoyed and smack me round the face occasionally, and stuff like that. But on the whole, I can look back now and say, 'Good effort, Mum.'

She did alright. I was quite close to my Mum. She turned into an old woman, started to get more Irish. She turned into *her* Mum and, on reflection, I must have driven her mad with the antics I used to get up to, turning up with bottles of whisky for Dad and the two of us getting legless. I was outrageous all the time and, of course, Mum believed everything she read in the papers. I'd be splattered all over the front pages with some hooker or a police car, or fighting or whatever, and I'd tell her not to believe it. But she kept insisting, 'It's alright for you, Cameron, you don't have to go up the Co-op, where all those people point at me.'

Mum worried to death about me all the time. She worried to death about my drinking, my behaviour and, funnily enough, she never knew that I'd stopped drinking. She would have been really pleased at that, pleased as punch that I'd packed up drinking. Dad, for his part, would have been pleased I'd started again.

Once, I said to him, 'Dad, I'm really drinking too much.'

I used to feel rotten all the time and I was drinking about a bottle of whisky a day.

'Here's what you do,' he said – and Mum thought he was going to say something really wondrous. But then he went on to say, 'Drink *gin*,' as if that doesn't count. 'Women's drink,' he added. 'Drink *gin*.'

Around about the time of Mum's going, I had to decide what to do for a summer season and although I wanted to go to Torquay, as I'd been there so often and I couldn't really bring myself to go anywhere else,

Laurie came up with another suggestion.

'What about playing Blackpool?' he said one day.

Oh, no. I *hated* Blackpool. It's just so tacky and awful. But playing a summer season means you've got twenty weeks' work there.

So, I thought to myself, well, I'll put a little band together and we'll do a few songs, so I don't have to stand up there on stage all on my own, and we'd have a bit of a laugh.

My driver Tom Reid had gone off parachuting, so I called up a guy called Mick, a Welshman who used to train the SAS in unarmed combat. He was not a *big* bloke at all but all the SAS guys said, 'He's the *best* personal bodyguard in the world, truly amazing.'

I got a shitload of lights, a PA system and a band and I thought, 'Right, we'll open with a song called "The Boxer". Then I'll do "W.O.L.D.", by Harry Chapin, which I do quite well. And I'll finish with Pink Floyd's *Dark Side of the Moon*, the last two tracks. That'll *really* piss off these fucking Blackpool people.'

And it did.

The jokes were fine. It was a really good show. The sound and the band were fantastic. I had them all dressed in *Star Trek* uniforms and Smudger, who played the banjo, was dressed as a Klingon because he just looked awful in the *Star Trek* uniform.

Me, Mick, Kevin the driver and Brian my gay friend, who's a dresser, took this big house in Blackpool and settled in.

Mick was a revelation. He wouldn't drink and if there was any trouble, he whisked me out of the way straight away. We'd finish work at 10 o'clock, go the pub, leave the pub at 11 pm, come home to this house, drink a bottle of red wine or two, have some cheese and basically eat whatever there was in the fridge. Well, after about two weeks of this routine, we thought we'd better start going training.

Mick and I went to the gym just to do some weightlifting and then when Mick went off to have a run, I'd fall asleep. After three months, that's about twelve weeks of going to the gym, I was pretty fit. I felt pretty good about the whole thing. Blackpool was still dull and boring but we just drank our way through it.

Our daughter Elsie was born during the summer season at Blackpool, so I never saw her being born because I couldn't get back in time. I had to go on earning the money, especially as I now had three children. I sang a little song for Elsie on the night she was born. Instead of singing 'Sing a Song for Maggie', the old Irish song, I sang it '... Elsie ...'

At the end of the Blackpool run, we came home. And what did we do then? We went on tour. Yeah, we went on tour for October. Off we went on tour again. There's a video of it called *To Boldly Go Where No-one Has Gone Before*. Two truckloads of equipment, and that band from Blackpool, went out on tour one night and I've never felt so ill in my life. I decided that I really wasn't well and that I had a problem with drink. I couldn't eat and I just felt rough.

I kept thinking, 'Oh God, I've got to do the show tonight,' and I'd pace around all day in terror about going on stage with a hangover in the evening.

For lunch, I'd have a couple of pints of beer. We took caterers with us as there were about 25 of us on the road. We'd stay in four-star hotels, me and the band, and the crew would set all the equipment up in the venue.

When they'd taken the gear down, they'd pack it into the trucks, climb into this big coach which had sixteen beds in it, and they'd sleep on that. The caterers would follow round in *their* truck and cook for everybody. And then there'd be me, who'd let the side down a bit.

The buzz used to go round that Jim had actually *eaten a sandwich today* – wow, great. Everyone knew I was getting worse and worse and Mick was trying to keep me as fit as he could. But I just wasn't eating. All I was doing was drinking. I don't know why. I don't think I was that miserable. I was a bit fed up that I hadn't seen Tracy or the kids for ages. Although I felt it wouldn't have taken a lot for Tracy to say, 'We want to come and see you.'

The tour rolled on. We got to Bournemouth, where we shot a video of the show in front of an audience of 3,700 people. Our party, the resident crew and the film crew, totalled about 50 people. I got to the hotel in the afternoon and felt terrible, so I had a bit of a kip.

Then I got up, jumped in the bath and took into the bath with me all the vodka and orange juice I could find in the mini bar in my room. There wasn't much of it, about two bottles of vodka, little miniature bottles, and one of those Schweppes orange juices. So, I poured myself a vodka and orange and drank that as I sat in the bath. And then I poured another one ... but then I noticed as I was sitting in my bath that my vodka and orange had turned into a Tequila Sunrise ... and because my blood pressure was so high I suppose, through drinking, I was having a nose bleed – and the blood from my nose was dripping into the top of my vodka and orange, making it look like a Tequila Sunrise. Ugh. So, I couldn't throw the vodka and orange away, could I? Because there wasn't any left, so I just, sort of, scooped the blood out and drank round it.

If I hadn't had a drink, I wouldn't have been able to do the show. And that was the most important thing ... *do-the-show*. I felt so ill with all the drinking and the not eating that, obviously, my body had told my mind that it had better start to feel better – otherwise it was going to be in deep shit on stage in an hour.

I went over to the venue and did the sound check. You can see on the video how rough I looked. I hadn't been eating very much and I was sort of white and sweating all the time. I had long straggly hair and when I looked in the mirror, someone else looked back. This hideous looking, haunted man looked in the mirror, full of denial about the drinking and the lifestyle ... and Brad Pitt must have looked back and said, 'Go on son, you'll be alright!'

Then, I went off to try to do a bit of training, went back to the hotel again and wandered around, totally frightened to death, knowing that I'd *got* to put in a performance but feeling totally awful. I was backstage in the dressing room and the first half had finished and there were all these people around me with concerned looks on their faces.

Then I went into the bathroom and threw up all over the place. I tried to get some brandy down me and I was still just terrified of going on, absolutely terrified. And that terror was caused through a hangover –

not eating, not feeling fit. I was frightened. I wasn't frightened of dying on my arse, I was frightened of, 'Oh I don't have the *ability* to do this.'

I was *so* scared. I was planning to walk on the stage and say, 'Oh, fuck off all of you.'

I just wanted to go and lie down on the sofa. Of course, I grabbed myself the largest brandy in history and drank that while I was on stage *and* maybe a pint of Spritzer, white wine and Perrier water. I used to have them everywhere.

An hour and a half later, I came off to a standing ovation and everyone saying, 'Thank God for that. Hope he eats something.'

But no. Instead, I poured myself a large whisky and said, 'Come on, we're going out drinking.'

And we'd head off to the hotel where I had a couple of pints and maybe a beef and horseradish sandwich.

People talk about the pressures of show business. I'd just go out there, stand up and talk. I know loads of jokes and I've been knowing jokes since I was a little kid, since I stood outside by the gate with my guitar as people came up the road.

Showing off, I'd be the life and soul of the party. That's when I was the happiest. And what more could one wish for than 3,500 people cheering, standing up and applauding, with me telling jokes and singing songs that I liked?

Trouble was, the old cunning alcohol said to me, 'You're not going to be able to do this until you've had an old swig of me.'

I used to go on stage with a pint of Remy Martin brandy with Perrier water added, so it looked like it was a lager. I used to drink my way through it. Quantity-wise, I suppose I used to drink a lot when I was on tour. Brandy was only my *'work drink'*. My *real* drink was whisky. Brandy was to get me *on*, you see, medicine. And whisky was the drink I quite liked.

I'd usually fall into bed about 3 o'clock and have to get up about 10 am, feeling awful. It was silly really because the tour would have been great but I couldn't imagine having done it without any booze. I've done tours since, without any booze. I go on stage now without any booze but then it would have been a big problem. I just couldn't have done anything.

I was drinking partly because I felt lonely. You can always feel lonely in crowds. I just felt I didn't have a woman who wanted me. Although I was still married to Tracy I was no longer in a real relationship with her and I was searching all the time for a proper girlfriend.

I still am to some extent.

Two days later, we did another bit of filming down at Chatham and then our last gig was in Crawley Leisure Centre. Tracy and all her friends were coming. I went on stage that night and it was my birthday. I was forty.

The show went really well and I had a little cynical dig at Tracy. And afterwards, when we went backstage to have my birthday party, Tracy was with Kenney Jones's wife, and another friend of hers and all three of the girls looked alike. They had their hair dyed mauve, aubergincy, in a dark reddish tint. They were all in the corner together.

So, Tracy was with *her* friends and I was with *my* family, my touring family. As a birthday present, Brian, my dresser, had bought me a picture of some *Star Trek* people that he'd got signed. He'd sent the pictures to America and got them signed, *'To Jim'*. And they'd organised a beautiful cake, as well. I think Tracy's nose was put out of joint a bit by that. She just didn't join in the party. I felt we just didn't know each other any more. And, of course, I was a bit pissed and was making it obvious that she wasn't welcome. Not that she *wasn't* really welcome.

There was a guy there with a limo to take me and Tracy home. We sat in the back and a row exploded. She was annoyed that someone else had bought me a cake and she wanted to be with her friends and I wanted to be with mine. She just went on, like women do, saying, 'I've never been so embarrassed in my life' and 'You're not like a real husband' and 'I wish you were different' and 'I wish you'd stop drinking' and all that shit.

I wasn't having this. I got home, packed my stuff, phoned Kevin and Stuckey, two guys at work, and said, 'Meet me in Brighton.'

We went down to Brighton, I phoned up a girl I knew down there (I used to call her Barbie, like the doll) and we got ourselves all plotted up in the Grand Hotel, where we proceeded to drink ourselves stupid for about three days.

As long as I was drinking, I was fine. And when I *wasn't* fine, I used to sleep. And I was away from Tracy. She was away from me. She was back in the house and when I *did* go home, I just said, 'Hello' and went off to the pub. Eventually, one thing led to another, and I ended up getting that fateful shepherd's pie in my lap.

The momentous day I was admitted to the clinic, just after Christmas, on the morning of Tuesday, 28 December 1993, marked a deeply traumatic experience for me.

I was utterly exhausted, my body was awash with drink and drugs, I'd reached rock bottom and I was in fear of my life. The words I'd uttered on Tracy's bed the previous evening still haunt me to this day – 'I know you've every reason to hate me ... but unless you help me now I am going to die tonight.'

Over the next few days and weeks at Farm Place, the medication the clinic put me on surely helped. And, in spite of my initial resistance, so too did the many soul-searching one-to-one discussions with my counsellor Steve and the lively group sessions in which I took part with the other patients.

The written exercises they put me through, listing the damage I felt I'd done to others, for example, also helped me contemplate the desperate hole I'd landed myself in.

They were brainwashing me and telling me that, unless I got on the Programme, I was going to die. I was joining in, had stopped taking the Heminevrin and had settled into a routine. I used to cheat a bit, though. I'd sneak out and nick a newspaper from the staff room, then sit in the loo and read it. I'd also go and sit in the bath, *anything* just to get away from all those fucking people.

Some of the girls there liked me though. There was one specially nice girl there called Camilla. Camilla liked me a bit and I liked her *a lot* – but, of course, at Farm Place, no fraternising was allowed. Things came to a head one Sunday, in about the fifth week I was there. Joy the counsellor caught me putting my arms round Camilla. I was just giving her a hug. They teach you to hug everybody there. All alcoholics hug one another. But Joy got the wind up.

'What do you think you're doing?' she said.

'I'm not doing anything,' I replied.

'Your wife is across there at the family meeting,' said Joy.

'Oh. Alleluia,' I replied. 'Well, I've got nothing to hide.'

'Well, would you do that in front of your wife?'

'I'm only giving Camilla a hug,' I said.

'I wouldn't enjoy it if I was your wife,' she said.

'Well,' I replied, 'if you were my wife, *I* wouldn't fucking enjoy it!'

That was it for me. I'd been dying to fraternise. I fancied Camilla like mad. I'd heard lots of stories about *other* people shagging at Farm Place. Some of the staff would tell us.

'Oh, the group that was here before you, they were shagging in the bathrooms ...'

All I got was my roommate's snoring. And now I'd been accused of fraternising. Well, fuck it! I'd had enough.

I tore upstairs, packed my bag, put my Parker coat on and walked out into the drizzle, past the ducks, up to the little hut by the entrance gate ... and I saw that great line to freedom.

I put one foot across the line, then the other – and I kept walking. And walking. I'd escaped!

I was frightened to death. I didn't know what to do. I knew I was ill and that these people were driving me mad, killing me off. I *wasn't* fraternising. I was miserable and frightened – and I walked.

As I strolled along the road, a car pulled up next to me. At the wheel was Kinsa, the night nurse.

'Where are you going, Jim?' she enquired.

'I've had enough, Kinsa,' I replied, all choked up with emotion. 'I can't bear it. I'm not going to drink but I just can't stand being picked on any more. Don't try to stop me. I'm going home.'

She ignored what I'd said. 'Hang on a second,' she replied, 'I'll turn the car round and drive you back to the clinic.'

As Kinsa went to do a three-point turn, I leapt over the bushes at the side of the road and disappeared into the woods. The moment I reached the cover of the trees, I immediately went into fantasy mode. I imagined myself with my SAS chums, Minky, Snapper and 'JB'. I got my nose down into the leaves and covered myself up with twigs and grass.

Staff at the clinic came looking for me, but search as they could, they couldn't find me. So I had the SAS to thank for that!

I kept walking, past two pubs thinking someone there would be bound to call Tracy who'd come out looking for me. Someone even stopped and asked if I fancied a lift. But I walked on through the drizzle with my blisters … and seven miles later I got to my house. I walked up the gravel driveway to find Tracy in the kitchen with our baby Elsie.

'I've escaped,' I said.

'What are you doing?' replied Tracy, shocked and surprised to see me. 'You can't come in here.'

'Please let me in,' I pleaded.

I explained I wanted to get better but that I was frightened. Tracy must have heard it all before but she made me a cup of tea. I told Tracy there was there a man called Morris, an ex-patient of Farm Place, who'd visited us at the clinic and that I wanted to call him. We met up in Dorking and he invited me to an AA meeting in a church. I sat there, listening to people's stories and something happened to me. Suddenly, I understood the problem and what Steve had said about getting on the Programme.

I understood the need to have faith in the fact that I was going to get better, the need to have faith in the group, in myself …

And I left that Alcoholics Anonymous meeting with one thought ringing inside my head.

'Thank God I'm an alcoholic!'

Tracy woke me at 8.30 next morning. We'd slept the night together. Life was complete.

'I'm an alcoholic. Thank God,' I thought to myself again. I'd found a new club to belong to. I wasn't on my own any longer. I plucked up the courage to phone Farm Place. I spoke to my counsellor Steve.

'I'd like to come back,' I said.

'No way!' he replied. 'Have you been drinking?'

'I swear to God,' I said, 'I went to an AA meeting with Morris.'

'OK,' said Steve, 'call me back in ten minutes.'

I guess he then discussed it with the rest of the staff there and when I rang back, Steve said alright, I could return. Tracy drove me back.

I was welcomed with open arms. I told all the boys that I'd had a shag and they patted me on the back. Then I sat down with Steve who asked me why I'd run away. I explained that I didn't like the way some people were picking on me too. Then Steve said something that really helped me.

'You've got to remember,' he said, 'there are a lot of sick people here. Their minds are different.'

That made sense to me and it gave me food for thought. In fact, during the eight weeks that I spent at Farm Place, I found the clinic provided me with plenty of 'thinking space'. I had time to ponder my predicament, time to familiarise myself with the Twelve Step Programme.

Being thrown together with a strange group of people whom I'd never met before didn't make it easy to forge relationships. But I did become friendly with a vicar named Colin. He was the local vicar down in Ockley and he used to visit the clinic every Friday, sit in the room and talk to us.

Of course, everyone used to say to him, 'Come on, you believe in God because that's your job. He doesn't really exist.'

Well, I *sort of* believed in a God and I believed in what the Freemasons told me — that God was the great Architect of the Universe. There was this supreme being that made it all happen. I didn't quite know what it was all about … and then, one Friday, I sat there chatting to Colin.

The Alcoholic's Treatment Step 3 says, 'Know that the only person who can help you is God … and you're to hand your problem over to "God", as you know or understand Him — your higher power.'

And because Colin had this great faith in God, God became a great comforter to me. Another of the great clichés of Alcoholic Anonymous is 'Fake it to make it.' In other words, if you don't *really* believe, just go along with it and eventually you'll get it.

And I got it.

I sat there one afternoon while Colin was being bombarded by all the smackheads and I turned to him and I said, 'I think I understand what you're talking about now — that God is there for me and if I give my problems over to God then he'll help me.'

And it was like a load lifted off my shoulders. My eyes filled up with tears.

'I *really* understand what you're talking about, Colin,' I said. 'I understand where you're coming from and that God can be a great comfort to you.'

The AA programme said you'd got to hand your problem over to God as part of your rehabilitation — and I suddenly 'got' that. I wasn't frightened any more. I knew I wasn't going to die. Before, I was frightened to death because it said you'd got to hand your problem over to God and I didn't quite know how to do that.

But then I *did know* how to do it and I told Colin about it and he said — I'll never forget what he said — 'Well, Jim, I hate to sound like an old cliché but Hallelujah — you've got it!'

I became a changed man. I became the man that the counsellors used to want me to be.

One day, a girl in the clinic group was 'sharing' her problems, as it was termed. They asked us, 'What does the rest of the group think?'

She was a big tall beautiful model and she was going on about how she'd got on the Programme and how things were going great.

'I really am dealing with my problem and understand it,' she was saying.

Then the rest of the group had to give what they called 'oboes', that's objections. Everyone would turn to another guy in the group, who'd say, 'Oh yes, I think Sophie's doing *really* well. I think she's come on a great deal in the last week.'

And another girl would say, 'Oh yes, I think Sophie's changed and she's really trying hard.'

Then came my turn. 'I think you're talking absolute bullshit,' I said.

I was being opinionated, of course. I looked across at Steve, the counsellor, and instead of him signalling to me, 'Oh God, there's Jim being opinionated again,' he gave me half a wink.

And he realised that I had *got on the Programme*, as they said, that I had suddenly had this *spiritual awakening* and that I knew what I was talking about. I just knew that this girl was totally faking it, totally 'complying', as they say.

So I told her straight. And she burst into tears and stalked off. Then the rest of the group turned on me.

'How *could* you say that?' they demanded.

'Because it's the truth,' I shrugged. 'She needs the truth to get better.'

From that day on, I was suddenly looked upon by the counsellors as someone who was going to get better. *It was a miracle.*

Then, of course, they started to reprimand me for telling jokes.

'You don't *have* to get round it by telling jokes, you know,' they'd say. 'Don't cover up your grief by humour.'

They did encourage me a bit though and when there was a lull, I started doing impressions of all the counsellors. I used to get up after dinner, go into the Oak Room, where we'd all have our lectures, and deliver a spoof lecture myself, a funny one.

I did it once as Stanley Unwin – in gobbledegook. All that ridiculous talk. All the counsellors and everyone would have a laugh with me because they knew I was on the Programme and was just being myself. I wasn't doing it to draw attention to myself. I wasn't doing it to cover up the fact that I was about to die of this dreadful disease. I was getting better.

At first, I did not have any trust in the counsellors, I had no trust in this awful American Twelve Step Programme, and I didn't believe that God could help.

But then something happened. Now, I *do* believe that He can help, whether He's there or not. Some fucker has got my problems and it ain't me – and it's making me feel much better.

I enjoyed the last couple of weeks at the clinic in '94. You had to share a room there and, cynically, I used to say, 'I know why we have to share a room. It's so you can get twice the amount of money out of people by having twice as many people to stay.'

We used to get up at 7 o'clock on a Sunday morning so we could go to church. Those of us who were religious would be taken by Land Rover down to the little church round the corner form my local pub. Although I wasn't *that* religious, I used go because we were also allowed to stop and pick up the Sunday papers. We weren't allowed the *News of the World* though.

I used to listen to Colin delivering his sermons. The week before I left, I went to the church and they all took Holy Communion. I never did that. I didn't want to do that Holy Communion nonsense. *My* God was different to Jesus, the son of God. My God was just a God who would help me out.

But now, I went up for the first time in my life and I knelt down with all of them at Holy Communion. I didn't want a bit of bread and I'd already spoken to Colin about what happened.

'You just get up,' he said and placing his hands on my head, he added, 'God be with you.'

And God was that day.

I went back feeling fantastic and just went about my day. I felt bright and happy. I was the one to be around. I was the sensible one. I was the one that helped other people.

On Sunday nights, we used to have an AA meeting where people who had previously been at the Farm Place clinic would come back. All the old faces would sit round and we'd listen to someone tell a story.

Someone would do the 'chair', as it was called. They'd sit in the chair and tell you how their life was, what they did and how life was now. It gave you great hope.

Then I'd sit in the chair and I used to make them laugh. I'd talk sensibly but amusingly about things. Deep down, I quite enjoyed the fact that everyone laughed. I also thought that by telling my story I could give other people hope because I'd *got on the Programme*.

Unfortunately, my single room, a double room with only one bed, was now up for grabs. Now someone *else* turned up and the night counsellor said to me, 'Jim, we're going to put someone in your room.'

'Oh, *please* don't,' I pleaded. 'I'm really happy there on my own.'

A man turned up who was Iranian. He'd been brought from a psychiatric hospital and he'd been quite heavily drugged. I didn't know his name. He was a big, tall, gangly man, really scary. They told me he'd been given a drug they codenamed 'The Cosh' because it kept you really quiet.

So, for me, the place now turned into *One Flew Over the Cuckoo's Nest* and this guy was going to sleep in my room.

'You *will* make sure he doesn't get violent with us, won't you, Jim?' the counsellor said to me.

I didn't know why she was asking *me* – probably because I was the one who was getting better and I was a new man.

The new bloke arrived that afternoon and we all sat round chatting. It was obvious he was off his head. That night, he went up to sleep in the bed next to me and I was frightened to death. Before bedtime, I thought, 'I'm not going in there.'

So, I stayed up as late as I could until about ten o'clock.

'You must go to bed,' everyone said to me.

So I went up to bed but I was frightened to bloody death – all night he was howling like a wolf.

Next day, he joined in a couple of our meetings but was really odd. Then his wife came to pick him up because it was obvious that Farm

Place wasn't right for him. He wasn't getting any better and he was pretty drugged. We were rather frightened of him because he was tall and gangly and foreign.

'I'll carry your bag out, mate,' I said (to make sure he wouldn't get violent with anybody).

I put his bag in the back of the car and he turned round and gave me a hug.

'Thank you for being my friend,' he said.

I was now getting better and was now on Step Four, which means you write out everything you've ever done wrong in your life. Then you go and confess it to somebody. I was OK about that. I'd given my problems to God and I listened.

In my last two weeks in the clinic, we were allowed to go out to AA meetings, proper ones – which I loved.

'How are we going to get there?' said Steve the counsellor.

'Why don't I just get my car brought down here?' I said.

Steve agreed that was a good idea. 'Then you can drive people to the AA meetings.'

So, my blue Bentley promptly arrived and he said, 'Haven't you got anything less grandiose?'

'No mate, sorry, apart from a Ferrari,' I said, 'and I can't fit them all in that.'

So there I was with my Bentley full of alcoholics, heading off to some meeting somewhere. We drove to a Quaker's church in Horsham. It was quite refreshing to go to meet some *proper* drunks.

'Well, my name's Fred,' said one bloke. 'I'm an alcoholic. I had a problem with Higher Power, now I've sort of got it. Me and God are pretty damn good together. God and me have a deal in life. Life with God, for me, is like being in a canoe going down a river, with me paddling and God steering. And sometimes God lets *me* steer – but do you know what, I've never got *Him* to fucking paddle.'

'That,' I thought, 'is it in a nutshell.'

'Hello Jim, my name's Bill from Liverpool.'

Oh no, I'd acquired another new room mate! Good old salt-of-the-earth Bill with his drink problem had turned up and he obviously knew me from the television. He was chatting away in the next bed to me. I *hate* sleeping in rooms with people. He put his pyjamas on and I put mine on and we got into our beds and he said, 'Thank God you're here, mate. You're going to be a great help to me.'

Then he added, as an afterthought, 'Oh, and by the way, I snore ...'

I turned out the light and tried to get to sleep through the sound of a wildebeest with a blocked up nose. This man could snore the fucking paint off a wall. I didn't sleep for a week because of this fucker snoring.

In our group sessions, he'd say, 'Thank Heavens this man Jim is such a great help to me.'

I didn't know *how* I was a help to him. I had bulging eyeballs like Sid James's, the bags under my eyes were unbelievable. But even though I've never been a lover of Scousers – and I *hated* him for keeping me awake – somehow I got quite fond of old Bill. He always thanked me for helping him. I think I just gave him a bit of inspiration. I suppose he thought, 'If this famous comedian bloke can do it, then so can I.'

I was nearing the end of my time at the clinic. Tracy used to come and see me on Sundays and I'd sit round with the gathering there. I wouldn't be miserable or fed up and I'd be the first one to share my problems with the others and try to help them.

Suddenly, the heroin addicts and the booze people were the same as me. I didn't dislike them any more and I was learning to become a better person. I was starting to understand people's problems, even if they *were* arseholes, and I knew that they had problems as well.

When the big day finally arrived for me to check out of the clinic, I put on my suit and Tracy came to collect me to drive me home. I was a new man.

Obviously, I felt relieved to some extent that I was leaving the clinic behind. Tracy thought I was a bit odd though. Although my life was changing and I was getting a grip of my own personal character defects, my time in the clinic was to prove a major milestone in my marriage. As things later transpired, it was to mark, more or less I think, the end of the relationship between Tracy and me ... So be it.

As we drove away, it was only a few minutes' drive to reach our house. The lanes leading home that I knew so well were strangely reassuring. But I was also acutely aware that the journey ahead *in my life* wasn't going to be plain sailing.

When I came out the clinic in the early spring of 1994, after eight weeks of torture, I threw myself into my work and quickly rehearsed a new version of *Sinderella*.

We opened in the West End – and everyone was there – except Tracy. She was in New York.

'Why didn't you come to the opening night?' I asked her.

'You told me you didn't want me to.'

Oh. I probably hadn't made her feel welcome.

We were hardly together at all really.

To make matters worse, at around this time, I stopped being looked after by my agent Laurie Mansfield. We'd had a bit of an argument about how long we were going leave *Sinderella* playing in London when audiences started dwindling. As summer came along, all the tourists who turned up knew nothing about pantomime and nothing about Jim Davidson. So the place was empty, and we ended up losing about £400,000 because we kept the show on longer than I would have done. I fell out with Laurie for the first time in my life.

But I wasn't the old Jim who was drinking. I'd only recently left the clinic and I thought I knew it all.

'I must be right because I am not drinking,' I thought. 'My judgement is not clouded.'

So, ridiculously, I fell out with my best friend in show business over commission and money. Laurie wrote to me saying, 'If that is the way you are, it is best that you leave the office. We don't want to represent you any more.'

Funnily enough Richard Digance, my dear old friend with whom I'd gone to the Falklands, got the same letter from the office on the same day.

We were both sacked by our agents so to speak!

So I'd lost Laurie — and now I was losing Tracy. Losing people looked like it was becoming a bit of a habit for me. Even though Tracy helped me get into the clinic, it was inevitable that we would split up, of course. But, as the old saying goes, breaking up is hard to do and so we didn't.

Instead, we just plodded on. I tried superficial changes, like buying a new house. That'll be a good start. We'll buy a nice new house. In fact, we'll buy a house in London as well. So I bought a little house in Ponsonby Terrace. I thought it was lovely, but unfortunately Tracy didn't like it.

In an attempt to patch up our marriage, we bought another house in Surrey, which used to belong to Oliver Reed. I still live in the house. But all buying it did was give Tracy a bigger kitchen to hang around in.

It dawned on me that I didn't have a marriage really. I had someone who had her friends and the kitchen and her special friend Jackie and her Mum ... and that was it. However unfairly, I felt that she didn't want *me*.

The real final split up came at my 41st birthday party. We had about 400 people turn up and it was fabulous, a great party. I wasn't drinking, of course. Tracy and her friends, all with their matching purple hairdos, stayed together and drank champagne. As the evening wore on, everyone went to bed and I found two handbags in the front room. We opened up one and found it belonged to my mate Roger Swallow's wife.

The other one had, on the top, a load of slimming tablets, which I recognised from when I was a kid. People go to the doctor's and they give them these slimming tablets. I looked at the name on the bottle and it read, 'Tracy Davidson'.

I took the bag upstairs and said to her, 'Why the fuck didn't you tell me you'd been taking these all the time?'

She went mad. 'It's nothing to do with you,' she shouted. 'How fucking dare you?'

So I went downstairs with her bag and she came down in the kitchen in her nightdress in front of Stucky and me, and a few of the others who were still up, and she went even more berserk.

'Give me my fucking bag. How fucking *dare* you look in my bag?'

It was as if this woman now hated me and I hated her. It was 14 December, the day after my birthday and I couldn't wait to leave. I could not wait to get away from Tracy and as soon as a chance came, I took it.

I organised a photo shoot. I just phoned up an agency and said, 'Can you send me down a Page 3 girl. I want to have a picture for another mucky panto I'm thinking of doing called *Dick Whittington*.'

It never really came off but nevertheless, the girl turned up. She looked like a proper girl, very sexy and her name was Debbie Corrigan.

Afterwards, I said to her, 'Is there any chance of, you know, a date?'

And so she took my phone number. Later, I called her up and said, 'Do you fancy a hamburger one night?'

'Well, I don't know, I'm a bit busy. I'm going away for a couple of days …'

I flew off to Cyprus to entertain the troops. As I got off the plane, my mobile rang and it was Deborah.

'I wouldn't mind that hamburger.'

'Bit tricky,' I replied, 'unless we make it a kebab, I'm afraid, because I'm in Cyprus.'

When I got home, I started to see Deborah. Tracy was down at the Farm, of course. We had a new nanny then, Becky, the daughter of my mate Roger, from the brickworks.

Becky became Tracy's pal and I felt like the outsider. I'd now got *two* women to argue with. So I used to come home, sit down and have a beer. I'd sit in my room, while Tracy'd be in the kitchen. Then I'd get my dinner on my lap.

We never ate *together*. It was a lonely old existence. I'm not saying it was anybody's fault, it was just the fact that I was pretty lonely.

I used to enjoy sneaking away to see Deborah. We used to go to Morton's together. She could drink a bit but I'd stopped. Then we'd go back to my new place in London and carry on with our affair. I don't know if it was a death wish I had or what, but I think people do this when they are having an affair – they secretly *want* to tell their wife.

I was *desperate* to get Deborah to join this new tour of *Sinderella* I was planning. So I asked Tracy, 'What would you think if I got a Page 3 girl to play the part of the Fairy?'

'Yeah,' she said, 'that would be a good idea.'

'What about this one?' I said, and I showed her a picture of Debbie.

'Yeah,' said Tracy, 'she's good.'

'Right.'

I thought that was dead crafty. Tracy would never find out. Although I didn't give a fuck, I didn't particularly want to get divorced either.

And so Deborah Corrigan became the Fairy and off we went. I'd been seeing Deborah since about Christmas, in fact, since my party and I thought, 'Well, let's just have a mess around and not be too serious.'

But then I decided I was *so* unhappy and this girl was making me feel better.

And then, of course, it wasn't long before the Press found out.

Tracy and the kids were at home with Becky the nanny and Tracy's Mum. I was out on tour in Brighton, staying at the Grand Hotel with Deborah. In the morning, she wasn't very well, so I went down the chemist to get her some bad tummy stuff, and when I came back she said, 'You'll never guess what's happened. As I opened the door, I thought it was you coming back, but it was a reporter who took a photograph of me.'

'Listen,' I said, sensing a problem here, 'I'm going to go home. I've got to see the kids on Saturday.'

I was driving home when the phone rang and a man's voice said, 'It's So-and-so from the *Sunday Mirror*. I believe you're seeing Deborah Corrigan and having an affair?'

'No, I'm not,' I replied.

'Well, you *are*,' he said, 'because we've seen you coming out of her room' etc. etc. etc.

'No comment,' I said.

'Well, look,' he said, 'we're just on the way round to tell your wife.'

'*Why* would you want to do *that?*' I said.

'Well, if you're having an affair, it's only right she knows.'

And they did! They went round to my home and said to Tracy, 'Do you know your husband's having an affair with Deborah Corrigan and here's a picture of her. Look, we took this picture this morning in his hotel room.'

And that was that. That was the end of the marriage, thanks to the *Sunday Mirror*.

Now if the newspapers *hadn't* told Tracy, there is the great debate – 'Well, we *wouldn't* have told her if you *hadn't* done it.'

Fine. But maybe if Tracy hadn't known, that would have all blown over with Deborah and we would have tried to patch up our marriage. But the newspapers had decided it was time for us to be divorced. And that's what happened.

I then had to make a choice between Tracy and Debbie. Tracy obviously went ballistic and didn't speak to me – but that was nothing new because she wasn't speaking to me anyway. Deborah moved into London with me, Tracy stayed in the country – and the divorce proceedings began. My fourth marriage was well and truly over.

Reflecting on those times now, I'd say I don't think I am happy about my life – I don't think I have *ever* been. It's because the alcoholic in one says there *must* be something better. You know, everyone's got it better than you have and you want to be something you're not – and you can't quite put your finger on it.

All you know is that when you're drunk, life is better. And alcohol takes away more than it gives you.

I felt my marriage had been to a woman who didn't really *want* me and didn't really *love* me. I think the only time we made love was to have babies. There was no real passion between Tracy and me. She didn't fancy me and I didn't push her buttons.

Well, now we were splitting up. I had survived the clinic – but my marriage hadn't. I had got on the Twelve Step Programme and had vowed to stay dry. Life without booze was an epic struggle but I have always been a fighter. I was determined not to lapse back into my bad old drinking habits. I had struggled hard at Farm Place and now I didn't want to throw it all away.

But with my daily efforts to refrain from drinking, and the realisation that my marriage was over, life after Tracy and life after the clinic added up to one thing for sure.

This would be a brave new beginning.

10

A new set of rules to run my life

After my spell in the clinic, my new lifestyle meant that I no longer depended on the daily excess of alcohol as part of my routine. It was a struggle to stay dry but part of the void that the booze left behind was filled by something that had become an important part of my life – religion.

I do a bit of praying myself now and a lot of communal prayers in my role as a Freemason. In some of the degrees of Freemasonry that I belong to, like the Knights Templar and the Red Cross of Constantine, a lot of praying is involved.

When I was in the clinic, God did mean something to me. Not so much Jesus and the Bible but there was something 'up there' to give my problems to.

Since I became a Mason, I started to look at religion as a *history*. I took the myth out of religion and so now I look at it from my own little point of view.

My religious beliefs run as follows. I'm probably a Christian but I don't believe Jesus was the Son of God. I don't believe he died on the cross. So I would probably class myself as a Gnostic Christian, rather than an ordinary Christian. But a Christian nevertheless. Jesus – good bloke.

I've become closer to God and closer to Jesus since I took out the 'Son of God' stuff. I never really quite believed that I could really fill in the gaps that one has to do to acquire faith. And as for miracles, I didn't believe in them. Why would Jesus just want to cure *one* blind man? Why would Jesus want to bring just *one* man back from the dead? I mean was he showing off or what? And I'm sure he had much better things to do than just feed five thousand people with a couple of fish. And why isn't he here *now* to stop all the grief and suffering that's going on in the world?

So who was this Jesus? Well, I believe he was from the Royal House of David. He was a Jewish King and I learned about his brother, James, and his other brothers. And I believe that Mary Magdalen was a little more important than people let on. I believe that Jesus and Mary Magdalen were married and that they had three children.

I re-read the Bible and now feel that the Bible is a complete contradiction. The Gospels, particularly the gospel of John, are obviously written by two different people.

I think that *blind* faith is not a good thing to have. I have lots of friends who are devout Christians who believe that Jesus was the son of God, who believe the Bible like it's the be all and end all of everything. It's *not* – to me, anyway. It's very contradictory. I don't care who you are, Noah did *not* live for nine hundred fucking years!

I learn something every time I pick up a book. I read about things and it adds to my understanding of religion, my love of God and a great love for Jesus, although I said this to vicar Colin, when I met him again some time later.

'D'you know, Colin, I don't believe Jesus was the son of God and because I know this in my heart, it's brought me much closer to Him. What He says makes more sense to me. I don't think He died for our sins. I don't think He died on the cross. I think He survived the cross, in fact …'

And I went into all my little details of where Jesus was when He died and where His body now is etc. I was really excited but Colin the vicar listened patiently.

'That's all very well,' he said, 'but Faith is something you don't get from a book. Faith is something from "inside".'

'Well, what if the facts add up to that Jesus wasn't the Son of God?' I replied. 'That Jesus was just from the Royal Family of Jewish Kings?'

Colin sighed. 'If you took away that bit about dying and going to Heaven, and the Resurrection and forgiveness for our sins,' he said, 'then

I wouldn't bother. I truly believe that Jesus *was* the Son of God and that's my Faith. That's what makes me feel good.'

But it didn't deflect me from my 'great esoteric study,' as it was called. I've since read the Koran and I've read the Bible a few times. This mention of religion takes me into why I've become a Freemason really. It explains perhaps why it means so much to me.

I've been a Freemason for about eleven years now. It started off because I was just nosy and I wanted to find out what it was all about. Freemasonry gives me a set of rules to live by, which I quite like because one thing I *did* learn in the clinic is that I didn't know the answer to *everything*. There is a Higher Power, a group of people, or in this case the ritual and teachings that go back to the time of King Solomon, even to Moses. All these things Freemasonry teaches you.

Freemasonry is not a group of people sitting round trying to overthrow the world. It's like a church service. It's quite ritualistic. There's talk of great stories, stories that are not in the Bible, some that *are*.

I believe that some Freemasons don't understand *why* they are Freemasons. They miss the point of it. They get their little books and they read all the ritual and they sit in their positions in the lodge in the Temple and they recite their bits without really quite knowing what goes on.

Part of the ritual is they say to you, 'Where were you made a Mason?' and the answer that you are told to give is, 'In my heart.'

And that is true – you're made a Mason in your heart.

You suddenly become a different person. And you're basically with a load of blokes – and women have their own Freemasonry as well, their religious assembly. You're promising not to break the law and are promising not to be arseholes.

Well, if you've read this book this far, you'll know that I can be an arsehole. Now, if I didn't have my Freemasonry, I'd be an arsehole *all fucking day long*.

Freemasonry has also taught me that we are all equal and that death is the great leveller. Freemasonry's just like that. You can go and sit in a Freemason's Temple and find a Charlton supporter sitting next to a

Millwall supporter, it's where Hindu can sit next to a Sikh, or a Catholic can sit next to a Protestant. And they promise to get on well. When people say they don't like secret societies, what the bosses of Freemasonry have always said is, '*We're* not a secret society. We're just a society *with secrets.*'

OK, a very clever play on words. What I say, what I believe, and what I've told the bosses of Freemasonry, is that when these politicians and people ask, 'Freemasons – what's the big secret? Why is it a secret?,' I say, 'It is very secret. It's more secret than we've told you in the past. We're a secret society because we have the ability to make better human beings.'

The obvious question then is, 'Well, why don't you share that with everyone?'

The answer is, 'Well, because not everybody wants to be a better human being.'

The Freemasons' motto is to 'Make Good Men Better'. I don't know if that's a *great* motto. I wouldn't have chosen that because I've had my rows with some of the people in Freemasonry. My mate who got nicked for fraud was a Mason and he had to go to prison. When he came out, he went to see the bosses of Freemasonry. He was going to be thrown out because he'd broken the Law.

'Hang on a minute,' I said, 'are you telling me that you are going to take away this man's belief and throw him out of the Freemasonry because he broke the Law? If you're a murderer you get a Bible, if you're going to the electric chair you get a priest – and you're taking away the only thing this man believes in. You *can't* take his membership away because we ask, "*Where* were you made a Freemason?" and the answer is "In my heart". And it's in his heart. So you might throw him out of Freemasonry but you'll never take the Freemasonry out of him.'

I feel we have this great responsibility as Freemasons. You can take someone who's a bit of a shit and put him in with fifty or sixty blokes with whom he gets together, has dinner and listens to this fabulous ritual in the Temple. He says a few prayers, gets to grips with God, however he sees Him to be, and *then* you've got the cornerstone of the makings of a person there.

Freemasonry can do it. I've seen it change people – it changed me. You still park on double yellow lines and you still smoke the odd joint but it makes you want to be a better person.

Now I've been made Master of Chelsea Lodge, which is the show business Lodge. It was the biggest private Lodge meeting ever for Freemasonry in this country. I'm also immediate past-Master of the City of Westminster Lodge; I'm a Master of the British Forces Foundation Lodge; I was the Founding Master of that. I'm also about to become the Prior of the Knights Templar.

When you first go in with your trouser leg rolled up, your blindfold on and the noose round your neck, they tell you all these awful stories about having to shag sheep and they say things like, 'Let's hope the goat doesn't bite you.'

In fact, we wind them up *so much* in Knights Templar, you know, I got some initiates to write down their blood group because they had to sign up in blood. And I wound them up so much, we've put blood outside on the door where the initiates were coming in.

Outside the Temple, you don't know *what's* bloody going on and we told them, 'Wear clean underpants, won't you?'

We have also asked the initiates, 'You're OK with touching another man's genitals, aren't you?'

They went *white and pale.*

When you join the Freemasons in England and Wales, you become an Entered Apprentice. When you go back for your next ceremony, you become what's called a 'Fellow Craft,' which is the *second* degree. Then you go back and do your *third* degree and you're then called a 'Master Mason', which is what most people are. You get the proper apron and you're invited to all the 'do's. Most people stop at the *third*. The fourth degree is called 'Royal Arch' or it's known as 'Chapter', and if you join that, it allows you to go on to various other side degrees. It opens other doors for you.

I'll attend a Masonic function about once a month but I'll speak to people who are Masons every day. You bump into them all over. It's become a part of my life and I'd miss it dreadfully if it wasn't there. It's in my heart, you know. I could be a Mason on my own in a room.

There's been some publicity about the Masons but anything people don't know about, they tend to knock. If you can't join a club, you say, 'I don't fucking want to be in that *anyway*, stupid club.'

People don't understand Freemasonry but I would urge everybody, 'Take the plunge. Take a leap of faith. Go and speak to a Mason, and get yourself in. You can always leave.'

The Chelsea Lodge, of which I am now Worshipful Master, is the biggest Lodge in the country. The Lodge has 400 members. When I was initiated as Master, there were 750 in the Temple.

My Master before me was Roger de Courcey. Peter Sellers was in Chelsea Lodge. Tommy Cooper was in Chelsea Lodge. There are great stories of him coming in with his apron on back to front, gloves falling off, flies undone, pissed as a fart. Bernard Bresslaw, rest his soul, he was in it when I was there. He was very nice to me. Mick McManus, the old wrestler; lots of the young comedians as well.

I went over to a black guy once, a comedian called Ian Irving, and I said, 'Do you fancy being a Mason because a lot of black people think it's a middle class white thing and it really isn't?'

There's some really high-ranking black Masons and Indian Masons. It's totally non-racist, it really is. But it's not *politically correct* – you can still tell jokes about the black bloke – with respect and love – and he'll tell jokes about the white bloke.

When Ian Irving became a Mason, I was really pleased that a young black comedian got up for his acceptance speech and said, 'I haven't seen this many white people since last time I was in court.'

Great. You see, it is a great leveller.

The difference between the show business Lodge of the Masons and something like, say, the Variety Club, is that members of the Variety Club don't pledge to become better people. They join together to raise money for charity.

I think the charity side of Freemasonry, and they give millions to non-Masonic charities, is something that we don't really want to flag wave about. It's not the importance of being a Mason. I think that charity comes with being a Mason but you don't justify being a Mason by giving money to charity.

People say, 'Well, they do a lot for charity.'

They do it because, by the nature of what Freemasonry turns people into, you become a charitable person.

I always say Freemasonry is *a religion* – and the boss of Freemasonry, who is basically Lord Northampton (he's the one down from the Grand Master) is always bollocking me, 'Jim, you mustn't call it a religion.'

'But it is *to me*, your Lordship,' I said.

There's a few famous Masons about. Bob Monkhouse is a member of Chelsea Lodge. Crippen was a Mason. Winston Churchill was a Mason but the best one of all is the little bloke down in Dorking Station where I go and buy a ticket to go to London. The bloke in the ticket collectors' office. He was my boss at Knights Templar. There you go, it's for *everybody*. It's a great myth that it's for the upper classes.

Becoming Master of Chelsea Lodge in 2001 was quite something for me. I'll be Master for a year and then I'll hand over to someone else. Being The Master or being 'in the chair', as it's called, is a great honour – but it's hard work. You have to do all the ritual, word-by-word. That's twenty foolscap pages to be recited. And people say, 'Oh, you must be a great Master because you're good with words.'

But I'm not. In the past, I've always made up my own words. Now I have to quote stuff that goes back to King Solomon's time, so if you get *that* wrong, you know, it's a nightmare.

What I want to bring to Chelsea Lodge and what I want to bring to Freemasonry is a bit more openness, a bit more 'Let's own up.' In America, they have marches. Well, we don't want to go marching but I would like people to know all about Freemasonry and to come and have a go, just to open it up to people. Come and become a Mason.

I've never gained anything by being a Mason, apart from more friends and spiritual awareness.

I get strangers come up to me and give me a bit of a funny handshake, and so we immediately start chatting.

'What's your Lodge? ... What do you do?' and you share a few

Masonic anecdotes. But you don't say, 'How can I help you? Are you in debt?' and 'I'll pay your debts for you.'

It doesn't work like that. I wish it did sometimes.

Freemasonry helped me get through the clinic as well. Because what the clinic was saying was not a million miles away from what Masons talk about – become a better person and have a belief in God.

So, it gave me a set of rules. It gave me something else to do, and just by doing it, it made me become more aware of how to behave. And I think that, over the course of 1994, it all dropped into place. I became a Mason, I quit drinking and I became 40 – all round about the same time. All those milestones helped me and I think changed me *as a person.*

Turning forty has changed me in all sorts of ways. I think the main thing was that now I was letting the world know that I was taking care of myself a bit better. I quit drinking and I was doing very well in Freemasonry and that's all I can put it down to – just being older and wiser. And not punching people any more. Just generally putting the brakes on a little bit.

In the clinic, they told me that once you're addicted to one thing, you're pretty much addicted to *all* of it. And having sex is like having a drink – it makes you feel better. And if you haven't *got it*, you're going to go out sniffing around for it. Some people go out sniffing. They go to extremes for a shag – *I do.* I've driven *hundreds and hundreds* of miles for a shag – and as soon as I've done it, I've thought, 'What the *fuck* am I doing here?'

I don't know if I can ever be faithful, although I'd really like to be. I'd like to meet someone who provided me with everything, someone I could provide everything to. So far, that's not happened.

When I first checked into the clinic, they mentioned sex addiction to me. It wasn't a throwaway line. But there are clinics that specialise in sex addiction. I was going to go and wait outside the door for a girl to relapse.

I tried to add up once how many ladies there have been in my life. I've had *lots* of ladies. I haven't particularly had many *good* ones. I've had *some* good ones. But you have a division, don't you? You have a 'league' that you think of. So I've had better ones than Bert the window cleaner – but not as many nice ones as George Best. I've had *thousands* of women. Some, I don't even know their names. Some I've just bumped into and had sex within fifteen seconds of meeting them. Those were the days! WPCs are more fussy now. Shame.

I've been married four times and also engaged a few times. But, to me, getting engaged doesn't count. Getting engaged is just, sort of, 'nearly taking her prisoner.'

'You're engaged to me now. You can't go off with anyone else.'

When I meet someone I fancy, I think, 'I *want* that *now*. I've *got* to have that.'

And then you've got to work out a way of getting it. You've got to realise that all the ones I *really* want don't want *me*. If they're *that* gorgeous, they're not going to want a middle-aged ginger comedian, are they? They want the guy who plays for Arsenal. So I have to work quite hard to get it.

My heyday was in my thirties. I could pull a bird *out of thin air*. With girls, you can tell which ones are going to 'do it' – and which ones are *not*. Finding the really good ones though that 'do it' – that's the problem. *My* groupies are, sort of, funny people. You get the odd 'groupie,' the odd one dirty cow who turns up and shags everyone. That's good fun.

Once, we were on tour. It was the tour before I went in the clinic in 1993, and there was a girl hanging around the tour. Seventeen of us drew lots as to who was going to shag her. We drew lots with matches. So I said, 'Don't worry about that – *I'll* do it.'

The trick was that everyone would hide in the bedroom. This was an ordinary hotel room, I add, and there were *seventeen people* hidden in this room. I swear to God you couldn't see them until you *really* looked. They hid in the wardrobe, on top of the wardrobe, under the bed, in the bath, behind the curtains. They were all there and they all leapt out at one moment. You know, 'HELLO … SURPRISE.'

I'm not married now. What I really hope for is just nothing much … a Page Three girl a week will do me. Well, I'd sort of like a girl that I fancied, one that looks alright. I'd see her in the kitchen and think, 'Oh, I'd like to …'

So, there ends 1994, when I came out the clinic and went up to do my first summer season in Great Yarmouth for a while. I quite enjoyed that, and down the road was the Wellington Pier, which was really derelict.

I had played at the theatre on the end of the pier a couple of years previously. I went down there to have a look at it – and it was really scruffy and falling to pieces. I did a deal with the local council – but they would only give me the lease for the pier if I guaranteed to do it up.

I immediately formed a Charity Trust and applied to the Lottery Commission and the Arts Council for some money to do up the pier. And in the meantime, I was spending my *own* money doing it up. I think I spent about £750,000 doing out the theatre, thinking, 'Ah well, the Lottery will come along and I will get that back.'

Wrong.

The Lottery people wouldn't give us the money, so I ended up spending it myself and working the summer season there. Even this year, I've been doing Saturday nights there. Well, I never really made any money there.

The whole idea was to try and stop it falling into the sea. For me, it was a labour of love, like some people have an old locomotive or an old car. I had a pier and a theatre. It was great to see it full of life again.

Next to the pier are the fabulous Winter Gardens, made of glass. You can get 1,250 people in there. It was a completely derelict spot, so in Year Two of my owning the lease on the pier, I gutted the Winter Gardens, borrowed £200,000 from the Brewery and did the place up. We turned it into the most fabulous looking nightclub you have seen in your life – and it was then that I realised I had been in the wrong job all my life.

You have never *seen* so many women as there were in this club. Young girls. And because I was the club owner, they suddenly started being nice to me and I'd be buying them the odd bit of champagne and they'd, sort

Julie and I loved messing about in boats.
Not without a drink, of course. SUNDAY PEOPLE

*People say that Margaret Thatcher cheers up
when I enter a room — because I can be a
bit rude about people.* DAILY EXPRESS

(Opposite)
My first jump!

My favourite rock star and good friend, Keith Emerson of Emerson, Lake and Palmer fame. THAMES TV

Eamonn Andrews springs his famous surprise. 'Oh,' I thought, 'this is it. Fantastic. I've cracked it. About bloody time.' THAMES TV

*Mum and Dad outside our council house
at 118 Holburne Road, Blackheath.* SUNDAY MIRROR

Me and my SAS 'minders' (L-R) Mick, Nish, JB and Goose.
Alison felt comfortable in their company too!

Tracy and I in happier times. THE SUN

In my capacity as Chairman of the British Forces Foundation (I got the easy job).

Live long and prosper. Blackpool wasn't quite sure what to make of us when I got the band to dress up in Star Trek uniforms.

Sinderella's dancing girls have several points in their favour.

John Virgo's Big Break as Aladdin. BBC

Mum, my biggest fan.

The wonderful Deborah Corrigan — with her eye on my plastic.

Me, Russ and HRH Prince Andrew share a love of golf. CROWN COPYRIGHT

Meeting the Prince is always a great honour.

A proud day, with my brothers and their wives, after collecting my OBE.

Mel Stace had to make a cake, interview some people and perform a comedy sketch with me — and she was very good. BBC

At Home (and Away) with Kate Ritchie, Christmas Eve 2000.

We planned a game involving the Royal Navy showing us how to serve officers in the dining room when the ship is a little bit rocky. BBC

Lea Kristensen likes blokes with ginger hair. Stay tuned to this channel!

My all-star cast (L-R) Sarah, Cameron, Charlie, Elsie and Freddie.

of, *'crawl up my arse'* a bit. They knew I was Jim Davidson, the comedian, but now I also owned a nightclub.

I stood there one night with Kevin and these two darlings walked up to me.

'Can I help you?' I said.

'Yeah,' said one of the girls, 'we are looking for a sandwich.'

'Sandwich?' I said. 'There's hamburgers, steaks, anything ...'

The girls shook their heads. 'No. We're not talking about *that* kind of sandwich. We want a sandwich *with you.*'

Bloody hell. Thank you, God. I looked up to God and thanked Him. So I said, 'I see. Well, I am staying across at the Carlton Hotel, opposite the Wellington Pier, and when the club shuts, I will be over there in the bar ... and if you are still hungry, I will see you there,' and I strolled away, playing Mister Cool.

Then I ran over and got Kevin my Roadie. 'For fuck's sake,' I said, 'nip over there and hire me a room immediately.'

He tore over to the Carlton and booked me a room. I flew over there, set myself up in the room and I said to Kevin, 'For Christ's sake, bring those two birds over.'

'It won't happen,' I was thinking. 'This is a wind-up.'

But then came a little knock at the door – and in came my sandwich. These two girls decided that they would have their way with me. The bastards.

Best sandwich I have ever had!

I had done *Big Break* for the BBC for five years when, one day out of the blue in November 1994, I got a phone call from a woman at the BBC.

'Hello, this is So-and-So at *The Generation Game*,' she said.

Oh, yeah?

'Bruce Forsyth is sick,' she said.

'I *know* that,' I replied.

'No, he really *is* sick. He is in Spain, he's got tonsillitis and he can't come and do the show – and we are recording it *next Thursday.*'

Now this was on Monday night. And she said, 'We would like you to do it. Are you free?'

Now I immediately thought this was a Noel Edmonds 'Gotcha.' So I asked her, 'Is this a wind up?'

No, it wasn't, she assured me.

'OK,' I said.

I went in to the BBC the next day and had a meeting with these people and it was true, Bruce *had* gone sick and I had to do *The Generation Game* on the Thursday.

I went to the rehearsal room where they used to run through the show and rehearsed. I was going to turn up on the Thursday to do the show in front of an audience – a bit daunting but I thought I'd just do it. It was already set up with Bruce's script, Bruce's people, Bruce's everything – except instead of Bruce, it was Jim Davidson.

Then another woman phoned me up. 'Hello. I am So-and-So from the BBC casting department.'

Oh yeah?

'We would like to talk about your fee for *The Generation Game*. We would like to give you £10,000.'

'I am sure you *would*,' I said.

'What do you mean by that?' she said.

'Well,' I said, 'I think it is only fair if you give me what Bruce Forsyth gets.'

She turned frosty on me. 'We are not at liberty to tell you what Bruce Forsyth gets,' she insisted.

'Well, *I* know what he gets.'

'No, you don't,' she said.

'Ah,' I said, 'you have got to work out in your mind whether I know or not, so whatever you offer me, if it is *not* the same as that figure, I will be insulted.'

'Mr Davidson,' she replied, 'what you have got to remember is that Bruce Forsyth has being doing this show for many years.'

'He ain't doing fucking tomorrow's one,' I said, 'and *that* is the one we are talking about.'

So I 'umm-ed' and 'ahh-ed' with them and battled with them … and I got the money up *a bit* but I didn't get anything like what Bruce earned.

But nevertheless, I just turned up and went and did it – and I wasn't particularly good at it.

But it did have one effect – when Bruce Forsyth heard that I'd stepped in and done the show … it made him get better very quickly.

11

Welcome back, my friends, to the show that never ends …

I was sitting in what passed for an Officers' Mess, which was really just a couple of Portakabins bolted together. We were huddled round the television, watching endless videos, drinking lukewarm RAF tea and munching awful council house biscuits.

It was about eleven o'clock in the morning and, of course, it was cold and windy. The cloud base was about ten feet below us and I was in a place called Byron Heights on the West Falkland Island. I was at a huge early warning radar station, manned by the RAF and, as the title of this place suggested, it was perched on a fucking great mountain with a drop-off over one side. I had been given a UHF radio so I could speak to the F2 Tornado fighters who'd taken control over the airspace in the Falklands.

I was making a little film to be inserted into a video and I was speaking to a pilot codenamed 'Eagle One.' I called him up on my radio.

'Eagle One, Eagle One, this is Jim. Are you within our vicinity?'

The radio crackled back. 'Yes. If you look out to the west, you will see us approaching. We should be with you in thirty seconds.'

'Bloody hell,' I thought, 'they don't hang around!'

They had only just left Port Stanley. I looked up in the air trying to spot the two Tornados. Into my radio, I replied, 'I *still* don't have you in visual.'

And the pilot radioed back, 'Look *below* you – not *above* you!'

And there, maybe fifty feet *below us*, hugging the ground, were two fighters. They'd warned the cameraman this was going to be one to keep his eye on!

We turned over the camera and suddenly saw these little dots coming towards us. Within seconds, they had passed us. They had stood on their tails and just disappeared into the clouds, sweeping their wings back as they did it. It was the most fantastic sight! It was brilliant that the RAF could do all this stuff – and I was controlling it! It was such a great feeling of power and I thought our RAF must be the *best in the world* ... until I tasted their lousy biscuits and their lukewarm tea!

The Falklands trip of 1994 was a difficult one for me because I wasn't drinking. When everyone was up on the piss at three or four o'clock in the morning and trying to pull birds, I was trying to get some sleep because I was bored. For the first time, I realised that not drinking didn't allow me to fit in as well as I used to. I would be up earlier than everyone else walking around.

On this particular day, I was sitting in the Mess when they said there was a phone call for me from England. I thought someone must have died or something. I picked the phone up and it was Mike Leggo, the Head of Light Entertainment at BBC Television in London. He had promised to call me when the BBC had made a decision on whether they wanted me to take over *The Generation Game* permanently.

Bruce Forsyth had been doing the show for years. Previously, he'd left for a while and had been replaced by the brilliant Larry Grayson, confirmed bachelor. I admired *all* the previous *Generation Game* hosts. When Bruce started with Anthea, I thought they were great. And I loved the way Bruce did those plays at the end. You think no-one can follow that, and then Larry turned up.

You didn't quite know what Larry Grayson was doing but he was very camp. My Mum used to say, 'He's not gay, you know.'

'Oh, it's just an act,' she'd say.

I thought Isla St. Clair was probably the best hostess of them all.

Then Larry went off to do other things and Bruce came back in a blaze of glory. Then he buggered off again, and then came me. After Bruce had fallen ill that time in November 1994 and I had stepped in for him, the

BBC people were quite impressed. They knew I had the ability to do it and now Bruce was going to stop doing the programme.

Bruce went off to do other things for ITV and, in a way, I sort of agreed with him. We were moving into a time where it was fashionable for young comics to wear jumpers and be politically correct. There was Ben Elton getting laughs from God knows what! I thought it must be canned laughter because he never made *me* smile once.

There were a few people up for it. I bumped into Matthew Kelly, that big, tall, gangling bloke that does *Stars In Their Eyes*. He said to me, 'Good luck, may the best man win.'

What I had going for me was the fact that I had done it before and proved I could do it, although I could imagine the BBC were thinking to themselves, 'Hang on, Jim is a blue dirty comic ...'

I have *always* been blue and dirty; I've had wives; I've had drink driving convictions; I'm scruffy; I don't play golf with the 'in' set. They probably wondered if I was right to carry their flagship TV show.

But I was still in the Falklands. I stood there listening on the phone to Mike Leggo calling me from London to say that they would like to start negotiations with me for the job. I sat there open-mouthed and watched a bit of my council house biscuit drop into my tea as I had over-soaked it in shock.

'So, would you be prepared to take on the show, Jim?' he asked me. 'Would you be prepared to come in and chat about it? How much would you want for doing it?'

Now I had a great opportunity, but I was without the best agent in the world, Laurie Mansfield, with whom I'd fallen out, and I was stuck in the Falklands. My tea had turned into stodge, with the biscuits dropping in it, and I had a man on the phone asking me who he was to do *The Generation Game* deal with.

As luck would have it, I had a mate called John Ashby. It was John who'd suggested I go to Barbados for my holiday with Julie. He suggested that he would speak to the BBC for me as a mate.

So there I was trying to get a line to phone John in England. He would phone the BBC and the BBC would then phone him and then he would phone me back in the Falklands. But by then I would have left Byron Heights and would be somewhere else, probably in Goose Green, where the electricity is generated by a hamster running around in a wheel.

After four or five days, John said the BBC had made an offer. I don't recall how much it was, but it was quite a few bob. And it was to record twenty shows at the BBC that summer. Starting that summer and ending that December. So I had to spend six months recording the show, one show a week.

I was thrilled that I had been offered *The Gen Game*. It is very nice to be chosen above everyone else. It must be like becoming an MP. I wouldn't mind being an MP. I'd like to get voted in just so I knew that people wanted me more than someone else – but actually *doing* the job would be a bit daunting.

It was the same with *The Generation Game*. I was pleased but I thought, 'How the fucking hell am I going to do it?!'

As Mike was talking to me about this on the phone in the Falklands, I was already working out how I would do it. Did I *really* want to be compared to Bruce Forsyth? Could I follow Bruce Forsyth? ... who is *brilliant*, he is, *absolutely*, especially with *The Generation Game*. Bruce has had years of experience. People like him. He is a nice man. He would have been exactly what the BBC wanted, rather than this scruff who'd turned up!

Despite not having Laurie to advise me, my ego and their flattery got the better of me and I said I would do it, subject to the contract. I shared the same fears as Bruce that the BBC didn't take its light entertainment department seriously. It wasn't like the old days of Thames Television.

When I recorded *Big Break* at the BBC, you would never see anybody. You would walk round this immense ghost town. It was like being on the inside of a battleship. You almost felt the BBC was geared up to make programmes like *Panorama* or *Watchdog* or something boring. And when Morecambe and Wise left the BBC, well, that was it. There was no light entertainment left.

They liked *Big Break* because the public liked the game. And if the public liked it, that delivered good ratings – which enabled us to make a few more series. But *The Generation Game* was something else – the BBC didn't muck about with it.

And I didn't want to become famous as the person who'd ended *The Generation Game* forever.

But they *were* talking good money. I can't recall the precise amount but a lot of money. I was nervous about taking over. I wondered how I was going to do it and also questioned whether there could be some ulterior motive in them offering it to me.

When I returned from the Falklands, I went to see Mike Leggo. He was Mr Blobby's Dad, you know. Mike Leggo was the man who invented Mr Blobby for Noel Edmonds. Noel had staged a spoof, for one of his *Gotchas*, to catch out Will Carling and Mr Blobby, who then spoke a few words, was used to trap him. The idea was that Will had to teach Mr Blobby to play rugby. It was hilarious.

So I was discussing my future career with a bloke who'd invented *Noel's House Party* and Mr Blobby. I know! But Mr Blobby was hysterical. He made me laugh my head off, although other people hated him. I thought I *get the joke* – the others, they don't get it at all. To this day, Mr Blobby is my favourite entertainer.

I was introduced to the new *Generation Game* producer, Guy Freeman. We decided that we would change it all round, change the way things were done. I didn't particularly want to do those plays at the end that Bruce did because he used to do them so well – the final game where contestants used to come in dressed up as Kate O'Hara from *Gone With The Wind* and Bruce used to send it up. And when they got the words wrong, he would look down the camera and say, 'Bloody fine pair we have here, dear.'

I was wary I couldn't quite do that as well. But the BBC were adamant, they wanted to keep those plays.

'Let's make it film clips,' I suggested instead. 'We'll do clips from films. We'll shoot it wide screen and although I don't particularly want to be in it acting, I will join in and mess around.'

The other thing the producer wanted to do was to bring in the contestants in cars, which was really odd. The doors would open on the set and in would come the contestants in these old vintage cars, or real flash sports cars. I'd ask them questions, then we would do the games and the conveyer belt was exactly as it was before.

So there wasn't much difference, really. Everything was the same. The same crew, the same cameramen, a new producer who also directed it, and me.

Now we had to find a young lady to do it too. Because that was always a big thing in *The Generation Game*. So we asked dear Sally Mean. Sally had been the Weather Girl on one of those breakfast television stations. I used to tune in when I came in from the clubs. She was very good and we wanted her to be rather 'upmarket' and stuffy – and for me to be the little naughty boy Jim that I am. We thought the chemistry would work well.

With Sally there was never any sexual chemistry there at all but she was great. She is not a flirt and she doesn't give you the hint that maybe you will have half a chance after two glasses of port. There was none of that. We just got on with doing the show.

Sally was very career conscious, very professional and she let me do the jokes. I would explain to her how a joke worked and she'd say, 'Fine. You are the best there is, Jim.'

And I would think, 'Great.'

We went into rehearsals, we looked at the games, we worked out some funny material and I brought in Bryan Blackburn the writer, to draft my opening monologue and a double bit with Sally. It was really weird because, in the afternoon before we started doing the dress rehearsal, Sally and I stood and looked at one another and thought, 'Bloody hell, here we are taking over the flagship of BBC light entertainment.'

It was bizarre to be standing there on that stage, where Bruce had stood, doing a show that Bruce had always done, with his various dolly birds ... we were following in their footsteps. We were absolutely terrified.

The first series started recording and the first thing struck me. I knew something was wrong in the dress rehearsal and I wasn't happy. I came down onto the stage, and in my normal style which I have always done on dress rehearsals, I 'blued it up' a bit.

I put in a few jokes and a few rude words to try and get the studio relaxed ... and I didn't get any laughs. This new camera crew were not like the ones on *Big Break*. They were young lads and they didn't laugh *once*. The floor manager, the person who walks around and tells you where to go, was so engrossed in getting this show right, that he and everyone else seemed to be wrapped up in their own little world of uncertainty that change can cause.

But there was no atmosphere in the studio at all.

'Oh, oh, this is a warning sign!' I thought.

I bumped into Matthew Kelly again at Shepperton Studios where I was having lunch with someone a few days later.

'Congratulations,' he said, spitting venom, 'you have got the fucking *Gen Game*.'

I didn't boast about it. 'Oh, OK,' I just said, 'you can do it *next* year!'

The newspapers had printed a huge list of names who were allegedly in the frame to take over as host. One was Terry Wogan. Now I am not a big fan of old Wogan, nice bloke that he is. I think he is always too pleased with himself. I don't think *The Generation Game* is a show about being too pleased with yourself. You have got to try to get the best out of the people and Terry is not a comedian. I didn't think it was right for him.

Michael Barrymore could have done it. I thought it was either Michael or me going to get it. Michael would have been very good at it, I am sure ...

I think the papers made the names up but Chris Evans's name was mentioned. I don't think Chris Evans would have the ability to do it. To me, he is as funny as a fart in a space suit. I met Chris Evans at the BBC a couple of years ago and he was waiting downstairs to go and see

Mike Leggo about some programme or other.

'Hello mate,' I said to him, 'how you doing?'

'Better than you, probably,' he replied, cheeky git.

Julian Clary was mentioned by the papers for the *Gen Game* job. The trouble is with Julian, he seems very nice and very attractive but if I was him, I'd worry about being the token gay on the telly. There is always *one*, isn't there. There was always John Inman or Larry Grayson. I would hate to be the token gay person. These days, we have Dale Winton as the token camp person.

I love Dale Winton and Dale loves me too.

I don't see Bruce Forsyth that often now. I am not very good at talking to him on my own level. He is a big star, Brucey. I knew he wished me all the best and he'd said something like, 'Jim will do the show in his own way,' which really means 'No way is he going to follow me!'

And no way *could* I.

Now, and over the years on *The Gen Game*, I have always mentioned Bruce. I always regard it as if it really is Bruce's show, and I'm just looking after it for him, although people have forgotten now. They say to me, 'It is *your* show and you shouldn't mention him.'

But I love to mention Bruce. You can't mention 'Cornflakes' without 'milk and sugar'; you can't mention *The Generation Game* without mentioning The Great Bruce Forsyth.

Mr Blobby joins in too and comes on sometimes with an ill-fitting wig and does Bruce Forsyth impressions – but *The Generation Game* team all love Bruce Forsyth.

What *does* happen unfortunately at the BBC is that the bosses change a lot. When I was there, in the first series of *The Generation Game*, we called the sixth floor, where the bosses lived, 'The Crèche', because the bosses were all younger than us! Then they get promoted and become Head of Pencils, or someone else goes off to work for somewhere else and a new person turns up. Someone who was a Floor Manager is now your Head of Light Entertainment.

You always have to treat these people with respect – but also you have to keep your eye on them … some of them don't know what the fuck they are doing! They don't *really* know how to make a TV show. But they have to give the *impression* that they do. *You* have to give them the *impression* that they know more than you do. But deep down, they don't! They wing it – as we all do! Bless 'em.

You also have to know that *they* are the boss and they have *got to be* the boss – and they have got to be *seen* to call the shots. They have got to be *seen* to come down and nitpick and say, 'I don't want that bit in the show.'

Halfway through recording the series, even before it started to transmit, I started thinking to myself, 'I am not hacking this! I am not doing it as well as Bruce did.'

I was doing my best to make improvements, to make changes. I even had my hair done differently. I went to the barber's, the hairdressers in Bond Street called Stephen Ways. Stephen himself has since married Gloria Hunniford. He is a real nice guy and a great hairdresser and his salon's fantastic. There are always *great* birds in there, fantastic birds. But I had not-so-butch Pedro, the little Spanish man, to do my hair.

I hinted that I wanted someone else do it, hoping they would give me some beautiful little dolly. Who do I get? Herdeshi, a Japanese bloke who looked like a sniper. He had really long trendy hair and used to wear hobnailed boots. He wore a skirt one day and was really bizarre. I *instantly* liked him.

'I need a change of image. I want to look different because I am doing *The Generation Game* now,' I said.

'What you need,' he replied, 'is a "Relaxer".'

'That's very kind of you,' I said, 'but I have packed up drinking.'

'No,' he laughed, 'it's for your *hair*!'

He slapped all this stuff on my head and my hair went *dead straight*. Normally, I have wavy, curly hair but it went dead straight and swept back. I looked like a prick, quite frankly. So now I had this new hair style, a new show and I could see it all going wrong.

Even Chris Tarrant said on Capital Radio one day, '*What has* Jim Davidson done to his hair!?'

And as much as I combed it, everyday was bad day hair. I looked like Michael Portillo in a wind.

About three-quarters of the way through the first series, I had a brainwave which was to change *The Gen Game*.

Bryan Blackburn and I decided that it would be better if we changed the way the contestants talked about themselves. Bruce used to say to the daughter, 'So tell me about the story when you left the handbrake off the car.'

We thought, 'Wouldn't it be better if we have *Dad* telling the story about *daughter*, embarrassing her, and then *daughter*, pre-armed with the knowledge that Dad's going to embarrass her, will have her *own* story ready, saying, "Well, here's Dad when he set the house on fire ..." '

Then we took it one step further. 'In fact, here's a picture of my Dad dressed as a woman.'

Then we would get the embarrassment factor.

The producer was new, Sally was new, I was new and we tried to make the show new. It was slightly obvious and the Press picked up that it wasn't quite working. So the feeling was, 'Grit your teeth, let's get the series finished and then have a little rethink.'

I never really bothered when the ratings dipped because *all* ratings were dipping at the time. I was resigned to the fact that *The Gen Game* wasn't working in this format, that it needed a change. The producer was floundering in the dark as much as we were. But little did I know that *Noel's House Party* was about to change the way that *The Generation Game* was done – for ever.

At the end of that series, I took a meeting with Michael Leggo and explained to him that I didn't think it was working. It was time to go back to the fundamental rules of *The Generation Game*, I said, drop all the cosmetic surgery and all the silly cars coming on, and just go for it.

We'd also made the mistake of taking some of the games *outside* the studio. Contestants had to drive a tank round, outside. Sally and I had to go and watch the contestants drive JCBs round the BBC car park – again, it was change for change's sake. And it didn't work.

We had a problem. And Michael Leggo came up with the answer.

He said, 'I want you to meet someone.' And he brought into my dressing room this little man, who looked very much like Kenneth Branagh. 'I'd like to introduce Jon Beazley.'

He said Jon had been doing *Noel's House Party*, the great rival, the show that followed us. It was always a case of 'Who would get the most ratings? Noel or us?' And Noel was winning by a nose.

But I knew that all was not well on *Noel's House Party*. Noel could be very fussy about things and when things weren't going right, Noel used to get humpy. And let's face it, the BBC are not the *greatest* at getting things right. The sound department have the same speakers that were hanging up there thirty years ago! The speakers I talked through to do the *Gen Game* were the same speakers they used on *Dad's Army*, when it was in black and white! The same sound bloke who did *Steptoe and Son*, was doing me!

No-one thought the way the studio was laid out was worth a change. The audience were sitting behind a row of six or seven cameras, so they couldn't see. They had to look above their heads to a television monitor, and also sound came from behind their heads when I spoke from the stage. They couldn't see me because of the cameras and they were looking up, so they'd got sore necks.

It took *for ever* to move any of the scenery. The audience came in at 7 pm and didn't leave until 10.45–11 pm at night. They were bored to death. It stopped and started and it was a fucking nightmare. And, at the end, when I was waiting for the crew to move something, I just stood there looking at the audience like a dick. I said to them, 'This is piss poor, isn't it?'

And the audience all agreed!

The next day I was driving up to my theatre in Great Yarmouth when I get a call from Mike Leggo. He said, 'Jim, it's Mike Leggo.'

'Yeah?' I said.

'Last night was fucking *appalling*!' he said.

'We've got the show the way I wanted to do it,' I said. 'We've got it on paper. Fine. But the crew and everyone took *forever* to do it. Every time I did a joke, someone said, "Can we do that again?" Why??? The camera wobbled, the lights went out, the sets were not in the right place, the contestants were not ready, the make-up's taking longer and it was awful ...'

And I thought Mike Leggo had phoned up to *apologise*. Instead, he said, 'Can I just tell you something. What I witnessed last night was the worst thing I've *ever* seen in television.'

'I fucking agree with you!' I said.

'No!' he said, 'I mean the fact that you told that audience that it was piss poor. Do you realise that up to 200 people are working for you on this show and they're *all* pulling together? And let me tell you Jim, I was so angry with you, if you'd have come up to me and said, "I'm leaving," I would have held the door open for you.'

I said, 'OK Mike, I'll speak to you later.'

I hung up and I phoned Laurie Mansfield, who'd by then resumed acting as my agent.

'Tell them all to fuck off!' I said to Laurie. 'I'm not being treated like that. Not only do they not know what they're doing but I'm getting the bloody *blame* for this!'

Laurie remained calm. 'Well, that will always be the case,' he said. 'What you've got to look at in *The Generation Game* is this ... Either you go along with the way the BBC do things, and try to encourage them, and try to help them to change the way they do things – *or* you can moan like fuck and be Mr Difficult, and then when it comes to who they want to work with, they might choose Mr Easy. So, there are two ways of doing this, you can do it *your* way or do it *their* way... OR way three, which is even better, is do it *their* way but get them, by persuasion, to do it *your* way rather than moan.'

So, I learnt a great deal that day.

The ratings were going badly because we'd got the format wrong, my hair was sticking up with a new hairdo, and Sally Mean didn't look as if she was *ever* going to shag. Just kidding!

I was aware that the viewing figures had dipped and that the show might be scrapped – and that was *why* I was so frustrated, that on the opening night, with the new show, we *still* couldn't get it together.

I'd turn up to record some inserts and the set would be all wrong and I'd say, 'Excuse me, the lighting's all wrong here.'

And they used to say, 'Listen, what do you want then, Jim?'

And I thought, 'Oh my God, they're now treating me like one of these awful prima donnas.'

I'd try to explain to them, 'But it's not what *I want*, it's what is *needed* to make this work. If this doesn't work, let's not do it.'

So, now I started to get a reputation for being fussy. And then you get all these idiots saying, 'Of course, you're a perfectionist, aren't you?'

That annoyed me. 'What do you *mean*? If my mike is supposed to be on, and it's *not* on, and I *want* it on, is that *perfection* or is that just *fucking common sense?*'

It was becoming a nightmare. I knew that if I didn't get it the way I wanted it to be done, the show might have been elbowed.

But I wasn't going to give up and that pep talk from Laurie Mansfield, prompted by Mike Leggo's 'open the door' outburst, made me realise that the BBC system needed to be *worked*. You need to *coax* people into doing things. You know, praise in public, bollock in private. I learnt that my man management skills were zero because I didn't quite twig!

When I found out that Noel was having problems too, he became my mate.

'Oh yeah, Noel, you poor bastard, they haven't got a fucking clue have they?'

'No they haven't,' he said.

Jon Beazley was producing *Noel's House Party*, and the word around the camp fire was that both he and Noel thought the time had come to part ways. So now I thought, 'That cheeky bastard Mike Leggo's going to give me Noel's cast-off to produce my next show.'

But Jon turned out to be the most experienced, the best, the most hard-working, meticulous producer I've ever worked with in my life.

When Jon took over at the helm, we went back to the fundamentals of the show. 'Let's make this Jim's show,' he said. 'Let's get a new set, a new director and let's have some fun. Who do you want on your team?' he said.

'Christ!' I thought. 'I could work with *this* bloke.'

The first thing we did was, we had to find a new girl. Someone took Sally to lunch and said goodbye. She did very well, Sally, she was great. She was very professional, she's lovely and I really hope to work with her again. But it just was not working. I'm afraid she caught the short straw.

All the girls that do *The Gen Game* want to do more. They don't like the idea of just being the hostess and just bringing the person on. Whether the *public* want to see them do more is questionable. That is what the bosses have to work out. Sally and I are still mates.

In the meantime, John Ashby was looking after a young lady whose name was Melanie Stace. She was a big tall girl who'd been working in a show called *Cococabana*, which John Ashby had helped put together with Barry Manilow. It was a fantastic show and Melanie was one of the dancers.

One day I said to John, 'I need a girl for *The Generation Game*.'

'Why not use Melanie?' he said.

'I wonder if they'll accept an unknown girl,' I thought, 'a dancer who hadn't done any television before.'

The producer agreed to take a look at her.

We made a demo tape. Mel had to make a cake, interview some people and perform a comedy sketch with me – and she was very good. So the deal was done.

Then, the producer said, 'And while we're at it, let's use your *Big Break* crew, you like them, don't you?'

Ahhh! Bliss!

On the very first day in the studio, I walked into the dress rehearsal and saw my old crew standing there. I couldn't have been more pleased to see them – and I wanted them to know it.

'Thank *fuck* you lot are here!' I shouted out.

And they roared and cheered! My old cameramen were back, my old floor manager, Patrick Vance whom I'd worked with at Thames Television. Brilliant. I used to *run* to work. I couldn't wait to get to the studios – and then I just knew the show would be a success.

God bless you, Jon Beazley.

We'd brought in a guy called Rob Collie, who used to write *Have I Got News For You?* and shows like that. He would be writing the way I spoke to the contestants. He'd be making the jokes up about it. The team would do all the research on the contestants and find out about all the silly pictures they had.

The contestant stuff worked a treat.

We worked out a new way of giving people surprises. It was a bit like *This Is Your Life* in a way. And this was all down to Rob Collie, me, Bryan Blackburn and, of course, Jon Beazley, who'd make all these wonderful things happen. We had pulled a great team together – and we all felt things were starting to go right.

We'd spring surprises on the contestants by bringing on people they hadn't seen since their school days, and we'd really embarrass them. We also had another secret weapon – Mr Blobby.

Mr Blobby would come on a few little tags here and there. We laughed at him so much we thought we *must* get him on the team.

We also recruited some real dolly birds to come on just for the sake of it, in *St Trinian's* outfits. It was all mad. It was all going a bit more mad, and then something else happened that changed and improved *The Gen Game* even more.

We planned a game involving the Royal Navy showing us how to serve officers in the dining room when the ship is a little bit rocky. In the studio, they built this bloody great 'mock-up' ship on springs. All the crew were on the outside of it pushing it backwards and forwards, while the Navy were serving up.

When the time came for the contestants to do it, me and Mel played the part. I was Noel Coward and she was someone else and we were sitting there in the ship, waiting to have soup and spaghetti with meatballs and blancmange. Then, when the other contestants did it, I played the part of some German First World War officer with one of those silly pointed helmets and Mel was a Fraulein.

As the ship started to rock, contestants were spilling stuff everywhere. The crew were throwing in buckets of water through the port holes, and I threw stuff back at the crew.

Now Jon the producer shouted to the director, 'Show what's going on!'

So the camera pulled right back and we saw the crew *for the first time* in *The Gen Game*. I was throwing blancmanges in people's faces, the meatballs were tennis balls and they bounced out of the studio. We just totally wrecked this set. It was the funniest thing – I've never laughed so much. Melanie was weeping, we were falling over. I was putting custard pies in people's faces. It was complete bedlam and bliss. When we finished, we were all dripping and soaking wet.

We changed the conveyer belt slightly as well, so if the contestant got 15 prizes, they could have a holiday too, which made it more exciting.

That night we went to the Green Room after the studio recording was over – and we all felt a great sense of excitement and anticipation. We suspected we had pulled off something special, something new.

'Have we created something new and different?' we wondered.

With all the messing around with the crew, whom you could hear and see laughing, what had happened was, they'd become part of *The Generation Game* family.

The boss from 'upstairs', Michael Leggo, came down to see us next day. This was it. Verdict time.

'I saw the tapes last night,' he said. 'It's a bit different, isn't it?'

'So what do you think?' I asked him, my heart pumping.

'When that meatball bounced off the table,' he said, 'I just fell on my desk and laughed until I cried. This is brilliant!'

Alleluia! Inside me, bells, whistles and hooters all went off at the same time! We'd done it. And the viewing public started to agree with us in their millions. The show began getting better and better. There was more slop, more custard pies, more tricks with the television technology. Me and Mel came on once as little kids with funny voices. It was just brilliant. We were having fun and enjoying our success with the audience.

After all the trials and tribulations we'd been through, after all the rethinks and production meetings, after making all those changes and improvements, finally all our hard work was starting to pay off.

It's hard to put into words the tremendous sense of achievement that gave me. But proof, if proof were needed, that we'd hit the jackpot came when the series started to be transmitted – and our viewing figure ratings went through the roof!

Ahhhh ... the sweet smell of success at last ...

12
The Battle for Mr Blobby

At last, *The Generation Game* was soaring back up the ratings to where it belonged and everyone on the show was buzzing with pride at our new-found success. We'd all shifted up that extra gear to 'make it happen'. And everyone was dead chuffed, not only the bosses upstairs, but also all the researchers and the writers, the crew on the studio floor – and, of course, there was one other guy who was an integral part of our new-found success – the short stumpy guy in pink with the spots. We mustn't forget him!

The bloke inside Mr Blobby is called Barry Killerby. Barry is a fantastic mime actor with a great comedy mind. The physical ability and agility he uses to make that thing come alive are just superb, and his energy is incredible.

What Barry has done, with our help, is to bring about the growth of Mr Blobby. He's turned him from being this thing that just says, 'Blobby Blobby!' into someone that can speak English a bit now as well.

He's learnt certain things. The way I look at Blobby, and I think Barry does as well, is as a great big shaggy dog, who loves everyone. But, of course, he messes up all the time. He's so honest and genuine, he's like a big dog that leaps up on you with love but knocks you over. He wants to give you a lick so he jumps up on the table – and he sits in your breakfast.

On set, in rehearsals, Barry always wore Blobby's head but sometimes he didn't have his legs on. Mr Blobby would come on in the dress rehearsal with his little legs hanging out, so you'd see a man from the bottom and Blobby from the top.

Once we had a goat come on at the dress rehearsal – and the goat had shat all over the floor, with those little nanny goat pellets. And Blobby came on and went, 'Ooooooooooooooh!' and, just totally out the blue, he picked them up and started eating them. Yeah, 'nanny goats' chocolates', as my Uncle Bill used to call them!

I wrote sketches for Blobby in the later series, produced by Sue Andrew, who is now the producer for Lily Savage. We made Blobby a film star and I think it pissed off the people 'upstairs' a bit.

There was also one time when Noel's new producer said, 'There's no way you can use Mr Blobby on your show. You know he's for us, not them!' and a big row went on about that. We eventually got to use Blobby. But we didn't use him for about five or six shows, until the 'powers that be' upstairs decided that, 'We would like Mr Blobby to do *The Generation Game* as well, thank you.'

I felt that we used Blobby better than Noel did. Noel used to just push Blobby out the way where I used to *encourage* Blobby to do things. We didn't use him for a while and it was a bit of a rivalry that went on between the stars. I didn't speak to Noel. I didn't think it was my business. But I used to take the piss in the dress rehearsals, even though I liked him a lot.

The sound men knew I was pissed off with Noel's people, so they used to play *Noel's House Party* music for me. Instead of walking down to my own theme, they put *Noel's House Party* music on. It really turned into a great laugh. We got into this rivalry and we knew that we were beating him in the ratings.

On the night, they followed us. We were the lead to them and they got quite big ratings. But when Jon Beazley left them and came to work with me ... once those meatballs bounced off that table, and we started to act like little anarchists, our ratings soared.

There were certain things they wouldn't allow Blobby to do. I wanted him to get pissed once, just drinking pints. I just thought it would be funny to get him drunk. And they said he must *never* be seen to drink alcohol. Why not? It's a bit crazy. He can *eat nanny goat shit*, but he isn't allowed to *drink*?

As time went on, no-one really knew what was going to happen next on *The Gen Game*. You did not have a clue. Once, I even sang a song on the show. I played piano with Mel – we did anything we wanted.

We decided we'd stage various battles, Custer's Last Stand, the Red Baron against Snoopy, The Alamo, Zulu … and all these battles were just the crew dressed up as various people having a custard pie fight. It was totally mental. And Noel must have thought, 'My God, *my* show's becoming a bit predictable, compared to this.'

So I think *we forced Noel* and his people into changing their show around a little a bit. I think they made the mistake of change for change's sake. They didn't stick to what they knew worked and try to improve on it. They made dramatic changes and I think some of the changes were a bit too much for Noel's crew – and it upset Noel … and *that* was the end of *Noel's House Party*, really! It was a shame because Noel gave it his all.

Another thing Mr Blobby wasn't allowed to do was smoke. You couldn't give him a cigar. There was one famous sketch on the last series, the one that nearly killed me. We had a new producer on board and Rob Collie had written a fantastic scene. One of the contestants, years ago, had had a nanny goat that she loved and they hadn't seen it for years.

'Yes,' I said, 'well, nanny goats live dog years. They live until they're 500 years of age. And we've found the nanny goat and we've given it to a BBC person to look after.'

And the doors opened and this Greek music played 'dun-dun-dun-dun diddle-dee-diddle-dee' … and there's Mr Blobby with an unshaven face and a chef's hat, in front of a big kebab.

'Mr Blobby, where's the *goat*?' I shouted out.

And he said, in his new English, 'In there!'

And he pointed to the kebab – and as he rotated the kebab round, sticking out of the kebab was a goat's head!

We laughed until we cried. It was just the *innocence* of Mr Blobby.

Word came from 'upstairs' that this was *not allowed* and I've never seen my mate Rob Collie, the writer of all these great bits, get so angry.

He's normally so placid. He's a Charlton fan like me, you see, so he's used to a lifetime of failure! Anyway, he went *mental* that Mr Blobby wasn't allowed to cook this goat.

So, they had to take the head off so that Mr Blobby still said, 'In there!' but there wasn't any goat's head sticking out of it. We had to reshoot the scene and redesign the kebab!

Then there was another time where a woman contestant had lost her hamster or something, and Mr Blobby found the hamster – but unfortunately had run it over on the way in. And he brought in this hamster we had made specially.

It was the size of an LP cover and about as fat. Mr Blobby brought it in and threw it on like a Frisbee. We kept the scene in. We begged and begged and they said it was fine the way we'd done it because we brought on a real hamster later.

There was another time when some contestant's little puppy dog had died, or something like that. And Mr Blobby gave it the kiss of life. He brought it in – and it was now blown up like a football, this little puppy, which he bounced and then kicked out the set! Then we thought, 'Oh no, this is all too much.'

It was just that Mr Blobby, in his innocence, of course, did what came naturally to him. I got the joke. I got what Blobby was about. But Mr 'Powers That Be' perhaps *didn't* get the joke. Mr Blobby would cook the goat, not because he was awful, but because he thought that that was what he was supposed to do with it. Give everyone something to eat. He was 'in character' all the time.

I used to do impressions of people. I wanted to do Pavarotti in a dream sequence. I'd love to be an opera singer, imagine that!

First, I did Rod Stewart singing 'Sailing'. I did Rod with these funny trousers on and the big nose and the hair. He was sitting in a boat and I was miming to the music, 'We are sailing, we are sailing ...'

We shot it in front of a blue screen, and in the back of the blue screen we superimposed a beautiful loch up in Scotland.

Then, as the wind increased, in the song the picture changed to a choppy sea. Then, to these *huge waves*. Next, we switched on a wind machine on and we blew off Rod's wig to show that he was bald. He also had a huge big false nose on.

I got some wires attached to me so they pulled me out, but I was hanging on to this mast while singing 'Sailing'. All the crew were throwing buckets of water ... I was throwing buckets of water back – and, of course, the producer said, 'Pan back the cameras, let's see all this action!'

It was so good that we did it again the following week, when I was Pavarotti. Well, *this* time, when I blew up in the air, exactly the same as before, my trousers came off, right, to show that I had stockings and suspenders on underneath. And there was that nice Anna Rider Richardson sitting in the back of the boat, eating 'Just one Cornetto'. This time, we were on a gondola in Venice, but we ran the same routine. The water turned into choppy seas and poor Anna Rider Richardson got soaking wet. She didn't know anything about what was going to happen. It was just fantastic.

Then we did it *a third time*, with me as a Scotsman singing 'Mull of Kintyre'. We did all these really bizarre things. We sat down with a blank piece of paper and thought, 'How can we be mad here?'

I loved it.

Contestants come in all shapes and sizes but they all seem a little bit nervous. I've always been aware that people's top lips quiver a lot more than I thought they ever did in real life. Sometimes you can tell if there's a problem when a contestant comes on. It happened once.

This one guy was a bit flash and wanted to be the tough guy. He shook my hand a bit too hard and decided that he wasn't going to do anything and wouldn't join in. That happens.

We had a West Indian couple on, which was nice because we don't get a lot of ethnic minorities coming on the show. We should have a lot more. As you know, West Indian people have a great sense of humour. They love a laugh. When it came to the game about naming body parts, they got no marks at all! *Absolutely none!* ...and where she stuck the sticker for the coccyx ... well, I can't tell you.

Some people come on who really want to go for it. One guy came on and did some Argentinian routine, you know, swinging balls round his head and bouncing them round all over the place. This guy was so fantastic, he brought the house down. While others are just not really up to it.

What we had though, was a Blobby, you see. When we thought things were not going too well, we'd send him on. We also used to send him on in the last game. Soon, it became a tradition.

Do you remember on *Morecambe and Wise*, when Ernie was finishing the show and Eric would walk along the back of the set with his hat and coat on and his paper? Well, we used to do that with Blobby a lot.

I always try to make the contestants feel as relaxed as possible. I always go to the Green Room hospitality suite when they're all there and have a chat. The researchers make them do silly things and make them play games. I don't know Ring-a-Ring-of-Roses. I don't know all that bullshit stuff. I just go and say, 'Have a fucking drink! Have a couple of glasses of wine and relax!'

I always say to them, 'Look, don't worry about the prizes. The prizes are crap. What you're going to do is you're going to be watching tonight's show on video for the rest of your life. So, you've *got* to go for it! And if you don't know the answer, if you don't know how to make it, then fuck it up!'

We had a few visits, too, from Sooty, that little bastard. Sooty came on. As you know now, I love the idea of puppets like *Rainbow*'s Zippy and George saying and doing what they're not supposed to say and do. Well, Sooty, as you know, doesn't speak, but Sweep squeaks. He talks in a squeak but you can sort of understand it. I saw this funny man, hidden behind a wall. I had to interview Sooty and Sweep. In rehearsal, we were in a bit of a rush, running behind, so we winged our way through it.

On the night, I stood there and out popped Sooty and Sweep and I was talking to them. And I got a custard pie and stuck it in Sweep's face and we all had a bit of a laugh.

And then Sooty produced, *it said in the script*, 'a water pistol and squirts Jim'. Well, the force of the water that came out of Sooty's 'water pistol' was like a *water cannon* in Belfast. It hit me right in the eye and I couldn't see for about ten minutes! We had to stop the show and Sooty, Sooty got a cheer from the crew! Anything that went wrong for me, the crew all cheered. You know, as in 'That'll fucking teach him, fussy bastard.'

So I always tried to get my own back on Sooty. When he came on the second time, I got a bucket of milk and just poured it all over the person who was working Sooty behind the desktop.

So, the audience knew that whoever was working Sooty and Sweep was drenched in milk. It was another one of those great *Gen Game* moments on camera.

If anyone ever saw the dress rehearsals that had been recorded, they would have got bigger ratings. What the BBC should do is show *The Generation Game* at 6 o'clock on Saturday night, and then at midnight on Saturday night we should show the dress rehearsal of that same show. People would absolutely die laughing.

I think that's a brilliant idea, because you'd see me coming out in jeans, you'd see people walking on and off. You could edit it down to show behind-the-scenes material and I reckon it would be a best seller. I really believe that.

Nancy Lam is a Philippine woman who has this brilliant restaurant down in Lavender Hill. She's got this little West Indian husband who cooks. They're fantastic and if you go in to her restaurant late, she'll say, 'You too late! Fuck off!' and she throws plates at you. She throws food at you and she's totally off her head. It's the best night out ever!

Nancy came along to do a *Gen Game*, and in the dress rehearsal, she was very funny, putting the noodles between her legs, saying, 'saucy noodles'.

But on the night when we did the show, she went berserk. She was saying, 'What's that big stick you got between your legs, Jim?'

And she was just doing all this filth. You've never seen an audience laugh so much in your life. Unfortunately, that *did* end up on the cutting room floor! She is *so* funny.

We went to her restaurant for a party, all *The Gen Game* crew went, and Paul Jackson, who was the big boss, turned up. Nancy told him to fuck off because she thought he was the cab driver who had come to pick us up!

'We're not ready to go yet,' she shouted at him. 'You fuck off back to taxi!'

Word was that Jon Beazley had been moved up – and he had. When Jon left, it was a really sad day for me. I was happy for him because he'd been promoted and, of course, I knew I'd played my part in that because he'd done such a good job on *The Generation Game*. We'd worked together as a great pair but the time had arrived for him to move up the ladder. I was sad to see him go – and frightened, too, because I needed Jon to say 'Well done' to me.

I'd wanted to please Jon. He had been great to work with. His face had always lit up when he'd got a kick out of the way I could generate comedy out of bugger all. Now he was going and I was a bit scared that I would be left on my own and would have to make my own decisions.

But thanks Jon, and when you're the head of the BBC, please can I have a pay rise.

The new producer was a girl called Sue Andrew, whom I'd met as a researcher on *The Gen Game*, when I stood in for Bruce all those years ago. She was a researcher on *Big Break* too, when we first did the series. Then she turned up as the producer.

As well as being quite a glamorous girl, we used to call her 'the pushy woman with the nervous tic'. Even on camera we used to call her 'that pushy woman with the smoker's cough'.

Sue was very conscientious as well and picked up where Jon left off. He became the overall boss. He was the brigadier and Sue became the colonel. We just got better and better.

I think I took advantage of Sue a little bit because I wanted to push the show even further still. For instance, we had Status Quo come on and do a three-minute medley, just for no reason at all. I did a song on there with my son Cameron, and upstairs Paul Jackson decided that the show was becoming a bit too self indulgent.

I actually disagreed with him. Now Paul has gone, people still say to me, 'Oh, seeing your son on *The Gen Game* was fantastic.' But the BBC thought it was nepotism, meaning that I was using the BBC to further the career of my son. Well, that wasn't the case. My son and I were a generation apart and we sang about that on the show. I thought it fitted perfectly but they said, 'What's it got to do with *The Generation Game?*'

They missed the point. The new *Gen Game* could do whatever it wanted to. Its brief was not to be boring and if Status Quo wanted to do a song on the show, great!

Suddenly they knocked five minutes off the transmission time so in the second series that Sue did, series five for us, we had to knock it on the head a bit. We couldn't do as many sketches as we wanted to.

Then Sue left the BBC and became second in command at Carlton. And the bosses upstairs said they'd got a new producer for us.

'Oh no,' I thought. I wanted to produce it *myself* – and, of course, they wouldn't allow that!

The new producer was called Jonathan Glazier. Now I'd worked with Jonathan before. He'd recorded one of my favourite videos called *Jim Davidson Exposed*. He directed that and I thought this was going to be OK.

It turned it out to be a disaster but not of his making.

He turned up with his message from upstairs, saying there were to be no more comedy sketches.

'You've got to concentrate more on the games, and that's it,' was the message.

Awful! Although no fault of Jonathan's – orders are orders.

As a result, of course, the ratings dropped and I was so depressed, so despondent. It had all been going so well and now it was going horribly wrong and *The Gen Game* was dipping beyond salvage. I prayed for a little light at the end of the tunnel.

Now my light at the end of the tunnel was as follows. Paul Jackson was about to leave and Kevin Bishop had taken over Paul Jackson's job. So, I said please, please, please, if you're not going to let me produce, let's make Rob Collie the producer.

'OK Rob can produce the next series,' they said.

I was thrilled to bits.

But because Rob had not produced before, they said we needed an executive producer.

'Please can it be John Bishop?' I said.

And John Bishop eventually agreed to do it. Bryan Blackburn, the best writer in the world, would be writing it; and Barry Killerby (Blobby) would be on the team and ...

But then, disaster struck. Within a week of Rob taking his job at the office to start the series, the doctor called him and said, 'I've got the results of your test, you've got to have a year off. You've got an ulcer.'

So now, after I'd battled for six months to get Rob the producer's job, the cruel hand of Fate stopped him from being able to do it, because he had to rest for a year ...

But I knew just the right person to take up the challenge ... Me!

What you see on the screen now is basically down to *me*. I have a producer called Ben Kellet to make sure I don't spend too much money and to make sure that everything I want to do, happens. Ben's a great producer and, of course, I'm overseen by John Bishop, probably the most respected and talented producer since the days of Mark Stewart.

With Sue Andrew, we had ideas to do items where someone would sing 'I can see clearly now' and we'd fill the stage with smoke, so they *couldn't* see. And then the crew would come in as fireman and cover this person in foam. And we thought it would be much funnier if Melanie did it, because she was glamorous and beautiful – but she said, 'No, I'm not going to do that.'

'Why?' we said.

'I don't want to look ridiculous,' she replied. 'I'm a singer. I'm a serious singer and dancer, and I don't particularly want to do that – and I don't want a custard pie in my face, and I don't think I want to do this.'

Previously to that I'd asked John, if Melanie did *The Generation Game*, would it be possible for her to play in pantomime with me?

'It makes sense that I'd got John Virgo with me *and* Melanie,' I said.

We went down to Bristol to do the panto but Melanie preferred her own company to ours. She was marvellous on stage, was just right for the part and great fun. But as soon as she'd come off stage, she'd go straight to her dressing room, and at the end of the evening, she'd just bugger off straight to her hotel room. She'd never come for a drink with us, never come to a party. That was just her way. It was a shame because it gave people the wrong impression of her.

One night, John Virgo, who was also in the panto cast, said, 'We're having a party. It's the stage manager's birthday.'

'Oh, no,' she said, 'I'm not coming.'

We couldn't work it out why she didn't want to come to any of the dos. Even on the last night, when we had a party, she came off stage, got in her car, and drove home. It was the same in Manchester, the following year.

Maybe Melanie didn't like mixing with us, or was a bit shy. I never really got to the bottom of it. But it did tend to give people the wrong impression. John Virgo said, 'What's the matter with her? Is she a snob or what?'

'No, John,' I said, 'it's just the way Mel is.'

I'm sure if John knew Melanie as well as I did, he'd realise that there's no malice intended at all.

'Goodbye Jim.'

'Goodbye Mel.'

That was it.

She's a very talented girl. I wish her all the best and I'll be the happiest man in the world when I sit in the front row of a West End theatre and see Mel starring in a big, glamorous musical.

As for the long-term future of *The Generation Game*, I'm contracted to do this series we're doing now, and another series. Then we'll see. By then, I will have clocked up eight years on the show. I love the game so much and I like what the BBC light entertainment group are trying to do now – even though Greg Dyke's stopped the biscuits!

It's been a privilege to try to do something with the show and I hope to stay with *The Gen Game* as long as the BBC want me, which really is as long as the public want me. What have I brought to the show? Well, the producer Jon Beazley and I brought it unpredictability and Sue Andrew took it one step further.

Audiences didn't quite know what was going to happen next. There were no *rules* to it. We made it lively, funnier, and it became a vehicle for the *whole* team to have fun, rather than *just* Bruce Forsyth, who pulled that face at camera two.

It's all been about that unpredictability. I want people to sit at home and think, 'What's this idiot going to do next?'

This show is about the public. The public get younger and younger – and the presenter gets older and older! At the end of the day, if people don't watch the show and *enjoy* it, then there's no point in making it.

Meanwhile, I want to make *The Generation Game* the best it possibly can be. Hopefully though, the show will be around long after I've gone.

And who knows? Maybe Bruce will come back!

13
Picking the wrong women

When I look back, Tracy and I may have been happy when we tied the knot in 1990 but we had a marriage that *wasn't* really a marriage. That much I can say.

As soon as I bought the house in Ewhurst, and simultaneously the boat *Afghan Plains*, we started to drift apart. And, over the period of the next six or seven years, we just lurched from one split up to another.

Come Christmas, if I wasn't in two strange girls' beds, I'd be in Bosnia, entertaining the troops. Tracy would sit in the kitchen and I would sit in my den, the bit of the house stuck on the end, and watch my *Star Trek* videos constantly.

I wasn't gagging for a drink but I was angry at Tracy, although it wasn't Tracy's fault. Tracy was the way she is. It was just that I couldn't make her the way I wanted her to be. She was very happy on her own, not having to mix with anyone.

And then the rows started.

Of course, she'd have her own friends and they all dyed their hair the same, and they all went to the gym the same, and they all wanted to drive the same car, and had their own little routine, and ... I got in the way. As long as I paid, it didn't seem to be a problem. Tracy and I never had the greatest love life in the world. She's since told me didn't really fancy me.

I don't think I ever pushed the right buttons with Tracy. So, I just didn't bother in the end and we grew further and further apart. Plus, there was always a nanny. If it wasn't Tracy's special friend Jackie, it was my mate Roger Swallow's daughter, Becky.

Tracy would have a kitchen full of women and they'd talk about how nice *other* people's husbands were – and then there was me – this guy whizzing in and out, panicking about where the next quid's going to come from.

And, of course, when Deborah Corrigan turned up in 1997, it was just like a breath of fresh air. Deborah had a few surprises in store for me though! As it turned out later, some guys had taken her to bed ages ago and made a film of her with two boys that eventually nearly ended up on the Internet. There were articles about it in the newspapers.

I wrote to David Sullivan, who owns the *Sunday Sport* and said, 'David, please. This is causing a lot of damage. This happened a long while ago in Deborah's past and I know Debbie is a colourful character and she sells newspapers for you. But this is hurting a bit. It's hurting me.'

And he wrote back to me and said, 'OK, we won't do it again.' And he didn't.

Some people have had some bad things to say about David Sullivan. But not me, I have to tell you.

I had the house in Ponsonby Terrace in London, and Tracy was living in the new house in the country, The Farm, down near Horsham in Surrey. I lived together with her in the country and when I went to London, I'd stay with Deborah at Ponsonby Terrace.

Deb doted on me, but things were never easy. She used to know I'd sift. I'd open a box and she'd leave a little note in it reading 'Fuck off, you nosy bastard!' Dear old Deb.

Deborah knew exactly which buttons to press with me. I'd argue with her and split up because I just couldn't take any more in the newspapers. She'd shout and scream and I'd say, 'Oh piss off out of my life.'

Then I'd miss her dreadfully. I was terribly in love with her – probably more than all of them actually. Of *all* the other women, I've probably loved Deborah the most.

She'd vanish for three days, maybe four days at a time. I wouldn't know where she was. I'd be phoning her agent.

'Where is she?'

Then, out of the blue, she'd call me from Spain. I'd say, 'Where are you? What are you doing there?'

'I just had to get away. I borrowed someone's apartment,' she'd reply.

She's a girl from Manchester who had enhanced herself siliconely and was great fun to be with. But in all my life, I'd never seen a woman cry as much. And yet, I could also say I've never seen a woman enjoy herself as much as Debbie. She was everything. She was up and down like a bride's nightie.

During our separation Tracy and I argued and argued about what we were going to do and then we did not speak to one another because the money problem was beginning. I then realised that she was now seeing another guy. His name was Noel and she was quite in love with him.

Eventually, in March 1998, the divorce settlement proceedings began. The hearing took about three hours and was held in a little room at Somerset House before a woman judge. Lined up in front of her were Tracy, Tracy's lawyers, my lawyers and me. As if that wasn't traumatic enough, we then went outside into the corridor to share out my money, or what was left of it.

It was a sad day for both Tracy and me, and I found the whole experience pretty upsetting. Tracy left the hearing before me. Then I strode out of Somerset House on to the Strand and into the heart of London's busy West End. It felt like a chapter in my life had ended – and that's just what had happened. My marriage was finally over. I was single again.

But as for being a free man, well, I was divorced but, because of the repercussions of the divorce, I couldn't exactly say I was 'free'.

So that was that. The divorce was settled. I was granted the right to see the children. Of course, I'd have to send them to public school. I'd have to pay for that, which was fine. But I also had a huge tax bill to pay and I had been told by friends that Tracy had found a house that she liked.

I had to buy the house for Tracy. I can't go into how much but it was a substantial house. And not only that, I had to buy it *in cash*, as they wouldn't let me have a mortgage.

So, I had to scrape that money together with a bank overdraft and God knows what, to buy this house – and then also give her a lump sum of money to do the house up.

· And then we agreed to the money. It wasn't agreed that she should be entitled to a lump sum *as well*, because it was deemed that we were only married for a certain number of years. The marriage was deemed short enough not to warrant a lump sum and I didn't have a lump sum anyway. I had this house in the country, which had a bloody great mortgage on it, and I had a house in London, on which I had a mortgage too.

In the end, I had to sell the house in London because I didn't have any funds left to pay Tracy and the lawyers.

Today, I am still very much living with the effects of that divorce. My problem with that now is that I have to do that *for ever* – until Tracy gets married again, or at least until the children go to school. When I got divorced, I didn't feel I was a free man because I wasn't free. I am still paying for everything. That's why I feel so bitter and twisted!

It means I can't stop working for another ten years. And I don't quite know how I'm going to do that. It's not as though I'm someone who could go and pull turnips up for a living, or be a farmer, or even a window cleaner. Sure, OK, that work is always there. Windows don't suddenly go off you. Windows are not fashionable. But if I stop work for the BBC, or if I find that the theatres are not full any more, or if I suffer real hell, or start drinking too much again, then I don't know where her money's going to come from.

That's the worst bit. And I *am* bitter about it. We were together for a relatively short time. Yes, we had three children and I'm committed to looking after them. But I resent the fact that I pay her all this money.

What puts me under pressure is that I know that I have to earn a fortune for Tracy and it just gets me down. Sometimes I think, 'What's the fucking point? The Taxman's on my back, the ex-wife's on my back … hang on a minute, there's nothing left for me here.'

That type of pressure does get me down and the only way I can get round it is to focus on a project or something I am striving to achieve, like trying to write a new pantomime or trying to get *The Generation Game* right.

Take what happened at Christmas, for instance. I have very little time off because I do pantomime. I get Christmas Day off. So, I said to Tracy, 'Can

I come round and see the children and give them their presents?'

She didn't want that. 'No, the children come to your house.'

'But I've bought them things for their computers,' I said, 'and I've bought them telly and PlayStation games. It would be nice to plug them in.'

'Well you can't come here,' Tracy insisted, 'because Noel's here.'

Now, you'd think this fucking bloke would go away for an hour. 'Well, can't he go up the pub for an hour while I come round?'

'No.'

So, for the last two years, I've either met the children at the gate and given them their presents and cleared off, or one year, I had to leave their presents in a phone box up the end of the road and ring up and say, 'Look, the children's presents are here.'

That made me angry. Noel could have gone up the pub and had a pint while I popped down and saw the kids. Tracy could have said, 'Look Noel, Jim wants to come round and see the children.'

The children wanted to see me but it just didn't happen. I didn't want to go out drinking. When all this happened, I just wanted to rip people's heads off, really. But that feeling fades away. You count to ten and off you go.

So, these days, I really do not know what I am going to do. I'm at my wits' end because I'm getting tired now. I'm getting older. In two years' time, I'll be 50 and I've worked solidly for years to have *nothing* – because, if Tracy wants a full and final settlement, or wants to be paid for the rest of her life, then I'll have to sell the house. I'll have to sell everything I've got to make sure that she's paid for the rest of her life, and to make sure my children go through school.

So, that's fine. Tracy will get her money. But what it will mean is that the children's legacy might have gone. What this house would be worth to the children in ten or twenty years' time is astronomical. But because of the way this divorce settlement has worked out, it means I might have to sell it now to pay her.

I can still retire but if I'm not able to work, then no-one gets any money. I've just got to make sure that my children are looked after. That's the real problem. Sometimes I just feel like buggering off.

We never really had a marriage because I was hardly ever there. If I wasn't working, I'd be in Blackpool for twenty weeks and Tracy came to see me for five days. Or I'd be on tour and she'd never phone up. We never spent any time together. We slept in separate bedrooms for most of our life. And then there were the times we split up. We must have split up, with me going off to live somewhere else, six or seven times. And I was away for ages.

Well, life is strange, isn't it.

While all this splitting up was going on, all this turmoil in my personal life, things started to go well for me in my *professional* life.

I was named the Variety Club Personality of the Year and the Comic Heritage people also gave me the Showbiz Entertainer award. I'd just put together this little pantomime called *Dick Whittington*. I'd spent a fortune on the sets and had written a great script with Bryan Blackburn. I had a fantastic pantomime to do down in Bristol, and yet at this time, my private life was just getting worse and worse and worse. It was just falling to pieces.

Receiving those awards was great. But they didn't mean much at the time because the one person I really wanted to like me was my missus and she didn't really. I can't remember the days when I received the awards. I couldn't even tell you what dates I got them. I did take Tracy to one of the ceremonies. She sat having lunch with me – Deborah was round the corner waiting for me to join her in a nightclub afterwards.

I don't know why but I pick the wrong women. After having four of them go wrong, it makes you rather bitter and twisted. You tend not to like women very much.

I don't trust them. And Deborah, you know, I loved Deborah. I said to her, 'Now, you won't do any more topless work, will you?'

'No,' she said.

Next thing, someone says, 'Oh, I did this topless shoot with Deborah the other day.'

So I go back to her and I say, 'Did you do that?'

'No!' she says.

It's a joke!

This went on even when I started splitting up with Deborah and our relationship started to go a bit funny. After I had to get rid of the house in London, she came to live with me in the country for a while. She'd go into town, she'd want to keep on doing her modelling and so on. But she couldn't boil an egg! Certainly couldn't wash a sock. But she was great fun to be with.

Then, we split up and I said I wasn't going to see her. And she cried her eyes out. I'd be walking around miserable for a month, worried to death about her.

Then she started to go out with some famous rugby player. I bumped into her occasionally and she seemed OK. And then she binned him. There was a big story in the paper. She'd do a story, then *he'd* do a story and then, oh my God, I started to see her again!

But then Deborah and I stopped sleeping together. I kept on seeing her for about six months on and off, but we didn't have any sex at all. We were just friends.

But whatever Deborah chooses to do with her life, she'll always be my friend. We've shared too many good times together – and too many sad times really – just to forget everything.

I still get phone calls from Deborah even today, and she makes me laugh and I make her laugh. She's got a little flat now that she's quite happy with and a little dog. She's got various boyfriends and she's always out of the country and that makes me really happy. It's a load off my mind. This is the woman that I loved dearly, more than all the others. But I couldn't have her. She was so into her own life. She was such a free spirit.

So now, as I write this with Christmas 2001 drawing near, Deborah's gone, Tracy's still round the corner and I see my children quite often. I get on really well with them. Then Sarah, my eldest daughter, moved in with me down in the country. In fact, she moved in towards the last knockings of Deborah being here.

Sarah was working for Coombs, the betting shop in Plumstead, where she lived. One day, a man came in and stuck a shotgun under her nose and said, 'Give me all the money!'

To which any other man's daughter would have collapsed in a heap! But *Sarah* replied in broad Plumstead, 'You're having a fucking laugh, aren't ya? It's only half past ten and we haven't took any fucking money yet! What type of burglar are you?'

At which point this very humiliated man with his shotgun left the shop! But it quite traumatised her and she came down here sobbing and upset.

'Look, pack in work,' I said, 'have a year off work and come and live with me.'

So that's what she did. She's 29 now. Sarah, my little Sarah who was born all that time ago in Plumstead.

Sarah coming to live with me was great and it was nice to come home and have somebody there. But then again, nowadays, she is hardly ever in, or else she'll be in the bedroom on the phone. So I very rarely see her. She'll nag me a bit, which is quite good fun.

After Sarah moved in, we went out and bought a couple of horses. One's called Duncan, my old cob and the other's called Jardi, which is Sarah's hunter. And we went horseriding together. Deborah had already taught me how to ride. We went up to Gleneagles. It put me in agony for a bloody week, but we had a fabulous time.

Now Sarah's started trying to put together garage and house music. She wanted to form a little company with her friends and be an agent for house and garage music, which she knows quite a lot about as she was always going to these nightclubs. She's a good-time girl. She loves to party. But all that went horribly wrong for her and she's now working for me, doing the marketing for the pantomimes for the new company.

Sarah and her little team get thousands and thousands of leaflets printed and they're then out and about distributing them. She's a very hard worker.

At the beginning of last year, my son Cameron moved in with me as well. Well, Cameron still *officially* lives with his Mum, Julie. In fact, Sarah still *officially* lives in Plumstead but they spend all their time here. I think my kids would still have moved in with me if I had been a drunk. But when

I was a drunk I wasn't a *rotten horrible* drunk. I was just a drunk, a good laugh, Mister Party Animal.

Cameron turned 19 in August and he's now in his gap year. I said I would sponsor him to write and perform some music, which he's been doing in my recording studio. He writes these great songs, he plays guitar and drums and bass guitar, he's great. He goes into the studio and records all that stuff. We hope that he's going to have a career in show business. He's a very talented guy and a good-looking boy, as well. He takes after his Mum, Julie. He resembles his Mum a lot. He's much better looking than the old Jimbo.

Cameron came on *The Gen Game* and we sang a song together called 'Father and Son', which was the old Cat Stevens song. It was quite good. Once, when I was doing *The Gen Game*, I wanted to record an album of songs that I like. So, I got in touch with one of my heroes Greg Lake, from Emerson, Lake and Palmer.

'Yeah, sure, I'll produce the album for you,' Greg said.

I told Greg I wanted to do a track called 'Watching Over You', which he wrote years ago for his little girl, when she was about three. Greg offered to write a new version of it, which turned out absolutely fabulously. We went into the studio and recorded this song 'Watching Over You', initially, so that I could sing it to the troops wherever I was visiting. It was a nice little song to remind them of their families.

The song was so good, we did a few others. We recorded 'Father and Son' with Cameron and I took 'Watching Over You' in to the BBC and said to Sue Andrew, my *Generation Game* producer, 'Look, seeing as we've got these new rules that we can do anything we want, can I do this song on the show called "Watching Over You"?'

She said OK.

I had the idea of performing the song – and while me and the band were doing it, I'd superimpose some pictures of my children.

So, I went to the dubbing suite and phoned up Tracy and said, 'Can you lend me all your home videos?'

I got all her home videos and we watched them all, looking for footage. And by the end of watching all these home videos, I realised … that I'd never been there for any of the kids' birthdays. I was never there when it happened.

There were pictures of her and Jackie and her Mum ... and I just felt so melancholy and so hard done by and so upset. All those pictures of the children did break my heart. I would have found it an excuse to turn to the bottle and have a drink – not so much now, because I know I can see the kids any time I want really, so long as they come to my house and provided that Tracy switches her answerphone off and picks up the phone every now and then. She's pretty good like that.

I put the video together and it was wonderful. It was beautiful and I sent it off to Tracy. To me, the video was one of the highlights of anything I'd ever done.

Then I did pretty much the same with 'Father and Son' with Cameron. The audience didn't quite know who this kid was. And suddenly, I super-imposed a picture of him as a baby on *This Is Your Life* and then I blended the two faces together and they knew that he was my son. And everybody loved it. Everybody thought it was fantastic – apart from Paul Jackson, the Head of Entertainment at the BBC, who said, 'What's that got to do with *The Generation Game*? Make sure there's no more of this self-indulgent shit on there!' – or words to that effect, bless him.

But it's fun living with the two kids, although they're scruffy buggers and I haven't been in Cameron's bedroom for a year. I *daren't* go in there. There's things *living* in there, I'm sure. I don't know what 19 year-olds do any more.

Sarah's the martyr. Sarah says, 'I have to get up at six o'clock in the morning and go to bloody work and then come all the way back here to sort them horses out ...'

And then on the weekends, she just vanishes.

Ironically, it's since my marriage split up that my family can now all get together. They like one another and they call each other brother and sister, which is great. Before, I always thought that if I had the elder children round, it would upset the wife. One wife would be upset. Now, I don't have anybody living with me, and all the children can get together – much nicer. When I'm away from the family, I have often performed overseas for the troops. In about 1997 I went back to the Falklands. It must have been my fourth trip there. I wasn't charging any fee for my time, as I never do. If I do get given any money (because they say it's the Government's money so I can have it in any case), I always donate it to charity or to the Ghurka Welfare Trust or something like that.

When I got to the Falklands, I wanted to make a little film as well and to include it in a video later on. That was fine, and they got me those two Tornados to look after. But I noticed that the atmosphere was slightly different there. The troops were now living down in a place that they called 'Death Star', actually, they're the barracks down at Mount Pleasant airport. They're pretty much segregated now from the locals.

I could sense there was a horrible atmosphere and so I said to the bloke at the Officers' Mess, 'Something's wrong here. Have I pissed anyone off?'

'No,' he said, 'it's not that Jim, it's just that we're sick of fucking paying CSE.'

CSE is the Combined Service Entertainment, the followers of ENSA. CSE is a division of SSVC, which stands for the Sight, Sound, Vision Corporation, which is funded by the MoD to provide the radio and television stations. CSE used to be run by the wonderful Derek Agutter, father of Jenny.

In fact, the whole of the SSVC group was run by a man called Air Vice-Marshall David Cryes-Williams. I met him once or twice when I did a few showcases for CSE and he was charming and willing to help. He was also gracious enough to explain that he didn't know about show business – that was down to us, he said.

His way of running CSE started to cause me problems, although I didn't think it was his fault. I'd been told, 'We're fed up of CSE charging us money.'

I didn't understand what they meant. '*I'm* not being paid to come here,' I said. 'In fact, we're having to pay for our food and everything to be here.'

'Well, we had a certain group here three weeks ago,' the officer said, 'and they were from the Seventies and we had to pay about £50,000 for the privilege of seeing them.'

'Well it *does* cost money,' I said, 'and these artists have to be paid.'

'That's not the point,' he said. 'We can't watch the Rugby Cup Finals because we don't have any link to live television, yet we have to pay £50,000 for these has-beens.'

'Hang on,' I thought to myself, 'something wrong there.' So, I found out what had happened.

Years ago, CSE used to receive a grant so it could pay all its artists to go round the world and entertain various people. The dancers, the singers, the band, they all have to be paid. It's very expensive but it worked a treat and they knew where they were.

Now, under Mrs. Thatcher's Government, that lump of money was cut up into a cake and each slice of that cake was given to the various commanders of various garrisons. So, Mr Falklands Islands would get a slice of cake and he'd decide what he'd want to do with it.

He might decide he wanted to build that television link, which is part of welfare and entertainment. He might want to put a kids' playground in. He might want to put jukeboxes in or have more phonecards, more televisions in each mess, or whatever. As for Mr Has Been Group and Mr Has Been Comedian, in the past when they cost nothing, it was good fun. But now the fees were coming out of the troops' welfare fund.

'Hang on a minute,' I said, 'there must be a way that we can provide entertainment for nothing.'

I asked John Ashby, who was over in America, to see if he could find someone to put together a research project on the way Americans entertain their troops. They run the USO, the United Service Organisation. It turns out that they raised most of their money from industry. Coca-Cola gave them $100,000 dollars and so on, and they put these shows on, funded by industry.

I put a little dossier together about how we could raise money from British industry, how we could persuade artists to do the show for nothing, and how we could get sponsorship and put these shows on. And I sent a copy down to CSE.

David Cryes-Williams then invited me to lunch. He took me into this boardroom and showed me an audio-visual demonstration. He was understandably very proud of the fact that he could do all this and he showed me the brilliant work that CSE do – which they *do*. But they get it wrong. The PA systems are shite, many of the bands are people that no-one want to see, some of the artists are people who cannot get work in civilian life and they're getting paid a fortune to do this. And the troops are now having to pay for this and are getting upset.

So I thought my idea was much better.

We had a row.

'What makes you think you can provide something that CSE can't?' he said.

'Because, David,' I replied, 'I'm doing it *for free* and I believe the public would be on my side.'

'Look,' I said, 'why don't you become a trustee of my British Forces Foundation and I will raise money for you? So, I will raise the money but I'll still let CSE do the sharp end, as long as you give me a position with CSE to make sure the entertainment is provided correctly and we're not paying too much money for the entertainers.'

That seemed a great solution.

I then phoned up the Admiralty and said, 'I'd like to speak to Jock Slater please' (that's Admiral Jock Slater, the First Sea Lord). He called me back and agreed to become a Trustee as long as he was satisfied that everything was above board. I did the same with General Arthur Denaro and I also phoned up the wonderful Sir Rex Hunt, ex-Governor of the Falklands. I asked Laurie Mansfield to cover the show business end. We set up with our lawyers, finding a little office in London, the cost of which I shared with my own production company – and that was it. The British Forces Foundation was born.

The Prince of Wales was very supportive. He had a party at the Palace for all our people and our sponsors, bought them all drinks, and he played polo for us. He did the voiceover and a little bit of film for our television show we screened last Christmas (2000), *Homeward Bound for Christmas*, which was our first British Forces Foundation show. We put together a couple of polo matches for the British Forces Foundation and the Prince turned up and played. The money raised by the event then went to the BFF.

It's quite an expensive thing to run, because the sheer weight of the mail-outs and the typing is very labour intensive. It was set up with a marvellous man when we first got together. Admiral Jock Slater had recommended him. His name was Barry Leighton, a charming little Welshman. He got the CBE and was the Royal Navy's Director of Public Relations. What a great guy.

My hope is – and I make no secret of this to them all – that the British Forces Foundation will take over *all* the entertainment of the troops, and the CSE will come under our wing and eventually vanish. And I hope that David Cryes-Williams could run all of it – he'd be great. If I can raise money from the public to put on these shows for nothing, and if the Government will undertake not to cut welfare for the troops by the same amount, that would make perfect sense.

The problem is if I raise a £1 million a year, the Government will *take away* a million a year. So, I have to play a slight political game, which David Cryes-Williams is great at. He knows how things work.

Loads of stars have helped the BFF already. Bradley Walsh went up to Birmingham and did a fund-raiser for us. John Virgo went on HMS *Splendid*, which is one of our nuclear submarines off the coast of somewhere scary, which I can't go into.

I told John he was going on a submarine but I *didn't* tell him which one or where it was. He was then whisked off, courtesy of Sir Donald Gosling, by private jet to go and entertain these guys who'd been there months over their allotted time at sea. They were feeling pretty down and I told John that a nuclear submarine was rather like a five-star hotel.

'Will they have a snooker table?' he asked me.

'Yes, of course,' I replied.

He wanted to know whether to take his own cue. I said they probably had loads of cues on board. Of course, I was lying through my teeth all the way along.

When he eventually got 'in theatre', as it's called, his first visit was to a supply ship where the sailors asked him, 'What are you doing here, John?'

'I've come to entertain on the submarine,' he replied.

'Oh, splendid,' they went.

'Yeah,' he said, 'it is quite nice, innit?'

And then, every time he said to someone, 'I'm here to entertain on the submarine,' he received the reply, 'Oh, splendid.'

And he wondered why they kept saying that. The name of the submarine, of course, was HMS *Splendid*, which John hadn't twigged!

He spent a couple of days with them and, needless to say, soon found out that there was *no* snooker table. Without one, John just did a 'grip and grin'. They loved it. He was fantastic. John is really good at that sort of occasion. In fact, he's a big guy John and I think he was the tallest guy on the whole submarine. *He came back with a very stiff neck afterwards!*

In Germany we put on Status Quo. Now this was what I always wanted to prove to CSE – that we can put on bigger and better shows than they can. David agrees with this. We should deal with all the really big names, and he should deal with all the bread and butter.

I phoned Status Quo's manager and said, 'How would you boys like to come over to Germany and do a show for me for the troops?'

Without a moment's hesitation, the reply came back, 'Yes, we can fit it in on June 13th.'

Great, so I then asked, 'How much will it cost me?'

Now, can you imagine, Status Quo, who play to 20,000 people a time, especially in Germany, they said, 'Nothing.'

So, my dream was fulfilled and I had managed to get a huge name in show business, an *international* name, to give their time to the troops because they *wanted* to do it. It's not a political thing, it's just the fact that they feel the troops are a bit hard done by.

Another band that helped us out were S Club 7. They did *Homeward Bound for Christmas*, our major show on HMS *Invincible*, down in Malaga. When Barry Leighton left to carry on with his upwardly mobile career (good luck to him), a young polo player whom I'd met a few times called Mark Cann took over. He was a major in the Army and we suggested that he took over the job of Director. He agreed and we sat round the table and chatted.

Wouldn't it be nice, we thought, if we had a televised British Forces Foundation show, to let everyone know what we were doing.

So, we had planned a show with the Ministry of Defence's blessing on HMS *Ocean*, our brand new 20,000 tonnes helicopter carrier. This great beast was going to come as close in shore as possible in the Adriatic or the Mediterranean and we were going to go down there. The BBC was going to film it – all very exciting.

The Prince of Wales agreed to do the Introduction to it and we had a slot on the television just before the Queen's Speech. We arranged for my favourite comedian Bradley Walsh to appear, Sir John Mills, Martine McCutcheon, S Club 7, Atomic Kitten.

This was looking superb and my friend and now executive producer from *The Generation Game*, John Bishop, was putting the whole thing together. He found a fantastic young lady to co-star with me called Suzy Perry. I met her for the first time at the airport on the morning of us going out there.

But while all this was being planned, the Ministry of Defence had *other* plans. Our design guys had flown to HMS *Ocean* and measured up the aircraft hangar to build our set. They'd worked out how we were going to get all our crew there, and so on. The plan was that she was going to come alongside into Malaga in southern Spain. With two weeks to go, the artists were booked, everything was ready to leave.

Suddenly HMS *Ocean* sailed from the Mediterranean to *Sierra Leone*! We did *not* have an aircraft carrier and we had nowhere to do the show. Disaster! So I sat in my bath upstairs and watched the news as *my floating stage* fucked off. Bloody Labour Government, I thought!

So I called up the Director of Public Relations, Royal Navy, and said, 'Would it help if I went to the First Sea Lord and begged please to allow us to do the show somewhere?'

And they said, they'd 'have a think.'

'Where is *Invincible*?' I said.

'She's in Malta,' they said.

'Well, can't you whiz across?' I said. 'Can we do the show on *Invincible*?'

'Well, she's making her way to Palma in Majorca,' they said, 'let us speak to the captain and if the captain wants to go ahead, you can have it.'

Now, I'd met the captain once before. His name was Rory McLaine and he was a great guy. We had a British Forces Foundation dinner on the ship when she'd come up to London. She'd weighed anchor in between the Dome and the Naval College and we went along and had dinner on board. This captain was the most outrageous, wonderful man you ever met in your life. I've never met an officer who's been loved so much by his crew and I got on famously with him. I hoped he would be favourable to having us on board – and he was!

Within three days, they were alongside and we arrived two days later. The ship's crew and our television company built the new stage, all the artists turned up and Capt. McLaine went on stage with his typical address to his troops.

'Listen up, you bastards. We're going to have a good time. Please welcome Jim Davidson...'

And on I went.

The TV show was just fabulous. We were dead chuffed. It got great ratings, everyone had a great time, and I fell madly in love with Suzy Perry. I ended up getting pissed and dancing with her in a nightclub until three o'clock in the morning, when I had to go home. I wrote her a love letter and tucked it under her door.

In the morning I rang her up and she said, 'Have you seen your letter?'

'No,' she said.

Good. So, I went down and promptly tore it up in front of her and apologised. And we've been friends to this day.

What I hope is that these young artists, who entertained the troops the first time, will want to do it for the second time.

When I was at last year's Royal Variety Show, Ben Elton came up to me afterwards and said, 'Jim, if you're ever involved with this troop stuff again, I'd love to do it.'

And I thought that was a great thing for Ben because that really does prove that entertaining the troops is not a political thing. It crosses the political divide. I told Ben I'd give him a call. And I did give him a call to come to Germany but he was in Australia, lucky old him.

Turning out for charity is not about doing it for the cameras. But sometimes it's important to have the cameras there because it lets people know that these things exist. In fact, we were there to highlight the reality of how hard our service men and women work and how proud we should be of them. They are the benchmark which other armed forces aim for.

There is, of course, one elite corps of which that is especially true – the SAS. I'm lucky enough, over the years, to have met and known lots of guys in the SAS. But it's also amazing when I meet other people and they say, 'That guy there was in the SAS. He was in the Iranian embassy siege.'

Now, the Iranian Embassy siege in 1980 primarily involved 'B' Squadron. In fact, they all had T-shirts made with 'B' SQUADRON SMOKE EMBASSY written on them.

When the Iranians broke in, 'B' Squadron were called in to go and sort things out. I know lots of the guys who did that. About seventy of the guys took that building out. But according to all these soldiers of fortune, who always say they're in the SAS, there was a lot more than seventy. I've met a thousand people who've said they were on that Iranian siege.

The one thing I've learnt about the SAS over the years is that these are not great big monsters who can punch holes in walls, although some of them can. You're talking here about the quiet man, whose eyes are intensely watching what's going on around him. Someone with a firm handshake, who's got a good body but not over-sized, someone who will read the *Daily Telegraph* as well as the *Sun*, someone who is interested in life.

I think the fundamental difference between the Special Forces soldier and the ordinary soldier is that in all cases, the SAS and SBS, they *want to do it*. They *want* to be soldiers. They don't moan too much like your Mr Squaddie does. They do it because they like it.

When soldiers train for the Paras, you get these corporals shouting at you and beasting you. But the SAS training staff say, 'Look mate, if you want to pack it in, just pack it in. Do your best, here's your grid reference, it's 60 miles away, you've got 24 hours, pack on your back, off you go, mate. No worries, if you want to pack up, just sit down and a lorry will come and pick you up.'

They play hard alright though. Some of my old mates, 'Minky,' 'Snapper,' 'JB,' they all tend to play hard. But they all work hard too.

'Snapper' is one of my favourites. He wrote a book called *Soldier I*. His was the first of the SAS books. He's a great chap.

Snapper had been sent to Hong Kong to train the Ghurkas in unarmed combat – but he had a punch-up in a pub and became the first soldier ever to get the cane, or rather he was the last British soldier to be publicly flogged. He said he didn't think it would hurt much – but then the biggest Chinaman he'd ever seen in his life came out with the longest cane in history. The caning put him out of action for three months. He got six cane strokes, and now he claims he's the only sergeant with 12 stripes, three on each arm and six on his arse!

I don't do a show for the SAS now. They're operational now so often and they're away. So I don't get to see them much. I've still got a few friends involved with them and, of course, I bump into them all over the world. The problem is, let's say you're in, I don't know, Macedonia, and you're in a hotel having a drink, and there's two of your SAS mates up at the bar having a drink. You don't talk to them.

This happened to me once. I thought to myself, 'I won't say hello to those guys because they're obviously doing something here, so I'll just ignore them.'

So, I didn't make eye contact with them, I just went to bed. The next night, I was there again and they grabbed me as I walked in and said, 'You were fucking ignorant last night, weren't you?'

What? 'I was trying to not blow your cover,' I explained.

'You silly sod,' they said, 'we're here on leave!'

But they do some scary things and I get to hear some of the stories. 'Scouse' told me a story once of when they were down in the Falklands. They were on a mountain, overlooking Port Stanley, doing an OP – Observation Post – and they'd seen this white building where Argentinians were going in and out quite regularly. It was maybe 600 or 700 metres from the outskirts of town, out towards the west, towards the mountains.

They decided that this was where the Argentinians were having meetings and plotting operations. So, they radioed through back to Hereford and they said, 'Why don't you attack it with some Milan missiles?'

Now the Milan missile is an anti-tank piece of kit that's infantry fired. It's carried and you fire it and it leaves a wire behind and you direct the missile by wire. It's called TOW, targeted on wire. Now, at the time, I think they were about £20,000 a shot and this guy, a Scouser, had never fired one before.

'Well, tonight,' they said, 'when there's a bit of a row and a barrage goes up, have a practice with one. Fire it at a rock, and if you hit it, you can use it.'

So, they fired a couple at a rock and successfully blew up this rock. That's forty grand done. So, the next night they decided to hit a proper target. They fired six Milans into a building, which is £120,000-worth, plus tons and tons of small arms fire and grenades, launchers and mortars, and they blew this place to smithereens.

Two days later, when the surrender of Port Stanley happened, they went over to take a look at their handiwork … and the building they'd hit turned out to be the gents toilet. It was the most expensive demolition of a toilet in history!

Paul Hill, who was in the SAS, became one of my great friends. But, sadly, Paul died of a heart attack while he was on holiday. He was actually on leave somewhere exotic having a bit of a break. I was told while I was in the Oman, entertaining civvies. And, of course, a few troops turned up and I was on stage feeling really as sad as hell. I phoned a few friends in England and had a good cry, self-indulged myself. I noticed a guy in the audience in civvies and I knew him to be an SAS man and I hinted to him to come and have a drink. I got a note to him.

He was a Scotsman named Eddie. I'd known Eddie from Hereford and I took him aside and told him the sad news.

'I'm afraid, mate, Paul Hill died today.'

We sat down and we had a few beers and Eddie was pretty sad obviously because Paul was a fellow SAS man gone. I was pretty sad because he was my pal but me and Eddie bonded a little that night because we both knew Paul.

'How do you guys cope with the fact that your mates get killed?' I asked him.

'Well, you've just got to go on,' he replied. 'I was in the Falklands, as well. I was on a mountain patrolling in a team one night when we saw four guys in green anoraks with droopy moustaches. I shot one, the others scuttled off. When we got there, it turned out it was an SBS guy that I'd killed. His name was "Kiwi", a New Zealand bloke. I'd killed one of our own blokes, and that's what you have to live with.'

Eddie was visibly moved. 'I felt terrible about it,' he continued, 'and, on the way back, I went into their SBS mess. The SAS guys came in initially to apologise. It eventually got into, "You shouldn't have been there." It ended up, we had a bloody good old punch-up over the whole thing.'

But that's what they do, you know. If you're in the SAS, you say goodbye to your wife for twelve months and off you go. It's bloody hard work. An infantry regiment like the Paras are bloody shit hot. The Marines are shit hot. The Guards are shit hot. But the SAS and the SBS – they're something else.

I go to Hereford when I'm working at the Leisure Centre or the theatre up there. I always nip by and go to see Paul's grave. They have a little plot there round the back of the church and he's got a few friends down there, Paul.

Now, all the guys who do my security are ex-regiment, SAS members. If I've got two guys with me when I tour, or if I'm doing the summer season, there's always one guy with me and someone in the crowd. The protection is there just to make sure people don't get too excited, fuck the show up. They're not big guys, like I said. But if you want to spot an SAS man, look at the eyes. Just watch the eyes, not the muscles. Just the eyes.

I will never forget when the Iranian Embassy siege happened. I was watching the snooker, like everyone else. Even the SAS guys were watching the snooker. Bang! I saw the two guys leap across the building and I thought, 'Fuck – someone's blown the building up!'

I didn't realise it was the frame charge they'd put on the window.

I know that guy who was the first one in. Everyone fantasises about him, you know, like in women's magazines. He was the most fantasised about person you'd ever seen. If you were to see him in real life, he'd frighten children. 'Mel' is his name – a great bloke.

So, over the years, I have done a lot of things with the SAS. I've jumped out of bloody airplanes with them, absailed down buildings with them, I've been out on the piss with these blokes – and I've seen what they're like with hangovers! But I tell you what, they're truly fantastic guys, each and every one of them.

In 1999 I made a decision. I hadn't touched a drop since 1994 but I decided that I'd have a go at drinking again. I went up to Manchester to meet a friend of mine, the musician Rick Wakeman. We'd decided to do a musical about Harry Houdini and we met in the Midland Hotel up there to talk about it.

Rick doesn't drink, although I don't think he is an alcoholic. We sat in the hotel lobby and I asked Rick, 'Would you like a drink?'

I had my normal Diet Coke at the time.

'Thanks, I'll have a Kaliber,' said Rick.

'Oh,' I said, 'that's a bit dodgy, isn't it, having Kaliber?'

'No,' he said, 'there's no alcohol in it.'

'But,' I said, 'won't it make you want to have one *with* alcohol?'

Rick laughed. 'Don't fucking worry about all that nonsense,' he said.

So I had one. I sat there with a cigar and a pint of beer, just like old times. It was great.

Then I went over to Thailand with my mate Stukey to play golf for three or four days and to fondle Thai women. In fact, we had eighteen holes a day ... and then we played some golf.

On the golf course, at every other tee, there's a little bar, and I picked up some light beer every now and then. I grabbed a low alcohol beer ... and then I found out it wasn't *quite* low alcohol – and I quite enjoyed that, although I didn't get pissed. But I quite enjoyed the taste of it. And then things gradually progressed from there.

I started to drink pints of shandy and I thought to myself, 'Well this is OK.'

One night, my daughter Sarah brought a lovely Chinese takeaway home and I just thought to myself, 'I'm going to have a glass of red with this.'

And I did. And oohhh the taste of that Chinese food with that sip of red wine was just the absolute bollocks. So, I thought, 'Right! That's it!'

And, like a typical alcoholic, I made rules for myself. 'I'll only have a glass of wine with my meal. I won't do this and I won't do that …'

Now, I can go into a pub and have a pint of beer, just one though. I've never been able to manage to drink two. Or, I can have a whisky before dinner, or I can have wine. I can go out all day down the Polo Club and drink too much wine and feel awful the next day. But somehow, it's not how it used to be, not *yet* anyway.

I keep a serious eye on myself. I don't tend to look on this as a relapse, although I have to say, if I was going to have to stop drinking again, I'd have to knuckle under and restart the Twelve Step Programme. I don't think I could just stop, although drinking hasn't caused me too many problems.

I still feel rough when I drink too much and I think that keeps me on the straight and narrow. Now, I keep a very strict eye on my drinking.

Of course, everybody started saying, 'Oh, he's drinking again,' and, 'Ooooh, you shouldn't.'

That used to piss me off even more. I hated all those comments from all those interfering fuckers who know nothing about it.

But, so far so good. Wish me luck!

'A bridge to normality,' said Steve, my counsellor at the clinic.

Well, let's hope it's not a bridge too far …

14
Jim Davidson, OBE

'Bollocks to this! I'll just have the *one* beer. This'll be fine.' I was hot, tired and thirsty.

In fact, I had a shandy rather than fuck it up, the equivalent of a Macedonian shandy. I had flown out to Macedonia to entertain the troops in 1999 and had been out on one of our long 'grip and grin' tours. I got back to the hotel pretty whacked, and all I wanted to do was get my feet into some hot water and have a soak.

But first, we headed for the bar where we got chatting to various journalists and I had a beer, I think, for the first time since I'd been in the clinic five years previously. I felt OK about it. And I had just the one.

In the late 1990s, Slobodan Milosovich had different plans from ours and Yugoslavia found itself being pounded by the Yanks, who I'm sure were just getting rid of all their old bombs because their use-by date was up.

It seemed pretty pointless, really, bombing people. I don't think you ever bomb people into submission. I mean look what happened in the Second World War here. The more Hitler bombed us, the more the country rallied together.

And the Brits, with their backs against the wall, are a formidable opponent. I'm sure that the brave, proud Yugoslavian people felt the same. I never forget when they all drew targets on their chests and stood on the bridges.

But duty called and we now had a couple of brigades in Macedonian, lining up to go and kick Slobodan's butt in Kosovo.

I had phoned up and offered my services and off I'd gone to Macedonia for a tour. CSE and David Cryes-Williams had said how pleased they were that I had agreed to fly out – and I was excited because this was the first trip that the British Forces Foundation and the CSE had planned together.

I'd also come up with the idea of having a Forces newspaper. I'd decided it was a great idea after a handful of people came out see me at the Lakeside Country Club one day and said, 'Look, we have this newspaper called the *Forces Echo* and it's really good. It goes out once a week to all the troops all over the world, the Navy and everyone. And it's gone skint and the bloke wants to sell it. Will you take it on?'

So I'd spoken to Mark Cann at the British Forces Foundation.

'Why don't we, as the British Forces Foundation, buy this newspaper?' I said.

'We can't do that,' he replied, 'because of the articles of the charity. They don't really allow us to trade as anything and make a profit.'

'Well, *I'll* buy it then,' I said. 'We'll set it up and I'll put the profits into the British Forces Foundation.'

And, so that's what we did. We set up our little offices down in Aldershot. I went down there and I became a newspaper baron! Brilliant! We had a launch in London and, of course, the Government people didn't turn up. But nice Ian Duncan Smith did. He was Shadow Defence Secretary then. He turned up to offer his support and even Norman Tebbitt wrote, in his own newspaper column, 'What a good idea.'

Little did I know that all the other people at the Ministry of Defence were getting anxious. They called me in to the MoD and said, 'Look here, Jim, this newspaper you're going to print, whose voice will it be?'

'Whoever's reading it,' I said.

'No, no,' they said. 'When the regular Forces papers are out, they are, sort of, sponsored by the MoD. Yours is an independent one. We don't want you going slagging everyone off.'

'Well, I *won't*,' I said. 'You'll just have to trust me.'

'Oh well, fair enough,' they said.

The name of the paper changed to the *Forces' Weekly News* and the first copy rattled off the presses on 3 March 2000. We started shipping it out to the troops everywhere and I thought it would be a good item to take out to Macedonia. I'd planned to walk into the NAAFI and distribute it there.

I'd come to Macedonia with a little dance troupe and we performed a few shows. I was the comedian and we entertained all the brigades that were getting ready to go into Yugoslavia.

Out there, I also bumped into General Mike Jackson, the Head of British Forces. I didn't know he was in our hotel. What a man!

In the corner, I saw a little light brown feller sat there with his anorak up. He had a pair of those famous eyes, darting everywhere. He was, I guessed, a bodyguard for some important person but it was obvious to me he was also from the SAS. So I went up, sat down and chatted to him. We talked about old friends and inevitably the names of 'Minky,' 'Snapper' and 'Taff' cropped up in the conversation. He told me he was minding General Jackson, who was holding court with a number of journalists.

Much to my surprise, the general then walked over to me, and personally shook my hand.

'Bloody good of you to be here,' he said.

I looked up at this man, who had a face that looked like it had worn out five bodies, and I thought, 'Here is a *real* soldier. This guy's not a desk general. This man is a warrior.'

He invited me up to Headquarters the next day to see exactly what was going on and to meet some of his staff. When I got there, I was struck at how determined this man was. Here was a general who knew his troops and whose troops loved him. He was just waiting for the order to go and I *knew* that if he did go into Kosovo with his troops, outnumbered as they were, that he would be victorious. He just had this air about him.

A few weeks later, after I'd said all my farewells and flown back to England, those forces *did* go into Kosovo and I felt helpless again. So, three or four more phone calls, and off I went, back into Kosovo. This time, I headed up to Pristina and I took with me a beautiful woman called Jane Omorogbe, who's better known to you all as Gladiator 'Rio', all six foot four inches of stunning female, really tough and absolutely gorgeous.

In the back of my mind I thought, 'Mmmmmm, I wonder if I have half a chance here.' But of course, I had *no* fucking chance!

Jane and I flew out with our little entourage of people who were taking us there and the next day, we jumped in our Army vehicles and drove the four hours to the Grand Hotel in Pristina. We got to the hotel and it was full of people, packed. In my bedroom, I found a little camp bed. And when I ran the bath, it was *cold* water. When I unplugged the bath, the water ran out all over the floor. I didn't know if this was some Macedonian way of cleaning the bathroom floor, but I couldn't get to grips with that at all.

We drove up to our first little 'grip and grin' place. We visited the Royal Engineers, who had disarmed all the local bandits and were making safe all the weapons. They discovered all sorts of stuff, including some weapons from the Second World War, like Spandau rifles. Even a Winchester rifle that John Wayne would have been proud of!

To my dismay, instead of wanting me to 'grip and grin,' they also expected me to do a little show for them, with no microphone, no nothing. It was now 9.30 in the morning and there were eight rows of 16 chairs put out for the guys who were sat there. So, I had to do an impromptu show. I got to the next place, and there was *another* impromptu show for me – and the place after, and the place after that all wanted the same.

By the end of that trip, I had done *18* shows in two and a half days. Rio loved it. She drove a tank and was the life and soul of the party. She really is a fantastic person. Her energy was superb, while I was totally flagging. She realised that I was worn out and that I wasn't prepared really to do a spot in front of all these people, specially not 18 stand-up concert spots. So, she helped out. It was great and I ad libbed my way through it.

I went up to see the Royal Artillery, who had their six guns pointed at the Yugoslavs over in Kosovo and I said to them, 'Christ, is this all we've got?'

They seemed confident enough. 'This is all we need,' they said. 'Don't you worry about that.'

'How many guns pointing back at you?' I asked.

'About 60!' they said.

'Ten to one?' I said.

'Yeah, but ours fire *further* than theirs.'

I was proud to be among them.

I was totally knackered by the end of the trip but we'd had a fantastic time. Pristina looked like the worst Saturday night that one could have in a town with hundreds and thousands of people strolling around with no money and nothing to do. Stolen cars everywhere, anarchy, total anarchy on the streets. A lot of the buildings had been damaged by the Yanks and us.

I saw a young British soldier from the Green Jackets, 18 years of age, out on the streets, with as much authority as you could possibly have, acting like a man of 30 years of age. They really did save a lot of lives out there and sort out all the mess.

It was great to see and although I was exhausted, having done 18 shows, and trying so hard to get into Jane's pants – with no effect whatsoever – I came back feeling that I'd done my bit, once again.

Back home, in 1999, about three years ago, my spell with *The Generation Game* was going from strength to strength. Jon Beazley, my old producer had moved on but Sue Andrew had taken over. Things were going just great. The crew were fantastic and the BBC also wanted me to do three stand-up shows.

'This could be good,' I thought.

I was told I had to cut out all my mucky material, which I did. The shows went down quite well and everything was rosy.

Tracy was living round the corner and although there was friction with me seeing the children at Christmas, everything seemed to be more or less fine.

I started to go down to my beloved Charlton Athletic again and spend some time on the terraces. I still couldn't drive past Mum and Dad's house though because of my memories.

I didn't want to get myself melancholy. I've not really *really* grieved over Mum and Dad since they died, apart from that time in the clinic when the counsellors got me to read out a letter to them. Phew! I just don't want to go and heap that on myself. Maybe one day, if I get a girlfriend or a new wife or something, I'll take her there and show her where I was born. Or, I'll take the kids back there one day and maybe knock on the door and ask if I can have a little look inside. But that would break me up a bit.

Nevertheless, it was good to get back to south east London.

Cameron was now well settled into the Farm in the country and was in the studio, writing and recording his material. Sarah was still battling around, trying to put shows on here, there and everywhere, with her beloved garage DJs. In fact, she even took a season up at the Winter Gardens, where she decided that Great Yarmouth was ready for garage music. She reckoned that the theatre and the nightclub would be full. Well, three months passed and it was disastrous. The only garage they like up there is the one they park their tractors in.

They're fabulous people in Great Yarmouth and I love them to death. In fact, anyone from Norfolk has a little place in my heart. But when it came to garage music and house music – forget it! They were still very much into Lulu and YMCA and without me saying, 'I told you so' *too* much to Sarah, she came back home with her tail between her legs, thinking there must be something else in life other than garage music.

We sat down one afternoon last year and I said to Cameron, 'Will you do me a favour? Nip up to the fax machine and see if there's a fax for me from the office. I'm expecting one.'

It was to do with my itinerary that Sam, my PA, was going to fax through to me. Cameron brought me back a fax that had originally been sent to me at Brooklands Close, Sunbury-on-Thames. I thought, 'Well, hang on a minute, what address is this?'

It was the address of my old warehouse, where I used to keep my sound equipment. In fact, we had moved out of that warehouse over a year beforehand.

This letter was from Downing Street and it looked very official. It read, 'Should her Majesty the Queen deem it, we have put your name forward for an OBE. Would you like it? If you would like to accept it, would you fill this form in.'

It also said I'd got to fill it in one month before a certain date. I immediately thought, 'Oh, my, God, what's the date?'

And the date was nearly passed. The idiots in the Government had sent my 'Would you like an OBE?' letter to a place that I hadn't been in for a year. And if it hadn't found its way back to me via various faxes all over the world, this private and confidential 'Would you like an OBE?' would never have reached me.

I thought this must be a ruse by the Government and by Tony Blair, who must be really fed up with me slagging him off. He must have said, 'Oh well, if we *have* to give him an OBE, let's post it to somewhere where he won't get it in time to accept it.'

But I got it, and I wrote back and said, 'Yes, I'd love to accept it.'

And then they told me, 'Well, you have to pick it up on 12 March.'

I thought that was quite a co-incidence as it was around that time that I first appeared on *New Faces* – on 9 March 1976. I don't know if this OBE was a present for 25 years of people putting up with my dreadful stories or was being given to me because of my work with the British Forces or was due to the fact that I'd now turned 40 and had got my life together a little bit.

On reflection, I think this was for services rendered. My initial reaction to the news was that I thought it was a wind-up by Noel Edmonds! But then, I just felt dead chuffed.

I found out that I could take three people to the Palace with me. Who should I take? I couldn't take my five children, so I thought it would be fair just to take the three eldest, namely Sarah, Cameron and

Charlie. At the time, Sarah was 29, Cameron, 19, and Charlie was 12. Cameron suggested that we wore kilts from the old Davidson clan to the Palace.

Great idea.

The first thing I had to do was to try and persuade Charlie to wear a kilt! He knows nothing about his Scottish heritage and can't remember his grandfather at all. So, we managed to persuade him – or blackmail him – and this poor little 12 year old got kitted out with the Davidson kilt. Cameron got his kilt made and the three of us whacked our kilts on. Sarah wore a nice outfit too and off we drove to the Palace.

'What a great day this is going to be,' I thought.

As we arrived at the Palace, we were ushered into four little groups. You got the *knighthood* people at one end, who thought they were better than the next ones down, who were the *CBE* people. And then, next to the CBE people, was us – the *OBE* lot.

And to my great pleasure, I found out that OBE is better than an *MBE*. So, I wasn't bottom of the list! And all the little *MBE* people were down the other end of the corridor. We all looked down our noses at them – and the CBE people looked down their noses at us …

And the knighthood lot looked down on *all of us*!

So, there I was in my kilt. Sarah, Charlie and Cameron were ushered through to the viewing area, in this huge great hall at Buckingham Palace, one of the most magnificent, grandiose, ornate and beautiful buildings in the land. I was knocked out just being there.

I got in line and we were instructed by a very posh brigadier as what we should do. He said, 'It's the Prince of Wales giving you your medal today, as the Queen's busy.'

I was pleased the Prince of Wales was giving me this medal because I'd worked with him in the building up of the British Forces Foundation and I'd met him a few times. I was just dead chuffed it was him – without any disrespect to Her Majesty.

This was exactly as I would have wanted it. So, we all got in line and I stood there and I waited for my turn. I felt very proud that I'd been given an award. I thought it was not so much a way of congratulating me for what *I'd done* but congratulations for what *I was doing*. Like a sort of pat on the back. 'Keep up the good work.'

It was numbing, really. I didn't quite know what it was going to mean to me. It was nice to think I would have some letters after my name but I just wanted to get the medal on my chest. I couldn't wait to be invited to a dinner, where I could wear it at some occasion where medals should be worn.

So, I stood there in the line at the side of the podium and spotted the Prince, who was in his Naval uniform, as was his Equerry. Then my name was called out and I walked forward, knowing that there were 200 people watching, sat in the viewing area, all the friends and relatives of the other people getting medals.

I stood to attention in front of the Prince and he took the medal and he hung it on the little hook (in advance of getting your medal, they stick a little hook on your suit). And the Prince said to me, 'Jim, I'm *so* pleased it's me giving you this medal today. It is very well deserved.'

'Thank you very much, your Highness,' I replied.

Then he asked me, 'Is Tracy with you today?'

'No, sir,' I said, 'I have my children with me.'

'Fabulous,' he said. 'I've never seen you in a kilt before.'

'No, sir,' I said, 'I'm wearing it as a tribute to my father, Jock.'

And the Prince said, 'Oh, lovely. Is he here?'

'No, sir,' I added quickly – I mean, I didn't want to say 'he's *dead*' – so I just said, 'He's *up there*,' pointing as I did to Heaven.

And the Prince, who's a lovely man, smiled sympathetically. 'Oh,' he said, 'I *am* sorry.'

'No sir,' I said, 'he's not dead. He's nicking the lead off the Palace roof!'

To which he laughed. And he even turned and shared the joke with his Equerry!

He shook my hand, looked me right in the eye and smiled and took one step back. I stood to attention and it was the proudest moment of my life. Not just proud for me because I'd got this OBE but I felt as if here was some little part of the country to make us all feel proud. There was my Prince before me and if he'd said to me, 'Come on Jim, we're off to war', I'd have been the first out the door with him. I'd have done *anything*.

If they'd said, 'You've got to work the rest of your life and give all the money you earn to the Prince's Trust, or you've got to be an MP, or doing anything, go and run a mile, go and become whatever', I would have done *anything* at that moment.

I was standing there ramrod straight and I'd never felt so proud of my country in all my life.

I walked off, sat down, and watched the rest of the ceremony. Everybody got their medals, people much more deserving than me, I'm sure. But I didn't care. I had mine.

I went outside and had photographs taken with the children in our kilts, and Sarah in her lovely outfit. Then we jumped in the car and sped off to the Lanesborough, the most fabulous hotel in London, on the corner of Hyde Park. I'd booked a little private dining room there for lunch, with my brother John and his wife Barbara, and my brother Billy and his wife, Billie.

Sad to say, my sister Eileen had passed away and wasn't there. My other sister Jean, of course, was in America. But I also had a couple of friends with me. I had Laurie Mansfield and his lady, Mandy, and Peter Elliot, whom I'd known from ages ago – the guy who'd had to pay off the ponies because Liz Fraser had sacked them! Dear old Peter with his big glasses and his grey hair.

And to crown it all, I asked the wives. Obviously, Alison couldn't come. I didn't know how to get in touch with Alison, or whether she'd want to come or not. She lives in America now. But I invited Sue, Julie and Tracy, the three of them.

Tracy's Mum came as well. It was just fantastic – until I thought, 'Hello, which wife should I sit next to?!'

So, I sat them in reverse order. I had Tracy next to me, then Julie and, a bit further down, Sue at the end. They all got on really well and I made a little speech and all the girls cried.

'Look, we've had our ups and downs and I know that it's all a bit of a laugh being the wife of a comedian,' I told them all. 'And you're open to having the piss taken out of you for having had a husband who's been married four times to various other women. But I know it took a lot for you girls to be here and so I really appreciate that today.'

And I truly did. Everyone all had a little cry and I, sort of, filled up a bit as well. And we drank to 'absent friends', Mum and Dad and Eileen and had a fabulously good time and posed a lot with my little medal.

There you go – Jim Davidson, OBE.

It was, of course, the first time that the three of them had been together in the same room. They'd all met one another individually but not the three of them together. *I was cacking myself*! Well, it could have gone horribly wrong. But I thought, 'I'll lead from the front and get everyone together.'

It turned out that they were all charming together. We enjoyed a great lunch and it was quite a bizarre occasion for me, looking back at it now.

Here was me from south-east London, with my brothers and my wives and people who had known me right from the beginning. I'd met Sue when we were 17. It was different with Julie and Tracy, because they knew me when I was famous. They'd married Jim Davidson. But everyone else there knew me by my original name, Cameron Davidson.

But we were all dead chuffed.

I decided I wanted to go away with my children but the problem with taking *all* the children on holiday, especially the three little ones, was that they were going to miss their Mum. So, I thought, 'Well, I'll ask Mum to come along as well.'

So Tracy came. And then, I thought I'd better ask her Mum to come too because she was going to want someone to talk to while I was out down the nightclubs, and off fishing and playing golf. I couldn't just leave her with the kids!

So the five of us got on a plane and off we went to the most wonderful place in the world, Dubai, and we had a great time, although I didn't go out with them much. I'd have dinner with them of an evening and then, when the kids were asleep, I'd bugger off into the night with my mates from Dubai.

I'm not usually 'good at holidays'. But I'm good at having holidays *in Dubai* because there's always something to do. They have the most fantastic golf course, the Emirate's golf course, which I love. The place is brilliantly run and the hotel complex where I stayed is down in a place called Jimara. There's a hotel there called the Jimara Beach, which is shaped like a wave. It's a five-star resort hotel with 27 restaurants, 15 swimming pools, and everything you need.

Next to that, they have a set of beautiful Arabic-styled 'Mediterraneany' bungalows. And on the other side of that, along this causeway, stands the Burj Al Arab, which is reputed to be a *seven-star* hotel! I've stayed in it a couple of times. In fact, I brought Tracy and the kids back from Dubai, which I had to do after two weeks because I had to fly to HMS *Invincible* in Newcastle to do a show for the captain.

I'll tell you why I like Dubai. First of all, there's the sunshine. The next thing you realise when you get there is there's no graffiti, no yobs and no drunkenness in the streets. You can have a drink in the hotels and the staff there are just the best. They recruit from India and Bangladesh and the Philippines and everyone is just so happy and smiley.

My new best friend lives out in Dubai. His name's Steve Lamprel and I met him down at the Polo Club here, which is owned by Kenney Jones. Steve is a fabulous bloke, always laughing his head off. He is larger than life and his lovely wife Gilly is great too. They don't have children but what they do have is *tons* of friends – and I can see why. They are the nicest couple you could ever wish to meet.

I frequently bumped into Steve, who runs a very successful company that builds and repairs oil rigs. And whenever we met, we'd click up and be great mates. So, he invited me over to Dubai.

I flew over for one night to play in his golf tournament, stayed on his boat. And now I just can't *wait* to get back there. Now, every time I have a few days off now, I just want to get down to Dubai. I just love it there.

Well, now that I'm nearing the end of this, my life story so far, and now that I've clocked up 25 years in show business since I started out on *New Faces* back in the Seventies, I suppose I quite often look back at the journey I've taken and how I've come a long way since I started out as a young stand-up trying to get my career off the ground.

Nowadays, I quite often bump into young comedians and they ask me, 'Tell us, Jim, how do you become a star?'

Well, that's a hellova a question and I always give them the one answer. 'Allow people to make money from you,' is what I tell them.

'No matter how good you are, you're only going to be good if *other people* in the business earn money from you.'

That means if you fill a theatre, it's no good taking all the money from that theatre. You've got to let them have a bit. You've got to let your management have a bit, your record company have a bit. You're there as a product to make money for other people and I'm afraid that's the way it goes.

The problem's always been to try and stay one step ahead. If you're *just* a comedian and you *just* go on and tell jokes, that's fine. But as soon as you start to earn money, things happen. There's an old saying in showbiz, 'Where there's a hit, there's a writ.'

And where there's success, there's lawyers. There's the tax man, the VAT man, the girls, the newspapers, and then, of course, your ego wants you to have a *better* car than Brian Conley, a *bigger* house than Bobby Davro – especially me. I want it, and I want it *now*! I've got to have this big, grandiose lifestyle around me.

And this last six months have proved to me that when you move into business, and you do things like trying to look after your own finances, you're not necessarily as good as you are at telling the jokes that generate the finances in the first place!

For example, my company Effective Theatrical Productions – my

Chief Executive Officer Barry Stead and I – decided that this year again we'd be staging nine pantomimes. That's three for Butlin's and six up and down the country.

Because there was nowhere to put me in the rather big and bulky and expensive *Dick Whittington*, we decided between us that it was time the pantomime came to London. So, we went into the Dominion Theatre. It was a very expensive show and was critically acclaimed – everybody loved it. Everyone who came thought it was the greatest thing they'd ever seen. But, unfortunately, not *enough* people went to see it.

So Effective Theatrical Productions went into voluntary liquidation. It's embarrassing when you get this list of people to whom you owe money.

But the lucky thing is, the people whom you owe money are the people whom you've made money *for* over the years. And people know this business is a risky business. If the public don't come to see you, no-one's necessarily done anything wrong.

But the public have their own ideas of what they want to go and see. Then, of course, there was also the train strike and the train crash and the fact that you can't drive to London. You can't get into London now unless you drive in a fucking Challenger Two main battle tank. It was a nightmare.

Of course, word spins round the business, 'Jim Davidson's gone skint.'

Well, that's not so.

'Why don't you put some more money in it?' I was asked.

Well, the fact is that I have a person who works closely alongside me, called the Taxman and now, as you read these pages, I've paid the best part of £1 million in the last eighteen months.

Some is back tax from my divorce settlement for Tracy. If, let's say, *hypothetically*, and we have to talk *hypothetically*, if I bought Tracy a house for £500,000 cash, then I'd have to pay at least £200,000 tax for the privilege of doing that. And so, that's all started to catch up on me now, and that's more pressure. With the company being wound up, I then have to go to the Inland Revenue and say, 'The profit I was going to get from Effective Theatrical Productions is not there. Can you give me a bit more time to pay the money that I owe you for the last two years?'

I have to say that the 'Tax Person' has been pretty good. I had an interview with a woman and I thought, 'Oh now, here we go, this is shades of the divorce again' (like the woman judge I faced!). I thought this tax inspector woman was going to look down her nose at me. But she was very fair.

But then, being a woman, she changed her mind again and said, 'I want all the money now.'

So, you never quite know where you are with the Taxman.

I want to say to the Inland Revenue, 'Look, hang on a minute. I'm not trying to fiddle you. I don't have any offshore companies. I just need a little bit of time to catch up after the losses of certain pantomime productions, the costs of setting up the company and the cost of running a family.'

But, as I say, they've been very fair so far, unless, of course, I'm dictating this text from HM Prison at the moment.

Anyway, I must finish there as it's time to slop out!

When I'd made it on *New Faces* in 1976, once I'd passed that audition and once I'd beaten the band called Canned Rock who were so good, I knew I'd cracked it. And I knew that I'd be able to deliver. I also really knew just about everything that has happened to me now. I had a fair idea that this would happen. All I needed was for that door to be opened for me. And it *was* opened for me.

With Laurie Mansfield's guidance, it has been fabulous ride for me. I've been able to deliver, *against all odds*, it has to be said! Going on stage when Mum died, going on stage knowing that my daughter was being born back home, going on stage when Dad died, and when Eileen died, having to carry on performing when I knew Tracy was running off, carrying on with the show when I didn't know where Deborah was – all these were pressures, pressures, and more pressures.

On top of that, I've had the financial pressures and all the bureaucracy that I don't really understand because my mind works in logic.

Although outgoings always put me under pressure, my *incomings* don't seem to. They don't bother me that much. It bothers *my agent* and the people who look after me. But the most important thing about signing a *reputed* £2 million deal with the BBC is the fact that they want me to do the job – not that they're going to give me £2 million. I'm not telling you buggers reading this precisely how much I get. I've kept the book cheap, haven't I?! That's all you need worry about!

I read in the papers that 'Jim has signed a new contract with the BBC reputedly worth £2 million.'

One paper I read reported that my contract was worth *£3 million*! But then again, every day you pick the paper up and it reads, 'So-and-So signs the *biggest deal in history* with the BBC' – so it all means Jack Shit really.

What it *does* mean to me is that the BBC want me to make programmes for them. So that means there's a little bit of life left in me and I know they only want to give me that money because *I'm* making *them* money. I'm aware of that. When I *stop* making them money, I'm either going to need Lorraine Heggessey, who's the boss there, to be my best pal, or for me to be her 'bit on the side' for the contract to continue!

But, at the moment, Lorraine and her team are saying, 'We want Jim Davidson at the BBC and we want him to carry on with *The Gen Game*.'

She's the Controller of BBC 1 and so that means more to me than having the money. If all the money stopped coming in, it would affect Tracy, and the people around me, a lot more than it would affect *me*.

When someone as important as the Controller of BBC 1 commissions me for a show, it makes me feel wanted. It doesn't make me think 'Thank God, here's my money.' Nor do I think 'Thank God, I'm back on the television.' It's more a case of 'Oh. Someone who knows what's what *wants me* and what I can offer.'

Very pleasant!

I think my long-term future at the BBC depends on how *The Gen Game* is going to develop itself in this new millennium. It got a kick up the arse when Jon Beazley and I gave it a shake-up and I think it's time for it to grow again now. If I can make the programme and bring it in for the budget that we're given for doing it – and the public like it – that's fine.

I know I have the ability to make the public laugh – and what I've got to do now is make sure that my bosses at the BBC know that too. And they can only do that if the ratings are good. So, please put this book down now and switch on BBC1!

It's ten years now that I've been at the BBC and it feels like it because I've seen so many people come and go. I've seen the floor managers leave and become directors, big directors become bosses and move up to the sixth floor.

I quite like the people at the old BBC. They have their own way of doing things and I think that's because it's *public money* that they're spending. And I think they're very wary of that. I read a lot in the Press about public money being squandered on this and that. But you try and get an extra fucking camera into Studio One – absolutely *no way*!

Personally, I'd like to see the Licence Fee *raised*. I think it's a cheap price to pay to have decent television and the BBC do turn out decent television. Plus, there's the bonus that you don't have to put up with those crappy adverts!

If we had *more* money to spend on making programmes, then the programmes would be better. In my view, it's as simple as that.

Although I love the BBC, and I'd like to be part of the BBC forever, of course I'd never close the door on ITV.

It's more a question of whether ITV want to open the door to me. At the moment they do. In the last year, they've been nagging my agent *like mad* for me to come over to them and do a similar version of *The Generation Game* on Saturday nights. Everyone on television seems to be battling for that Saturday night slot, and the edge has gone off *Blind Date* a little bit for now and they're looking for something else to put on. Ant and Dec are filling a hole at the moment, and everyone is looking for that magical programme, for that 'Noel Edmonds slot', the one hour programme at 7 pm on Saturday nights, the show to grab all the audience. And ITV believe that I have the ability to do that.

But the BBC believe that I have the ability to do that as well. At the moment, I'm quite happy with the BBC and ITV have talked about offering me a lot more money. Well, they ask every year, 'Is Jim signing another contract with the BBC?'

And every year Laurie says, 'Yes.'

And every year, they up the money a little bit more.

But what the BBC are offering is an ability to make more programmes. I can do the stand-up shows; I can even do a situation comedy if I want to, so they've told me. I can do a bit of acting but, most of all, is the fact that they've trusted me now to look after *The Generation Game* and to get it back to where it was in the heady days of producers Jon Beazley and Sue Andrew. And that's what I'm going to do.

Of course, the great battle there is when you're on your own with a microphone. You know what you're saying, what's going to come next. You know how to structure the act. And when you're making a TV show, I'd give it the same set of rules. It's exactly like telling a joke. I have 200 people I have to convince that we *must* do it my way because that's the way it works. I need to achieve that without them saying, 'Oh, he's a fussy bastard.'

Now *that* is the thin line you tread, that *everybody* treads. And I'm really happy to do that at the BBC.

There's talk of my making a situation comedy at the BBC, although I'm not particularly fussed about it. There's talk about my hosting a chat show at the BBC, which I wouldn't mind doing. There's probably other people much better at it than me. But I think what I'd like to do is just get on with *The Gen Game* and *Big Break* – the shows that people like. People *love Big Break*. And what the BBC are also allowing me to do is remind people what my job is.

I'm an adult comedian. I'm a 'past 9.30 at night' comic. You give me a mike, a couple of cameras, and a 10.30 slot – and off I go!

I think the BBC sees me as a light entertainment person. The great thing about me, which people realise, is that I can do so many different things. I can be the *mucky* comedian at 10.30pm, and I can be the *kids'* comedian at 6.30pm. I understand the whole product. I understand that there's a beginning, middle and an end and I understand about budgets and how television works.

Don't forget, I've been doing it for 25 years now.

15

Close to the edge

When I look back and reflect on the professional journey I have taken, I feel I have achieved a great deal in my career and come a long way since I began over 25 years ago.

But I do have one big ambition left. My ambition would be to take *The Generation Game* to America – and I'll tell you why that is.

When we have American guests who come over to appear on the show, like the US Marines who performed that wonderful silent drill, throwing guns at one another, they *all* piss themselves laughing at *The Generation Game*. They tell me how absolutely wonderful they think it is and they say how great they reckon it would go down in America.

Now, that's one thing I really would like to do. I absolutely have the ability to do it and I wouldn't even be nervous. I'd take my production team over there, work with some American writers and put that show together in no time. I think *The Gen Game* would be a *wow* in America, I really do. I wish I owned the format to it because I'd be off there tomorrow.

I know other people have tried their luck over in America and not been terribly successful. But *The Generation Game* is a big enough show to travel anywhere in the world – and America is the place I would like to front it.

It's always exciting working on *The Gen Game* but, as this book goes to print, I've just been through one of the most exciting chapters in the show's history ... and her name is Lea Kristensen!

God, did we wrack our brains trying to find a new girl for the show. We also have a new producer and a new executive producer. Once the word goes out that you are looking for a new assistant to be a presenter on *The Generation Game,* all the agents send in their stuff. We had tapes and tapes and tapes.

I spoke to Suzie Perry, the girl who now fronts *Superbikes* for the BBC. She said she would do it but she wanted to get a lot more involved in the show, to introduce items and interview the contestants, which I didn't think would be right. She might have been very good at it but we didn't want change for change's sake. We'd made that mistake before.

I even asked Tara Palmer-Tompkinson. I had lunch with her and she was wonderful. She's the 'it' girl, you know. And I could see immediately why – because she's definitely got 'it'. She was a most charming creature. But unfortunately the people at the BBC seemed to think that she didn't have enough experience under her belt. That was sad but at least I got to meet her and share a lovely lunch.

Then one day a photo landed on my desk. The caption said she was Lea from Denmark. I'd never seen her before. The photo looked lovely, so I called her agent, who's a friend of mine.

'Look, you *must* see this girl, she's wonderful,' said the agent. 'She's working with Bruce Forsyth in Leeds at the moment…'

'Oh, fuck,' I thought. 'I don't know whether I can see her,' I said, 'because I'm off to play golf in Scotland.'

'Well, she'll fly down and meet you at the airport then.'

So as I was waiting to fly to Gleneagles to play golf, I popped in for our pre-arranged meeting to Harry Ramsden's fish and chip restaurant at Heathrow Airport Terminal One … and in walked this beautiful, tall, bubbly and charming Danish girl called Lea. We got chatting.

'Do you want some fish and chips?' I asked her.

'No,' she said.

I felt like saying, 'Do you want to come to Scotland for a week?' but I didn't. And then she went on her way and I went off to play golf. Meeting Lea totally put me off my swing, I can tell you.

There were a few more girls in the frame. We even thought of asking Rod Stewart's beautiful girlfriend Penny Lancaster. She's wonderful but the word round the BBC was, 'Why would she want to do *The Gen Game?* She's got Rod and she lives in Los Angeles.'

We decided to give it to Lea. We got her in for a screen test, to see what she looked like on camera. And she looked even better on camera than she does in real life!

We phoned her up and said, 'Don't tell anybody the news for two weeks.'

There was a General Election going on and we wanted to let the newspapers get through all that nonsense before we made our announcement. The photocall was of me and Lea together.

As we stood there having our picture taken, I said to her, 'Be prepared now, Lea, life's about to change. All your past will come out, every picture there's ever been of you in a bathing suit will start appearing, every boyfriend you've ever had will come out of the woodwork.'

'Well, don't worry,' she said, 'I haven't had a lot of all that ...'

And lo and behold, the very next day, topless pictures of Lea were published in the *Sunday Sport*. Not posed pictures, though. They were those long-lens paparazzi photographs, showing her with her ex-lover Mick Hucknall, from Simply Red.

Still, that's a point in her favour, come to think of it, because it shows she likes blokes with ginger hair! ... Stay tuned to this channel!

As this book goes to press, we have recorded two *Gen Games* with Lea and I've got to tell you that she is just perfect for the show. Lea has turned out beyond all my expectations of what I hoped she would be. Everyone in the studio loves her, she has great comedy timing and she is just a joy to be with. I haven't known Lea long but she is probably the nicest girl I have ever met in my life. ... And before you ask, readers – no, there's *no* romantic involvement – although I wish to Christ there was! Let's see how things develop ... on *The Generation Game*.

Well, I've talked a little bit about the pressures of my business life and the pressures of show business in particular but sometimes I think pressure can be of your own making. If I didn't want to run all these other business ventures, and I didn't want to have tax problems and marriages and all that, I guess I shouldn't have taken it all on. I shouldn't have … but you do.

At the end of the day, I went into the clinic because I couldn't control my drinking or my excesses and my personality defects. I learnt a great deal in that clinic and I spent six and a half years not drinking.

Now I drink again. I don't drink *tons*, like I used to. But sometimes I still have one too many. Not that I fall over and get pissed. But I have one too many glasses of wine at dinner and I feel awful the next day.

But whereas I used to drink four *bottles* of wine, and feel awful, now I drink four *glasses* of wine and feel awful. So I keep on the straight and narrow. I don't know why I started drinking again. I think it sort of just crept in. I had that Macedonian shandy, didn't I! And I've had the odd glass of port and I'm afraid it was a bit like, 'Oh, the one won't hurt.'

But there again, they told me in the clinic that the AA programme is just a bridge to normality and so is it normal to want a drink? Mmmm interesting.

I still believe that I'm an alcoholic and that I have to watch the amount I drink. Yet, I believe I have much more control over my life now. Perhaps I don't have more control over my drinking because I think *alcohol* decides how much of it I should have. But I have more control over my *life* and I haven't got on anyone's tits yet through drink.

There was a period where everyone thought, 'Oh, he's drinking, you know. It's all going to go horribly wrong.'

I think that's gone now. People realise that I'm older and wiser. If I hadn't had that break in the clinic, and if I hadn't learnt what I learnt from Steve and from Colin the Vicar, then I think I would be in a bit of a mess.

When I first started drinking again, I felt a bit guilty. 'Oh, bloody hell,' I thought to myself, 'I went through all this and now I'm having a glass of wine.'

But I sat down with a Chinese takeaway and a glass of red wine and I thought, 'This is *wonderful!*'

Now, I don't drink to alter my moods, although sometimes, if I'm feeling a bit tired before I go on stage, I'll whack a glass of wine down or a vodka and orange or something, but I won't have too many. I won't go guzzling and I won't go out on the piss all the time.

I'm drinking spirits again. I'll drink anything that comes along. But I won't drink *gallons* of it any more. I'll have the one. I don't know, I suppose I drink like everyone else does now, I think. Bit odd that, being the same as everyone else. I never liked that. I might have to stop again!

I didn't feel 'down' when I started again. The only thing that *is* sad, is that now I can't go back to the Farm Place clinic on a Sunday. I used to like that, going back to help out all the other people who drink. I can't really now. Well, I suppose I *could* do, but I don't want to be a hypocrite. I couldn't say, 'This is how you stop drinking – and look at me, I've started again!'

But my life is much more manageable now and it's much more manic than it ever was. There are so many other things to do, which I cope with so much better now. Although drinking doesn't help me relax, it makes me feel a bit more normal.

When I came out of the clinic, Tracy said I was 'like a robot'. I was a different person, like a zombie. But that goes after a while and you drift in to getting used to not drinking. At certain stages, I couldn't have had a drink if someone had put a gun against my head. But it crept back in as life became more normal, and now I'm used to being on my own, whereas before I didn't like it at all.

These days, I don't panic and miss people. I went through a difficult time when my relationship with Deborah ended and I still didn't pick up a drink. I didn't pick up a drink because I needed to get myself into my fantasy world. Now, I can get my own warm rosy glow around me by *not* drinking, by just feeling better.

If you like, I wouldn't say the clinic has taught me how to drink correctly. And I'm still wary that, if alcohol has it's way with me, I'll drinks gallons of it. But I do keep an eye on myself now.

When I started drinking again and the newspapers first found out, suddenly I was front page news. In a way, I was quite pleased when that headline came out. Because at least it showed that the spivs still know about me! It's a big deal that I'm drinking again. Great. If it just sort of crept in and no-one had mentioned anything, I would have almost been disappointed.

The other night I went to a 'do' with some young model on my arm, and *no-one* took a picture. *No-one* wanted to ask, 'Who's the new girl in Jim's life?'

I was well upset! I'm fed up about reading about Gerri Halliwell. Perhaps I'll have to start going out with *her*!

It didn't bother me all that they ran headlines like, 'JIM'S ON THE BOOZE AGAIN.'

You get these people phoning up, asking, 'Oh, I'm so sorry, are you alright?'

Hah! 'Yeah, *of course* I'm alright. I'm fine.'

Nothing lasts forever, does it? *A day at a time*, they say in Alcoholics Anonymous. *A day at a time.* And I had six years of '*a day at a time*' – and now my life is not 'a day at a time' at the moment. My life is, I don't know, my life is … my life!

If I want to have a drink, I *will* have a drink. I've made myself no rules there now. But I also know that if the drink gets the better of me again, I can go back to Square One. I said to the newspapers that the Farm Place clinic had a permanent bed there ready for me and that will always be the case. No-one's going to say, 'You bastard, you've let us down by drinking again.'

No-one's going to say that. And if ever there's a problem, or if ever I feel that I can't cope with life and my drinking, then I'll go and get my head back and restart the old Twelve Step Programme.

My social habits have slightly changed now, mind you. Nowadays, I'll tend to go to a restaurant, rather than to the pub. If I go in the pub and drink a pint of real ale, I'll only have *one*. I can't drink any more!

Actually, I don't think it's the *amount* you drink that matters. I don't think that's got anything to do with it. It's how you behave that's important and how you feel *inside* and *why* you're drinking. That's what I've altered, not the amount. I could still go and drink a bottle of whisky now but I'd want to drink it because I like the taste of it and everyone's having a good time and we're all pissed and we're all dancing – not because I want to feel morose, or I want to feel different, or I feel I can't carry on with life today.

I've still got loads of my mates from AA whom I speak to. There's my mate Alfie. A great bloke – and he doesn't drink. He decided to stop drinking. He knows that I was on the wagon for six years. And he knows that I have a drink now – and he doesn't bollock me about it! He knows that this is what I do.

There are certain people in Alcoholics Anonymous who think I've left the club.

'Oh, we must get him back in,' they say.

What the fuck do they know about me? I know as much about alcoholism as anybody, I guess. And what I do know is that it just doesn't go away.

At the moment, as they would say on *Star Trek*, 'it's cloaked'. My alcoholism is 'cloaked'. It's not surfacing itself. But, then again, if I want to go down Churchills's one night and have a couple of dances with a lap dancer and dance to YMCA and leap about, then I'll do it.

That's one thing I've started doing – dancing! It's really fucking embarrassing. That's a good enough reason to stop drinking, isn't it!? When I start drinking, I start dancing. I love it. It's ridiculous, isn't it? And I dance like your Dad dances at a wedding.

I'm not going to make any rules for myself because rules put me under pressure and pressure I don't particularly like. I don't make any. I'm not going to forecast how I'm going to feel tomorrow. And, if I don't feel up to life, I don't want a drink to feel better. It doesn't *work* like that now. If we're going out for dinner tonight, I'll have a glass of wine. If not, sod it. I'm not bothered.

I'd say I've been 'off the wagon' and drinking again now, I would imagine, for about two years. Not bad, eh? No headlines yet!

I don't think my drinking will *ever* be 'under control.' But I don't have any problems with it yet. And, don't get me wrong, *I* will not be the first person to say, 'I have a problem.'

Someone *else* will tell me.

Brandy is the thing I won't drink now. I used to drink *gallons* before but I've just gone off the taste of it. It wasn't a great taste. Brandy used to make me feel better. It was a great 'kick in the arse' medicine – get yourself on stage, get awake, feel better, stop throwing up. But I don't need all that now.

In the past two years, there have been times when I've still really overdone it. The first time I had *a lot* to drink, I was in the Ukraine. I'd gone out to do some research on a musical I was planning to do. I went to a restaurant and had some caviar and I poured out a half a pint of water from a jug – and it turned out to be neat vodka! So I drank that, and afterwards I couldn't sleep.

The sweat was pouring off me. I was shaking and trembling and I had to have another vodka in the morning for breakfast and I thought, 'Oh no, I've gone back … I'm back … I'm an alcoholic again … I'm in the gutter.'

I phoned up Sarah and said, 'Get an aircraft and come and get me. Take me to the clinic.' And Greg Lake, the producer of my album, was there with me doing this research.

'What's the *matter* with you?' he said to me.

'I feel awful,' I said. 'My life's ended. I got drunk last night and I've got this awful hangover and I feel exactly how I used to.'

Then he said something which took me right back to the clinic. 'Alright,' he said, 'you drank some vodka. You feel ill. You haven't slept very well and you've now got a hangover. Keep it simple, that's all it is. Your life hasn't ended! You'll feel better later.'

And he was right. I felt better later.

And I learnt a lot from Greg that day. He was a great saviour for me then because I thought, 'Well, if I feel rough, no bother. People feel rough.'

But I'd mistakenly imagined, 'I feel rough. I won't be able to *cope with anything* because I'm not completely on the ball.'

Greg got it. 'Keep it simple,' he said, which funnily enough is another cliché from Alcoholics Anonymous. KISS – Keep It Simple, Stupid.

So, I'm keeping it simple.

What I'm fed up with is justifying it to people. I'm fed up with justifying that I'm being pigeonholed. He doesn't drink. He's taken the pledge – and everyone goes, 'Phew, thank God for that – Wow!'

And now – 'Oh, he's drinking again. Shit!'

At the end of the day, it's my own business, quite frankly. It's *my* life. No, I'm doing alright. I'm doing OK, really.

In two years' time, I'll be 50. I *wanted* to retire but we'll have to see what the financial situation has to say about that later. I'm really not in control of that. Other people influence that.

So really, my destiny is not in my own hands. On the one hand, I'm being put under pressure to do certain things to provide money for people. And on the other, there's me wanting to battle against what they're doing and to plan my own future, or however much of me there is left to have a future – because everything I have to do is for so many other people.

I'm under quite a lot of pressure, too, from my charity work, which keeps me pretty busy, too. As Chairman of the British Forces Foundation, I'm quite committed in the diary. Lots of people from a variety of different charities write to me and ask, 'Will you come along and do our charity show? *We'll pay you.*'

And I tell them, 'How can you *pay* me if it's a *charity* show?'

'Well, we need you to sell the tickets,' they reply.

'Well, I'm sorry,' I say. 'So, if I go and charge you, you'll say to the papers, "We're from Such-and-such charity and Jim Davidson's charging us £10,000."'

Then, everyone will say, 'What a rotten sod – with all that money he's got!' ...

So I just tend to work on my own charities. I do a lot of Masonic fund-raising for charity and I do a lot for the Forces, plus the odd event for mates, if someone phones up.

The other evening I went to the David Shepherd Foundation, the animal foundation, and helped to raise £175,000 for them. I could open a garden fete *every afternoon* if I wanted to.

With all this chasing about, I also find that down time is very important. The thing with show business is that you are *always* in the public eye. That's a pressure. Wherever I go, there's people seeing me for the first time and they stare at me – just like *I do* when I see famous people!

Of course, when show business goes wrong and you've got no money, when you've got to get on a bus to go to work, you're *still* that famous person, which is even more embarrassing. That is the most awful thing – to be famous and poor at the same time.

In my down time, I play a little golf. I'm not very good and I don't think I'll get much better after playing for 20 years now. I don't play that often these days and I have a golf handicap of 18-ish.

I might go out and play with John Virgo and Rocky Taylor, the stunt -man, or occasionally I'll turn up for a charity golf event but I don't do as many as Bruce Forsyth or Jimmy Tarbuck. I just like to play.

Ever since I was a child, I've enjoyed fishing. But it's not just a matter of grabbing a fishing rod and going off. You've got to plan it and, as I say, I very rarely have a couple of days to myself now. You need one day to sleep and the other day to fish. But frankly, I must admit that I do find relaxing as hard *work* as working.

Nowadays, I am teaching myself to work under pressure. And there *are* always so many pressures. Like the pressures of, 'Christ, this microphone's not very good,' or

'The PA system's bad,' or

'They can't see me,' or

'They can't hear,' or

'They're pissed,' or

'This room's crap,' or

'They've heard my jokes before.'

Then there are the pressures of, 'Oh shit, there's someone else who wants to take my job at the BBC,' or

'Oh shit, there's someone who wants to run off with my girlfriend,' or

'Oh shit, she likes her special friend more than she likes me,' or

'Oh, shit, I can never see the children,' or

'Oh fuck, where's the next penny coming from?'

And talking of pennies, my financial worries and pressures, sadly, involve a lot more than pennies. After four divorces, I couldn't *afford* to get married again now. I've got no money. I've got to work for the rest of my life to pay for certain things. At the moment, I couldn't retire. In five years' time, I wouldn't be able to retire because I still have to keep paying Tracy and the kids. It's a lot of money. So no matter what, I'm not really in control of what I want to do with my life.

Right at this moment, I'd like to be able to pay for my house and everything and then have no debts. I'd like to work when I want to work. I'd like to live in Dubai and fly home to England to do *The Generation Game*. I've got a lot of mates in Dubai. It's a wonderful country.

There's nothing really here for me now. The children are growing up, and the three little ones know I'm their Dad but their home is with their mother and whoever their mother ends up with. They're quite happy. I see them as often as I can.

If I were to go out now and find a girl, there is no way I could get married again. I just wouldn't have the money and I have five kids. I don't have a girlfriend right now. I have *a few* I see, and some I like more than others. Some I phone up just to have a bit of 'How's yer father,' but I think people realise that I am not really out for a relationship at the moment.

I have always lived beyond my means. I've got a huge mortgage on my home, and I have a business to run.

When I started as a stand-up, I was earning a few quid a night. Now I can get £15,000 a night, £20,000 a night. But the money just vanishes. You pay 20% commission and 40% in tax. You are still left with a few bob but there are bills to settle, the house to pay off, security expenses.

When I go on tour, the costs of going on tour are *phenomenal*. When I toured the show before I went in the clinic, the *costs* were about £50,000 *per week*. That's £50,000 a week I was paying other people.

When I put on the pantomimes, it's a similar story. This year, this Christmas, I have the best part of a thousand people working for me, all earning money. This year, I have got eleven pantomimes on. I've become a businessman now, as well as an entertainer.

What I *want* to do is create a multi-purpose media company where we can produce. I want people who work for me and produce pantomimes, touring shows and West End shows. I really enjoy that.

It's a juggle and a struggle – and it all adds up to one hellofa lot of pressure. But I've discovered that I've just got to look at all these pressures in a positive way.

I am what I am. I'm a comedian. I make people laugh and I'm successful at it because the theatres are full, because the ratings are pretty good, because I still have the ability to create things.

I can still write and produce pantomimes.

I can still direct pantomimes.

I can make people and myself a lot of money.

But I have to be on the ball for that. I can't just bugger off to Spain and play golf with Jimmy Tarbuck, which I'd love to do. I have to keep ticking over.

It really is like walking the knife edge. It's like standing on the edge of a cliff with the wind blowing you off the cliff and you're hanging on because you really, really, want to hold on to what you've got.

And although I do feel real pressure, I also realise that what I do is something that I really enjoy. When those people out there laugh, or when *The Generation Game* is going well, and when I see that final product and think, 'I'm really proud of this,' then it makes it worth hanging on for.

When I'm up against the wind, sometimes, I *do* feel as if I just want to let go. And bugger off. Go and live in Spain or, in my case, disappear to Dubai. Just take the pressures off.

It's what they said to me in the clinic, after all, all those years ago. 'Give it up, Jim. Pack up your job. Just dump all the pressures – and then you'll be happy.'

But honestly, I don't know about that … It's certainly tempting. And

I can tell you, it is a very fine-edged line to walk down. It's a terrifying tightrope I am perched on. I have to keep all my wits about me and my eyes peeled. All the time.

But when all's said and done, I guess I'm up there on my tightrope because I'm where I like to be ... Close to the edge.

Wine is strong;
A king is stronger.
Women are even stronger.
But Truth will conquer all.

The Book of Esdras